The medium of Leonora Carrington

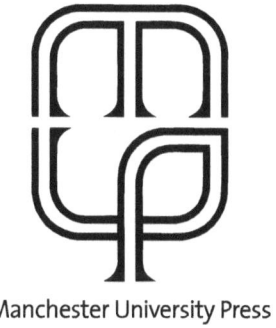

Manchester University Press

The medium of Leonora Carrington

A feminist haunting in the contemporary arts

Catriona McAra

MANCHESTER UNIVERSITY PRESS

Published by Manchester University Press
Oxford Road, Manchester M13 9PL

www.manchesteruniversitypress.co.uk

British Library Cataloguing-in-Publication Data
A catalogue record for this book is available from the British Library

ISBN   978 1 5261 6123 9   hardback
ISBN   978 1 5261 7745 2   paperback

First published 2022

Typeset
by New Best-set Typesetters Ltd

Contents

Illustrations

Acknowledgements

It was perhaps inevitable that research for this project would involve an elaborate network and a long-term odyssey. I have been amazed many times by the serendipitous way in which, in spite of the odds, Leonora Carrington brings people together. I have met some marvellous "imagineras" (to use my friend Roger Shannon's word) on this journey, and wholeheartedly thank everyone who answered my interview call. The Leonora Carrington Foundation has been steadfast in its support for my research, and I enjoy spending time with Gaby, Paty, and Dan Weisz more than I can express. My intellectual friendships with Anna Watz and Jonathan P. Eburne have been crucial to this venture, and this book wouldn't exist without their rigorous feedback, lived politics, and sheer belief. Emma Brennan has been a long-term supporter of my work on Carrington, and I am so grateful to everyone at Manchester University Press, especially Alun Richards, for helping me realise this book. Special thanks to the Aridjis family, Stacy Klein, Lucy Skaer, Heidi Sopinka, Lynn Lu, and Samantha Sweeting, whose illuminating works feature in my content chapters. And to Kim L. Pace and Mayako Murai for inspiration. Thank you to Tim Walker and Alex Pasley-Tyler for allowing me to use the magnificent cover image. Thank you to Tracy Bohan and Susan Powell for arranging interviews with Ali Smith and China Miéville. And to Jo Mortimer, Karen Nash and Juanita Bullough. Much of this book was written within art-school environments where I was able to spend time immersed in practice, a term I have always suspected to be profoundly magical. I am grateful to colleagues at Leeds Arts University and the University of St Andrews. Thank you to the Westfjords Residency in Iceland who permitted my own creative solitude and perpetual search for the Arctic fox, especially Ingeborg Lossie, Guðbjörg Lind Jónsdóttir, and Janne Kristensen. Finally, very special thanks to my family, who have supported my distant excursions and "late-night internet booking" (Skaer) with tolerance and love. This book is for my cohabitors, Soren and Niall Campbell.

This research has benefited significantly from presentation at a variety of venues including: *Leonora Carrington Centenary Symposium*, Biblioteca de México; a keynote address invited by Roger Shannon, Michelle Man, James Hewison, and Ailsa Cox at Edge Hill University; *The Artist's Dining Room*, London invited by Marina Warner DBE and Yinka Shonibare CBE; *Visionary Artists, Visionary Objects*, The John Rylands Library, Manchester, invited by Naomi Billingsley and Lieke Wijnia; *Surrealism in Britain, 1925–55*, The Hepworth Wakefield, organised by Hilary Floe and Rachel Stratton; International Society for the Study of Surrealism (ISSS) inaugural conference, Bucknell University, Lewisburg hosted by Roger Rothman; and The Dada and Surrealism Group Seminar, University of Edinburgh led by Patricia Allmer. Select material presented here appeared previously in different guises: *Leonora Carrington and the International Avant-Garde* (Manchester University Press, 2017); *The Space Between* (2018); *Gramarye* (2017; 2020); and *Leonora Carrington: Living Legacies* (Vernon Press, 2020).

Introduction

Patience. Slow-burning fuses make big blasts.

—Susan R. Suleiman (1990)[1]

Pilgrimage

She expired and the world seemed to shift on its axis. I received the information via text message while walking up University Avenue in Glasgow towards the conclusion of my doctoral studies in May 2011.[2] The shock of that moment gave way to resolve. For I suddenly realised that the future of my research, everything I had planned, my whole approach to doing art history, would now need to be conducted in an entirely different manner. This study is the result of that revelation; the need to meet a range of creative intellectuals who did know her, and to consider, in detail, how they have both channelled and replied to her. Thus, the project has become anecdotal, combined with political and theoretical edgework. It operates at the point of overlap between creativity and scholarly historiography which I define as both feminist and curatorial. The notion of "legacy" is paramount here, as is the Barthesian concept of "the death of the author," which forms a well-worn yet necessary citation, borne out through practice.[3]

Research for this book has involved a series of pilgrimages. Along the way, I have found it strangely comforting when I see copies of *The Hearing Trumpet* (1974) for sale in Heathrow Airport. I have sat for hours on the Paseo de la Reforma (a major boulevard in the heart of Mexico City), contemplating the gigantic, bronze sculpture *How Doth the Little Crocodile* (2000). This crocodilian ship, with lizards for passengers, seems to be ferrying the imagination to an alternative reality or underworld seeped in Mexico's mega-diversity and Latin American culture.[4] Ironically, I have found myself travelling many thousands of air-miles to meet critics and theatre-makers that live her eco-politics, and to go on residencies and writing retreats in search of conditions conducive to writing this book. This has become a deeply reflexive self-criticism—how to square the carbon footprint of research with the headspace necessary for making it happen? This book attempts to answer this question, with an awareness that the very approach to studying and engaging with the English/Mexican artist and writer Leonora Carrington (1917–2011) is always already a series of contradictions.

Her story has been widely documented. In sum, Carrington was an imaginative artist and writer from Lancashire in the north of England, who rejected her wealthy background, impressed the surrealists, and ended up in Mexico City, where she became one of the most unique and uncompromising creative figures of the second half of the twentieth century. While her journey, bravery, and youth are striking, especially given her rebellion against the debutante conventions of her time, her progressive femininity and eccentric persona have often been presented in the scholarship as more mythical than her own pictures. Yet, it is in her work that we need to look for the most compelling evidence of her power. Throughout her career Carrington sought to investigate the hidden facets of knowledge in order to represent a terrific and astonishing archaeology of the imagination. Her curiosity for ancient cultures and alternative belief systems was voracious and unparalleled.[5] Meticulously detailed egg tempera paintings comingle with her textual narratives and a wide variety of further media (often involving external fabrication), including epic tapestry, detailed printmaking, and bronze sculpture.[6] From a precocious age she was accomplished in both writing and painting, and would develop her abilities into a profound and personal mode of eco-feminist activism which has caught the attention of subsequent generations.

Even before her death, artists and novel writers had already embarked on the process of working through her legacy. Glasgow-based, conceptual artist Lucy Skaer queries the art world's obsession with international jet-setting, city-hopping and fetish for cheap, commercial flights: "when I arrived unannounced at Carrington's shuttered house (the address of which I had been given by a Texan collector), I was questioning the wisdom of my self-funded trip, based on a whim and some late-night internet booking."[7] Much of Skaer's account of meeting the elderly artist challenges this prospect of being in transit, and serves to de-romanticise Carrington's own historical adventure to Mexico. Scottish novelist Ali Smith's fictional account, *Artful* (2012), continues this transitory inquiry, enrolling Carrington within the meta-narrative of a lecturer's notes: "You told me Leonora Carrington was an expert in liminal space. What's liminal space? I'd asked you. Ha, you'd said. It's kind of in-between. A place we get transported to."[8] Such ambiguous thresholds are a useful way of approaching Carrington; a shape-shifter for the imagination, reawakening our values. It seems fitting that one recurrent motif from Carrington's *oeuvre* positions gravity-defying vehicles as complex metaphors for exodus or the departure lounge of the psyche.

In rethinking what might constitute a greener and more ethical pilgrimage, it is interesting to note that many of those who travelled to meet the elderly Carrington tend to document the authenticity of their encounters through the language of the medieval quest or spiritual rite of passage to meet a guru or mentor. Such "running-away-from-home" to meet a self-exiled, English avant-gardist in a faraway land became a project of fandom for those seeking so-called enlightenment and personal growth. Canadian-Ukrainian novelist Heidi Sopinka and American artist Anne Walsh narrativise their twists of fate through their preferred media of fashion photography, travelogue, and scriptwriting. Joanna Moorhead's journalistic story of her long-lost cousin, Prim, is explored through the medium of biography (2017), while Rosemary Sullivan reflects on her meeting with Carrington via homage-reportage (2015). English playwright Alice Allemano (2018) and Norwegian novelist Susanne Christensen (2019) have fictionalised or imagined similar pilgrimages to Carrington's door in Colonia Roma, Mexico City. Of course, any form of creative hero-worship quickly fell flat when seeking out the presumed wisdom of this primary surrealist. Sopinka describes the firm sense of self-cancelling she was greeted with, "a flat refusal—no!" A complete rejection of any celebrity status on Carrington's part; a denial of the wise-woman cliché.[9] Carrington was adept at eroding stereotypes in a revisionary manner. Silvia Cherem experienced a similar attitude: "She does not cooperate; it does not interest her."[10] This was true too for scholar Susan L. Aberth, who attempted to meet her thesis subject only to have their rendezvous cut short repeatedly until she brought the artist a cheque from her gallery, an errand that enabled a significant, historiographical foot in the door.[11] Again, Aberth describes this process resolutely through the liminal language of "initiation."[12] Sopinka further reminisces about her own highly aestheticised expedition with two creative friends, artist and writer Alisha Piercy and photographer Natalie Matutschovsky, to Mexico City in 2009, as "a pilgrimage to discover the inner workings of the last living Surrealist."[13] In Sopinka's account of searching for their subject:

> We did these performance pieces to try and conjure her. We used a lot of her iconography to make these picnics across Mexico City. It was amazing, we'd dress up in these costumes and conceive of what it would look like. Leonora loved it when we told her! We showed her some of the imagery. I think she felt it was about time! She was finally starting to get a bit of a taste of people seeing her and her work in a larger context.[14]

Possibly their sheer commitment to an aesthetics of séance in her honour managed to convince Carrington that her time had come. Whatever she

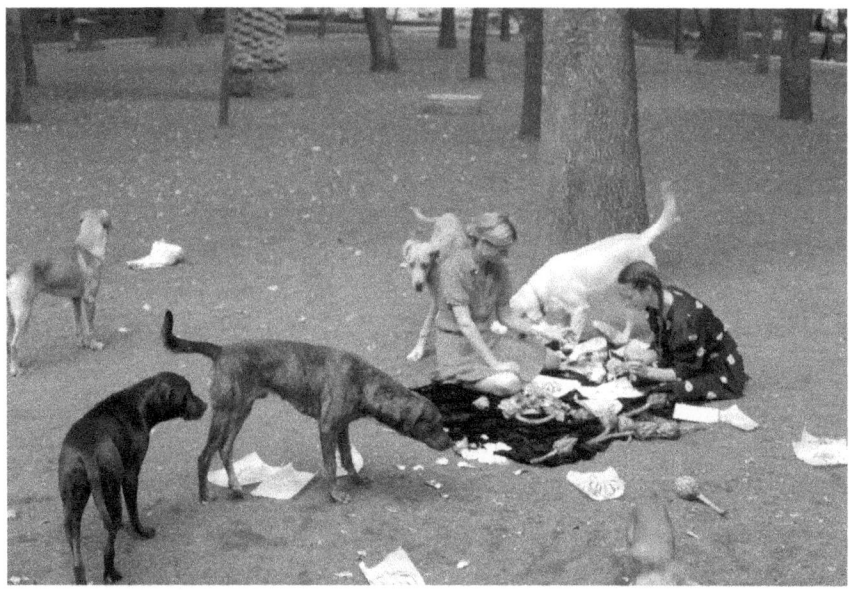

1 Photo by Natalie Matutschovsky, Alisha Piercy, and Heidi Sopinka, 2009

personally may have made of her cult following, certainly she and her work are now becoming seen within the larger, political context that this book will explore.

Quotation

There now exists an abundance of independent, creative responses to Leonora Carrington and her work, especially in the decade since her death. One might imagine such an increase to be a likely outcome of the perceived relaxation of copyright restrictions following an artist's passing, but this would be an understatement of her pre- and posthumous clout. The announcement that her recently reissued children's book *The Milk of Dreams* would be the curatorial theme for the 59th International Art Exhibition at the Venice Biennale (2022) curated by Cecilia Alemani seemed timely. It features respected contemporaries of Carrington, like Dorothea Tanning, and successive generations such as Paula Rego, Niki de Saint Phalle, and Lynn Hershman Lesson, to younger artists like Alberta Whittle, bolstering and renewing the power and potential of art by women to inform and transform art-historical understandings through a global curatorial platform.[15] In recent years, Carrington's name has also started to appear more regularly on variety of media channels beyond the art world, from television programmes such as *Antiques Roadshow* (PBS, 2014) and *University Challenge* (BBC, 2018; 2020), to the rise of social media outlets, especially Instagram, a digital photo-album and micro-weblogging platform, where, at the time of writing, @leonoaracarringtonestate has close to 80,000 followers.[16] As Natasha Boas points out succinctly in a recent catalogue essay: "Carrington is current."[17] Indeed, in the contemporary arts, it is striking how Carrington has been appropriated by a variety of emerging and established twenty-first-century artists and writers as a starting point, cameo, or catalyst for reviewing their own practices. Some of the most compelling examples to be explored in this study include the work of novelists Heidi Sopinka (*The Dictionary of Animal Languages*, 2018) and Chloe Aridjis (*Sea Monsters*, 2019), both of whom met or knew Carrington, and pursue her trailblazing eco-feminism through literary soundscapes and marvellous poetics. Their novels are quietly political and nestled within broader curatorial frameworks which variously involve art writing, exhibition-making, photography, in Sopinka's case, fashion designing, and in Aridjis's case, filmmaking. Meanwhile, the *Leonora* cycles of conceptual artist Lucy Skaer (*Leonora*, 2006 and *Harlequin is as Harlequin Does*, 2012) and Massachusetts-based ensemble Double Edge Theatre (*Leonora: La Maga y el Maestro* and *Leonora's World*, 2018–20) enable a fuller understanding and critical appreciation of Carrington's esoteric conceptualism and depth of interests. Elsewhere, Scottish artist and actor Tilda Swinton's performance work and highly aesthetic re-embodiment of Carrington's characters in the fashion stories of photographer Tim Walker (2013; 2017) toy with the mythologisation of Carrington's iconic status as a form of self-identification, albeit paradoxically, via disguise and costume. A collaborative performance installation by London-based artists, Lynn Lu and Samantha Sweeting (2011; 2016), made in the immediate aftermath of Carrington's death and based on her novel *The Hearing Trumpet*, also has much to say about the social dimension of her work and reach of her thinking in experimental art-making.

In no particular order, Carrington has been further evoked throughout the arts, and the range of media she and her work are referenced through gives room for pause: in **novels** (Ali Smith's *Artful*, 2012, China Miéville's *The Last Days of New Paris*, 2016, Michaela Carter's *Leonora in the Morning Light*, 2021, and Alyssa Harad's *Madame Creature*, forthcoming), **autobiography** (Deborah Levy's *Real Estate*, 2021), **short stories** (Fernando A. Flores's "The Performances of Liliana Krauze," 2018), **poetry** (Penny Sharman's *Fair Ground*, 2019, W. N. Herbert's *The Wreck of the Fathership*, 2020, Jenny Wilson's "The Little Carmelite," 2017, Deborah Harvey's "Oystercatchers," 2019, and Jean Taylor's "Alter Ego," 2021), **children's literature** (Leslie Sills's *Visions: Stories About Women Artists*, 1993, and

Michelle Markel's *Out of this World,* 2019), **illustration** (Emilie Seron's *The Hearing Trumpet,* 2005, Niklas Nenzén's *Down Below,* 2012, Melodie Stacey's *Leonora,* 2020, and Virginia Mori's *Surrealist Dinner Party,* 2021), **comics** (Tor Freeman's "At the Party," 2019, and Kelcey Parker Ervick's digital drawings, 2021), **animation** (Elizabeth Hobbs's *The Debutante,* 2021), **films** (Pamela Robertson-Pearce's *Gifted Beauty,* 2000, Aleksandra Niemczyk's *The Siren's Scream,* 2021, Chloe Aridjis and Josh Appignanesi's *Female Human Animal,* 2018, and Joanna Lipper's biopic, in progress), **painting** (Elizabeth Cheche's *What We Saw When No One Was Looking,* 2018, Anita Elias's *Leonora's Quetzal,* 2019, Rose Moon's *A Place to Dream Up a Storm,* 2019, and Simphiwe Ndzube's *As They Rode Along the Edge,* 2020), **fashion** (Ayka Yasis's *Darvault,* 2009, Tereza Rosalie Kladosova's *Muses,* 2020, and Maria Grazia Chiuri's *Le Mythe Dior,* 2020), **jewellery** (Anna Gunheim Benito's "Crocodile" necklace, 2021), **music** (Clara Engel's *Songs for Leonora Carrington,* 2017, Michael Begg's *Sonambulo,* 2019, Try Conditioner's "Leonora," 2021, and Project Blackbird's "Baby Giant," 2021), **podcasts** (Laura Marling's *Reversal of the Muse,* 2016, Jennifer Higgie's *Bow Down,* 2020, and Hannah Buckley and Gillie Kleiman's *The Rocking Show,* 2020), **choreography** (Michelle Man and James Hewison's *Imaginarium,* 2014, and Eldarin Yeong's *The Meal of Madam Candlestick,* 2019), **curatorial projects** (Helen Nisbet's *Houses are Really Bodies* at Cubitt, 2017, Constance Jones's *Leonora's Hands,* 2021, Jenna C. Ashton, Alison Duddle, Alice Kettle and Eleanor Mulhearn's *House of Opposites,* 2020–21, and Cecilia Alemani's *The Milk of Dreams,* 2022), **artist's books** (Anne Walsh's *Hello Leonora,* 2019, and Claire Dean's *House Book,* 2019), **puppet shows** (Caracola Producciones's *La Dame Ovale,* 2017), **performance** (Katharina Ludwig's *The Wound Lickers,* 2020), and more **theatrical productions** (Dirty Market's *The Hearing Trumpet,* 2017, and Alice Allemano's *About Leo,* 2018), to list only a selection.

The sheer number of above examples and diversity of creative practices represented may indicate that Carrington's story has become a tried and tested method, a distinctive persona ripe for annexation, an unusual historical precursor who justifies common aims and ambitions. Given Carrington's apparent cult following, the practical citation of her and her work offers a secretive wink-factor for an unofficial (yet rapidly increasing) "in-club," a communicative gesture for those like-minded readers or audiences already "in the know." Some highlight a collaborative instinct inherited from Carrington and her own contemporaries, while others point out that the sense of individuation and rebellion associated with Carrington's maverick approach to artmaking provides a model for the pursuit of niche interests.[18] This suggests Carrington's appeal is both heterogenous and contradictory, an ambivalence which recurs throughout this book. On closer inspection of the range of materials noted above, even more complex attachments or interplays reveal themselves, for many of these creative responses that feature in this book are made in media that Carrington herself did not use, or deploy an aesthetic that is entirely distinctive from hers. As Linda Hutcheon reminds us in *A Theory of Adaptation* (2006): "The adapted text, therefore, is not something to be reproduced, but rather something to be interpreted and recreated, often in a new medium."[19] Mieke Bal has long concurred with a related idea: "[b]y reusing forms taken from earlier works, an artist both carries with [her/him] the text from which the borrowed element has broken away and constitutes a new text with the debris."[20] Applying Bal and Hutcheon's ideas to the practice of quoting Carrington suggests that something radically new and politically innovative might be conjured, and that the medium is crucial to conveying this.

Of the numerous creatives cited above, as wide a selection as possible have been interviewed for this book (see Appendix), and their answers have come to shape my working understanding of Carrington's status in the contemporary arts. The interviews were conducted over a number of years in a variety of locations and communicative media. Often, I found the interview process constituted a séance of sorts, a dialogic formation that attempted to summon Carrington, not to ventriloquise but to tap into her existence. I interviewed Aridjis in her cosy London townhouse (July 2014) accompanied by a distinctive feline, a Carrington maquette and many books on magic, poetry, and archaeological nostalgia. Sopinka and I met in Fortnum and Mason for tea and crumpets during her UK book tour (May 2018), then subsequently in the Scottish National Gallery of Modern Art during the Edinburgh Book Festival (August 2018) for tea and scones and a viewing of Carrington's *Portrait of Max Ernst* (1939) which had recently been acquired. Stacy Klein was also interviewed in person in Ashfield, Massachusetts (June 2019) amidst her paraphernalia of puppetry, masks, theatre posters, and her small dog, followed by email exchanges. Further bespoke interviews with Skaer, Sweeting, and Smith nuanced the research but were increasingly conducted via email as we went into lockdown. These were followed up with a slightly more disciplined subset of four key questions which helped shape my approach to interviewing an even broader cohort of creative intellectuals. Each time, I found their words took my project in unanticipated directions, so that my own critical position on Carrington has become ever-shifting.

Until now, much of this potential network has remained curiously disparate and often siloed, no doubt due to the heterogenous and often grassroots characteristics of the contemporary arts. Through curating such responses together for the first time, it is hoped that a space for new proactive dialogues will be enabled, combining forces, pulling resources, and further galvanising the range of activisms Carrington herself espoused. To date, the scholarship on Carrington has arguably been more collaborative than the practice. That said, there have been productive crossovers, and a chief purpose of this study is to demonstrate some of the potential underlying resonances that might forge a sense of community. Double Edge Theatre have welcomed the scholarly input of Aberth, Tere Arcq, and Jonathan P. Eburne through organising discussion fora and commissioning interpretation texts as well as developing their archive. House of Opposites collective (named after a painting by Carrington) combines academic curators and textile artists (Ashton and Kettle) with puppeteers and illustrators (Duddle and Mulhearn) as a collaborative model of thought. Novelists such as Ali Smith, Chloe Aridjis, and Marina Warner, have each worked on Carrington with a critical as well as a fictional eye. The ever-increasing array of scholarly inquiries may also be understood broadly in this context as creative interpretations in that they often provide subjective representations and different versions of how we can understand Carrington.[21]

Why another book on this particular artist and writer? For one, I believe it is vital that we develop a better understanding of why Carrington, especially, has received this level of fandom. Why does she hold this exulted position for so many contemporary figures? What and how does Carrington and her work signify for these creative intellectuals? By unpacking the purpose and meaning behind this vast array of interpretations and adaptations, I seek to create a guidebook to her activism in the present tense. This study proposes that Carrington's significance to the contemporary arts has become far reaching; aspects of both her and her work have been pervading the cultural imagination since at least the mid-twentieth century. In avant-garde circles in Mexico City, Elena Poniatowska, Alejandro Jodorowsky, and Alan Glass were already recognising her hold over their creative imaginations. Then, in the 1980s, waves of appropriation art continued to shore up this notion of artistic and intellectual quotation. New media artist Lynn Hershman Leeson "became aware of [Carrington] in the early 1980s," and bought a small drawing by Carrington, *Woman on a Bicycle* (n.d.), which became something of a talisman for Hershman Leeson's creative thinking.[22] Sherrie Levine's readymade photograph *After Walker Evans* (1981) was perhaps one of the first to provide a next-generation, practice-based response to Carrington through reappropriating a photographic portrait by Walker Evans which Marcel Duchamp had used to represent Carrington in a surrealist exhibition (1942).[23] American novelist, Alyssa Harad, has also pointed out the "secretive" appeal Carrington held for creative women growing up in the 1990s, the scarcity of Carrington's publications and exhibition catalogues only heightening this sense of intrigue and cult value.[24] The Iranian-American novelist, Porochista Khakpour, seconds this view, explaining how women are "weirdly marginalized" in the contemporary literary scene for not writing realism, and that the existence of Carrington gives Khakpour licence to command her own selfhood among so many "normals."[25]

Secondly, I believe that a fuller, more practical historiography for the expansion of Leonora Carrington studies needs to be developed in order to appreciate the variety of cultural mechanisms and channels through which she has come to be known. This project is thus also a citational practice, at times densely but, given the extent of Carrington scholarship, necessarily so. As mentioned, I believe it is vital to more fully appreciate the creative potential of the scholarship, how theory and making inextricably inform one another (which is why an art historian and several curators have been interviewed for this project too).[26] The number of artists and creative writers who have looked to the scholarship for guidance on Carrington is telling in this respect. Aberth was already aware of Carrington's potential for appropriation as early as 2004: "In an ironic postmodern twist Carrington is being visually *sampled* by an audience who is still by and large unable to recognise her work."[27] Where previously Carrington was considered something of a cult figure, idolised in small, secret circles, over the last decade at least, there appears to have been an exponential increase in engagement with her and her work, leaving no doubt about her international cultural import.[28] Historiographical analysis is crucial as this provides key insights into the artist/writer's reception, and helps position our subject squarely within a revisionary context. This will be the task of Chapter 1, with necessary space to work through the multiple meanings of the term "medium." Beyond literal application (such as egg tempera paint), this book explores the poetics of medium, from Carrington's own interests in the occult to the idea of her and her work as conduits for contemporary makers, and as a timely model of eco-feminist thinking.

Thirdly, I believe the time has come to reinvestigate her legacy, to myth-bust some of the recurrent narratives around her. Striking though her personal mythology might be, the repetitions often amount to a sensationalism that has arguably obscured some of her more necessary contributions to the avant-garde as an intellectual in her own right. Clarissa Pinkola Estés has written of the wild-woman archetype which closely relates to Carrington's idea of the female-human-animal: "[s]he is an archivist of feminine intention. She preserves female tradition. Her whiskers sense the future."[29] The mythographer and long-term friend of the artist, Marina Warner, rightly claims that Carrington "has become a beacon for women artists and writers."[30] It is telling that the majority of respondents tend to be women from a variety of social, cultural, and ethnic backgrounds, suggesting Carrington could provide an intergenerational site of feminist cooperation. Yet Carrington's impact is not exclusive to women, nor should it be—writer China Miéville and curator Viktor Wynd indicate long-term interests in her work since they were teenagers. For composer Michael Begg, Carrington became the "subject" of his recent residency to Mexico, her paintings prompting his eerie and primordial soundscapes as well as reigniting his writing.[31] British-Nigerian artist Yinka Shonibare CBE (RA) initiated an Artist's Dining Room event in Carrington's honour hosted by Marina Warner (January 2018), while the South African-California-based artist, Simphiwe Ndzube, has made a vivid, assemblage painting, *As They Rode Along the Edge* (2020) (Figure 34), that borrows its title from one of Carrington's short stories and the compositional mechanics of Carrington's drawing, *I am an Amateur of Velocipedes* (1941) (Figure 35).[32] Meanwhile, Double Edge Theatre is refreshingly transparent about their land acknowledgement, the fact that they work on "the traditional homelands of the Nipmuc Nation and other Indigenous Peoples who have had a presence in western Massachusetts and travelled this land."[33] Such consciousness around diversity is apparent in Carrington's own *oeuvre*—think of her double Eve, a representation of a black woman and a white woman sharing the apple of knowledge in her famous poster, *Mujeres conciencia* (*Women's Awareness*, 1972) (Figure 2), or the person of colour at the cauldron in *The House Opposite* (1945) (Figure 8) as evidence of inclusivity. Moreover, I believe there is a decolonising agenda to be found within Carrington's ethos. While some Carrington respondents come from non-white, Latin American, and East Asian heritages, the present study is largely, but not exclusively, an Anglophone, northern hemisphere study. Yet, as I will show, Carrington and her artworks appeal to a broad range of contemporary and often explicitly feminist discourses and reassessments because they act as a force of disruption with which to question political realities.

The present book takes as its focus the very revisionary positions and marvellous practices of those that respond to Carrington. I would even go as far as proposing that it is Carrington, and not one of the central players like André Breton or Max Ernst, who is chief in keeping the surrealist message relevant today, by providing a younger generation of makers and thinkers with a strategy to unhinge and dislodge previously unchallenged discursive patterns and frameworks. With the exception of Carrington's contemporary, Frida Kahlo, whose work has been discussed at length in terms of its (mis) appropriation and adaptation, few feminist-surrealists have received such a following and as many creative tributes as Leonora Carrington.[34] Much of this may be understood as "quotations without inverted commas," an elusive notion promulgated by Roland Barthes.[35] The vast majority of responses are intertextual, implicit rather than explicit, active (nay, activist) rather than passive. Reflecting on existing tendencies in the scholarship to date, the artist's son, Gabriel Weisz Carrington, has been prompted to "wonder when

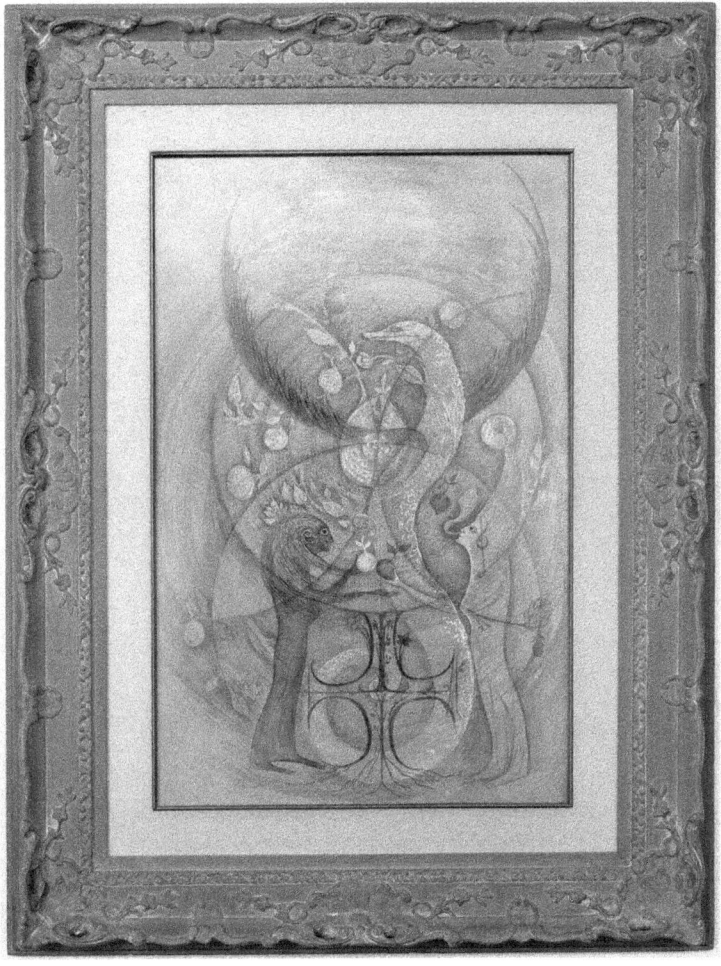

2 Leonora Carrington, *Mujeres conciencia* (*Women's Awareness*), 1972

will the moment come when her art will be the most important feature."[36] This book proposes that this moment is now.

Against influence

This is not a book about influence or imitation. Rather, it is a study of critically invested appropriations. Words like "influence" are highly suspicious in considerations of a cultural bricoleur like Carrington.[37] This was true too for her contemporary, Tanning: "Never underestimate this word [influence]. It is everywhere, favorite nib of the poverty-stricken pen."[38] As Caroline I. Harris rightly tells us: "influence rarely functions in the way art historians might want: as active transmission and passive acceptances. Rather hers is an oblique resonance."[39] There are two predominant trends: one being literal quotation at the level of iconographical re-creation (often best demonstrated through comparative image pairings); and two, a more conceptual and displaced re-embodiment of her core principles without any morphological equivalence or likeness (a body of work which comprises Carrington as a theoretical framework). Yet, the ongoing reality of responses to our primary subject shows that such trends sometimes overlap, and this study will offer a reconsideration of the political nuances and activism of such legacies and creative reincarnations. Joanna Moorhead notes in her biography of her cousin: "she has a band of very dedicated followers: once people fall for her, they are usually smitten."[40] "Smitten" is a gentle way of putting it; *possession* might be more accurate an assessment of the current situation. Many (myself included) would wholeheartedly confess to falling prey to the "fandom" associated with this subject, what Catherine Grant and Kate Random Love have recently explored as a "model for subjective and emotionally driven engagement."[41] Some of the artists/writers interviewed for this book were quick to remind me that they are "creative enthusiasts" rather than scholars of Carrington, yet again the two tendencies often align.[42] In his Oedipal study, *The Anxiety of Influence*, Harold Bloom emphasises that when one "falls in love" with the work of an artist or writer, they are automatically inclined towards bias or what he calls "poetic misinterpretation."[43] Any appropriation or idolisation of a precursor on a later artist or writer's part is, therefore, always already a creative interpretation or what Mieke Bal might term a "wilful misreading."[44] Such quotations are not to be confused with mere influence or likenesses, and the examples I have selected for this study make a concentrated effort to move beyond this by engaging more critically with Carrington. To be "under the influence" is to be intoxicated and under someone else's spell. While Carrington's enchantment and hold over the creative imagination is no doubt true to some extent, my examples retain a sense of active agency in order to query, as well as celebrate, Carrington's cult status beyond the biographical. Writing on Joseph Beuys in "The Twilight of the Idol," Benjamin Buchloh laments that "the cult and the myth seem to have become inseparable from the work."[45] However, reflecting on the achievements of feminist art history, Griselda Pollock recently claimed:

> Once I disowned the bourgeois myths of great artists and a mythic idea of personal creativity—you may recognise my perpetual war against the mythic Van Gogh and other idealised and thus betrayed white artist-men—I learned to see the world with and through art made across of multitude of situations, perspectives, bodies, minds, agonies and desires.[46]

By de-centring the artist, such "agonies and desires" will be brought to the fore here too. To use Angela Carter's term, this study attempts to "demythologise" Carrington, to dismantle those perpetual myths ultimately found to be unhelpful or restrictive to the feminist project (e.g. passive influence, romanticised biography), while demonstrating Carrington's re-embodiment through remaking and re-presenting, i.e. how a subsequent generation of artists, writers, makers, and thinkers have practically applied her principles.[47]

The practices to be explored here channel irrationality in a nuanced and self-critical mode. They become *active* embodiments—the next-generation maker is acting *on her* rather than merely following a model of passive reception. For instance, the media in which such quotations are made often present starkly different outcomes from the detailed visual narratives and aesthetic excesses found in her own art and writings. As artist and filmmaker, Aleksandra Niemczyk tells us, in working on *The Siren's Scream* (2021): "I didn't want to be literal and adapt the images as they are, but rather research ... as a whole and let it become an inspiration for the film I was creating."[48] Our subject has rather become a dialogic and marvellous *medium* to be worked in and through. This is consistent with Michael Baxandall's suggestion:

> "Influence" is a curse of art criticism primarily because of its wrong-headed grammatical prejudice about who is the agent and who the patient; it seems to reverse the active/passive relation ... If one says that X influenced Y it does seem that one is saying that X did something to Y rather than that Y did something to X. But in the consideration of good pictures and painters the second is always the more lively reality.[49]

Today, the artist's afterlife has been extended through her continued existence in the practices of contemporary artists and writers whose multiple perspectives enable an unmooring of fixed meanings, whilst presenting a strong case for her and her work as a force field in contemporary art, literature, and performance.

Previously I attempted to put Carrington's name in quotation marks and even tried to "channel" her, firstly through a séance-like exhibition (2016), and secondly by offering to speak on first-name terms (2017). Yet, these early experiments did not always achieve the effects I sought. Omitting her name altogether as a mini-"death of the author" ultimately became too mannered as a critical gesture and risked erasing her still further. Rather, a more slanted, detached view on our elusive subject has become necessary, what Katharine Conley has explored in other areas of surrealism as a ghostly anamorphosis ("'form,' *morph*, seen 'backward'"), and what Lucy Skaer has explored in practical terms as a mode of critical displacement.[50] More broadly, Mieke Bal's "preposterous" activity of "beckoning" or "quoting" history in the present moment provides a necessary model for millennial purposes.[51] Far from historicising Carrington (a tendency no doubt due to her association with the historical surrealist movement), such an approach seeks to further embed her in the contemporary, what Bal emphasises as "con"-current and "tem"-poral.[52] The term "the contemporary arts" is surely questionable in the early twenty-first century—here I use it broadly to refer to a set of post-surrealist, conceptual, and performative strategies that often involve interdisciplinary forays into literature and the curatorial. The related term "practice" recurs throughout this book, for the contemporary arts might be best characterised, not only by regular rehearsal or routine aesthetic commitment, but by the shift in emphasis from material end-product to *process* which occurred during the second half of the twentieth century and has been maintained in studio pedagogy and beyond. This approach has the benefit of disciplining a focus on how others have responded to and worked within Carrington's legacies. Such a critical experiment seeks to dislodge our reliance on teleology and test the strength of the legacies themselves, a mode of recalibration which places the emphasis on the inheritors and semantics of the resulting artworks. If nothing else, it encourages a more innovative pattern with which to write into and through.

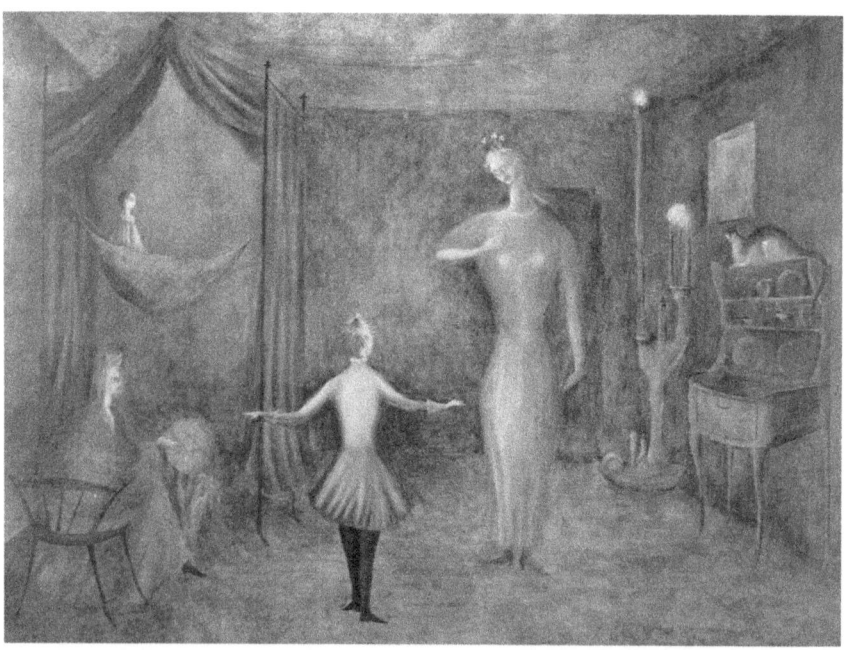

3 Leonora Carrington, *Night Nursery Everything*, 1947

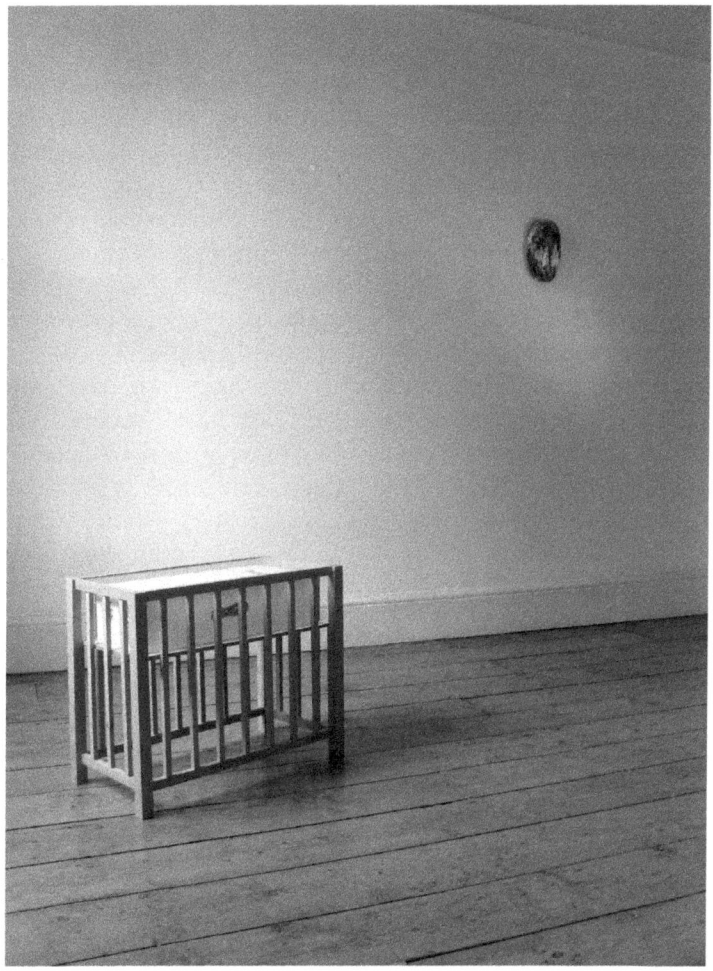

4 Kim L. Pace and Sarah Woodfine, *Mercurious*, 2019. Installation shot featuring (*left*) Sarah Woodfine, *Boy*, 2008; (*right*) Kim L. Pace, *Moth*, 2019

This book attempts comprehension of our subject through practice while aware that such a study will always already remain incomplete. What has become apparent to me is that any attempt to comprehensively map this trajectory will inevitably fall short because, even as I write, new responses to Carrington's work are ever emerging, in the process of being commissioned, and rapidly coming to the fore. Carrington's legacy is thus in a state of perpetual becoming.[53] Moreover, her hauntings are no longer limited to explicit examples alone. Indeed, I have begun to notice hints of Carrington's force in unexpected places—experiences which seem very in keeping with the surrealist notion of the marvellous. For instance, the conceptual design of *Pan's Labyrinth* (2006) by Mexican director Guillermo del Toro is highly reminiscent of characters and *mises-en-scène* from Carrington's paintings, most especially her goat/lion homunculus from *Who Art Thou White Face?* (1959). The overarching theme of the feminine against fascism concerns both Carrington and del Toro, and his child-eater character seems to have crept straight out of one of her pictures. In the realm of contemporary art, one carefully curated corner of a two person-show, *Mercurious* (2019), by Kim L. Pace and Sarah Woodfine, conjured Carrington's *Night Nursery Everything* (1947) (Figure 3) within a Georgian townhouse gallery. A cradle containing a rectangular lozenge with the paws of a wolf-child was positioned exquisitely under the watchful eye of a bark-like moon-mask ceramic entitled *Moth* (2019) (Figure 4). The spare but precise effect was that of a Carrington composition reinterpreted; a microcosmic response to Carrington's night-nursery lullaby pictures by two artists who are women. In another corner of the same show, Pace extended the canine imagery—a ceramic canopic jar with the head of an Anubis-like figure, a favourite Egyptian god of Carrington. Such imagery recurs in *Untitled* (2021), by Rachel Goodyear, a monumental yet meticulous drawing of a hyena on top of an antique desk. Goodyear reflects: "The hyena has not made an appearance in my works for many years though has always maintained a presence in my mind, and most often with a tentative homage to Leonora Carrington."[54] Carringtonian tableaux have occurred to me elsewhere, too—I couldn't help but feel her presence in the séance-like installation of Guðbjörg Lind Jónsdóttir's house in remote Thingeyri, Iceland, where a typewriter sat centre stage in Jónsdóttir's elegantly arranged, domestic environment, ready to receive the wishes of the beholder, which were then burned ritualistically in a nearby stove. Such ephemeral sightings or outright hauntings have become inevitable given the intertextual nature of this research, marvellous encounters amalgamated into the very fabric of reality.

The following chapters will take a necessarily selective focus, with close study of the mid-career, creative practices of Tilda Swinton, Lucy Skaer, Chloe Aridjis, and Heidi Sopinka, Lynn Lu and Samantha Sweeting, and Stacy Klein of Double Edge Theatre, those that have made work through the legacies of Carrington on more than one occasion. The chapters are arranged thematically through a range of different activisms, from eco-criticism to subjective identity politics, and through a series of unfolding notions: "maybe-ness" and narrative extravagance, esoteric conceptualism, creative solitude and hibernation, menageries, and, finally, edgework. Chapters 2 and 3 reposition Carrington's hold on the conceptual dimension of contemporary art, while Chapters 4 and 5 broadly consider the impact of the animal in her work. Chapter 6 then cycles back to the performative domain through a focus on sustainable theatre-making and eco-farming. As I will show, my selected creative women (Swinton, Skaer, Sopinka, Aridjis, Sweeting, Lu, and Klein) have much to say on the nature of contemporary culture and its recycling of avant-garde precedents. Finally, the Afterword considers individual exemplars, including responses to Carrington by those whom I consider feminist-men.

Carrington has long been associated with transgressive art-making, and it is striking how historical surrealist artworks by women in the 1930s and 1940s have become topical and instructive in the age of #MeToo (founded by American activist, Tarana Burke) and other campaigns of empowerment for marginalised voices, such as Writers Rebel (co-founded by Chloe Aridjis).[55] In 2007, Natalya Lusty was already aware that the literature of Carrington and photography of Claude Cahun "raise questions that although once considered more marginal to modernism are now at the center of contemporary theoretical debate and discussion."[56] Curators of *Leonora Carrington: Magical Tales* (2018) framed the exhibition similarly, with "themes which are opportune today like feminism and ecology."[57] In the catalogue, Aberth further emphasises the importance of this cause to Carrington: "During the last decades of her life in particular, it was the plight of animals in our increasingly fragile world ecosystems that consistently aroused her political outrage."[58] During the 1980s, the poet and animal rights activist, Homero Aridjis, involved Carrington in the environmentalism of the Group of 100, explaining that in Mexico: "writers and public figure whose opinions are respected … are expected to play an active part in the country's affairs, championing human rights and the environment, advocating social justice, and fighting corruption, whether through literature or through their actions."[59] Many of Carrington's own position statements in earlier pieces such as 'Female Human Animal' (1970) shore up her later involvement as a signatory of the Group of 100 (1985). From the very beginning of her career, Carrington was political, such as her early, rebellious reading of Aldous Huxley at Ascot or her debutante character's absenteeism and solitary absorption in Jonathan Swift's *Gulliver's Travels* (1726) instead of the social chore of attending her coming-out ball.[60] Increasingly, her feminist intertextuality appears to have turned "green," such as her aforementioned poster, *Mujeres conciencia*.[61] Boas rightly unpacks Françoise d'Eaubonne's 1974 term "eco-feminism" for Carrington studies, suggesting that "environmental intersectionality" might be a more accurate term for subsequent generations.[62]

My suggestion here is that, when it comes to Carrington, her feminism and eco-criticism are always intertextual, or, in other words, intertextuality is always political.[63] Mikhail Bakhtin's carnivalesque notion of the "dialogic imagination" was elucidated as *intertextualité* by Julia Kristeva in an essay of 1966, "Word, Dialogue, Novel," in which she claimed that "Writer as well as scholar, Bakhtin was one of the first to replace the static hewing out of texts with a model where literary structure does not simply exist but is generated in relation to another structure."[64] Kristeva's French feminist politics are noteworthy here too. The theory of intertextuality can be understood as a mid-twentieth century discursive phenomenon which had much in common with surrealism—uncanny projects of *déjà vu*—that also roughly correlates with the historiography of Carrington.[65] Anna Watz's research is particularly illuminating on such matters, demonstrating the importance of "an often overlooked intellectual historiography between women surrealists and the later feminist poststructuralist critiques," and reminding us that Carrington's lifespan overlapped with second-wave feminist theory, especially during the 1970s.[66] For example, Hélène Cixous's well-known manifesto (1975) sought to demythologise surrealism's beloved Freud, particularly his castration complex, by revising the figure of the beautiful, laughing Medusa.[67] Cixous's manifesto had much in turn to offer avant-garde theorist Susan Rubin Suleiman's notion of "feminist intertextuality" which used Carrington's novel *The Hearing Trumpet* (1974) as one of its chief examples, focusing on the playful figure of the mother in avant-garde literature.[68] In doing so, Suleiman insists on an intertextuality which is both gender-political and pleasurable. One might wonder if intertextual studies are still relevant given the three decades that have elapsed since Suleiman's writing?[69] Over the last decade, Mieke Bal and Michelle Williams Gamaker have started to integrate an activist approach into their own "theoretical fictions," suggesting the political dimension and purpose of intertextual studies has accelerated to another level, becoming more relevant and more widely dispersed than ever.[70] A feminist-surrealist revision of the movement is now reoccurring in earnest, building on the achievements of Gloria Orenstein and Whitney Chadwick, among others, during the 1970s and 1980s.[71] "Feminist-surrealism" is a term used in Watz's study of Carter's writing within the context of revisionist surrealism.[72] Watz's use of the term is situated within Suleiman's notion of a "double allegiance," a simultaneous acknowledgement and critique of historical surrealist formats and techniques.[73] One might compare the sizeable increase in scholarly attention that was devoted posthumously to Carter in the mid-1990s to the abundance of new critical attention currently being lavished on Carrington in the mid-2010s and early 2020s.[74] It is exhilarating for my generation to witness this groundswell of topicality and the extent to which Carrington's perpetual themes dominate the currency of feminist-surrealist artmaking. Her iconography has become a necessary blueprint.

Much of our existing understanding of "Leonora Carrington" owes no small part to this revisionist feminist context. Marina Warner's introductions and Angela Carter's anthologising of Carrington's short stories during the 1980s through Virago, the feminist publishing house, have been crucial to this revival of interest. Carter's *Wayward Girls and Wicked Women* (1986) recognised Carrington's "The Debutante" (1937) within Carter's own idiosyncratic mode of feminist literature, while Warner shrewdly describes Carrington's tale-telling as "a kind of black mischief Cinderella."[75] The more recent reissues of Carrington's short stories by The Dorothy Project and The Silver Press over Carrington's centenary in 2017 are testimony to a growing market of interest, and it is no doubt that these publications have significantly enabled and extended the readership. Such circulation and attention have undeniably contributed to the recent explosion in the scholarly domain, a new generation interested in the lessons of revisionary feminism and a necessary framework and language through which to vindicate such aesthetic "mischief" and "wayward" approaches. As feminist art historian, Amelia Jones, has pointed out, we have reached a point historically where many of the next generation of feminists are now "in positions to do something about [canonical oversights] on an institutional level."[76]

For intellectualism

You are trying to intellectualise something desperately and you are wasting your time!

—Leonora Carrington (2006)[77]

This book works against the grain of anti-intellectualism which has become a deeply worrying trend, especially in recent years with the onslaught of populism and neo-liberalism. One of the more concerning tendencies in this context is the recurrent suggestion that Carrington was too much of an outsider, rebel, and eccentric, and should therefore be excused from subsequent intellectualisation or academicisation by others.[78] While such a suggestion may be well-meaning in terms of respecting Carrington's own viewpoint and authenticity, I find this too limiting, constricting, and inaccurate an argument given the multitude of feminist possibilities that her work is now engendering. Moreover, this view denies the intellectual avant-garde context she was working in and through. As Eburne concurs, Carrington's "position is anything but anti-intellectual. Carrington's artworks demand participation."[79] We cannot deny her a dialogic afterlife. Even more troubling is the insidious, unconscious bias that perpetuates around her gender. While Pinkola Estés rightly warns against the patriarchal nature of the academy, suggesting that "over intellectualisation obscures the patterns of the Wild Woman and the instinctual nature of women," it is equally problematic to deny women such as Carrington the right to intellectual championing.[80] Certainly, we should remain alert to the institutionalisation and commercialisation of feminism—tendencies our subject sought to disrupt.[81]

The idea that Carrington and her work should not be intellectualised because she herself resisted explanation is, therefore, problematic for several reasons. Following Bal, I agree that the artist is not always master of their own house, certainly not always in control of interpretations of their artwork.[82] That refusal and denial was a common encounter for those who met Carrington only strengthens her appeal and exacerbates curiosity. Her self-cancelling can be seen as a dogged strategy of elusion and continues Pollock and Carter's de-romanticising of the artist which, again, I feel is vital to put into practice and commit to here. I would like to use this book to demonstrate that our subject was in fact a profoundly prophetic, political guide who insists that the viewer do some legwork and make up their own mind about how to interpret her, what to take from their encounter, and how to be haunted by her. Thus, her self-cancelling should not be misread as modesty but reinterpreted as an assertive gesture of empowerment. I therefore strive unapologetically to reposition her and her work within a range of theoretical encounters. I maintain that one reason why she, of all the surrealist-related artists, is proving so productive as a source text today is that subsequent generations, especially younger women and those who identify as queer and gender non-binary, have been enabled through her as an epistemological force, and as an embodiment of intellectual history.

Notes

During the worldwide Covid-19 pandemic, The Getty Museum Challenge invited domestic re-creations of famous artworks. A number of examples featured artworks by Leonora Carrington, such as *The Inn of the Dawn Horse* (1937), *Portrait of the Late Mrs Partridge* (1947), and *The Ancestor* (1968). While this study focuses on professional practice, it is noteworthy that Carrington's rich iconography was reimagined as a source of homespun comfort. The Dream App (2021) can be used in interesting ways to generate artificial, Carrington-like fantasy imagery drawn from digital details of her visual *œuvre* (grateful thanks to Ashley Good). Hashtags #LeonoraCarrington and #LeonoraCarringtonChallenge are useful in locating numerous tributes and pedagogical briefs, such as animated gifs of her artworks by Maizz Visual (2013; 2018): https://en.maizz.mx/leonoras-dream-gif-collection (Accessed 8 August 2020).

1 Susan Rubin Suleiman, *Subversive Intent: Gender, Politics, and the Avant-Garde* (Cambridge, MA and London: Harvard University Press, 1990), 171.
2 This marvellous occurrence is not unique. Dawn Adès reports a peculiar experience of hanging a picture on the day of Carrington's death, 'Testimonial,' *Leonora Carrington: Magical Tales*, eds T. Arcq and S. van Raay (Mexico City: Instituto Nacional de Bellas Artes, 2018), 446.
3 Roland Barthes, 'Death of the Author,' *Image, Music, Text*, trans. Stephen Heath (London: Fontana, 1977), 142–148.

4 Writing on this public sculpture, Porochista Khakpour wisely notes: "[s]omehow only in the casual chaos of Mexico City could Carrington look so incredibly ordinary," 'Surreal Talk: The Otherworldly, Magical Writing of Leonora Carrington,' *Book Forum* (2017): www.bookforum.com/print/2403/the-otherworldly-magical-writing-of-leonora-carrington-18463 (Accessed 23 April 2021).

5 Elizabeth Coonrod Martínez, 'Introduction,' *Lilus Kikus and Other Stories by Elena Poniatowska* (Albuquerque: University of New Mexico Press, 2005), 27; Lorna Scott Fox, 'Swimming Under Cemeteries,' *Times Literary Supplement* (May 2017): www.the-tls.co.uk/articles/public/leonora-carrington (Accessed 6 April 2021).

6 For example, Carrington's etching for *VVV Portfolio* was made at Atelier 17 (1942), and Susan L. Aberth tells us Carrington collaborated with Ricardo Rosales's family weavers on her tapestries (1948–58), 'Animal Kingdom,' *Leonora Carrington: Magical Tales*, eds T. Arcq and S. van Raay (Mexico City: Instituto Nacional de Bellas Artes, 2018), 259.

7 Lucy Skaer, 'The Transcendence of the Image,' *Tate Etc.* (September 2008): www.tate.org.uk/tate-etc/issue-14-autumn-2008/transcendence-image (Accessed 11 March 2020). Isla Leaver-Yap, 'Lucy Skaer: Drawing Close.' *Map Magazine*, 10 (June 2007): https://mapmagazine.co.uk/lucy-skaer-drawing-close (Accessed 21 May 2020).

8 Ali Smith, *Artful* (London: Penguin, 2012), 111. Like Carrington, Smith has a long history of using her own literary profile to promote environmental activism, serving as an important signatory for the Group of 100 and more recently offering a reading for Writers Rebel (2019), part of the Extinction Rebellion movement.

9 Interview with Heidi Sopinka. This is further borne out in Sopinka's novel when the Carrington character points out: "she mistakes me for wise and maternal. The truth is I'm neither of these things," *The Dictionary of Animal Languages* (London: Scribe, 2018), 120.

10 Silvia Cherem, 'Eternally Married to the Wind: Interview with Leonora Carrington,' *Leonora Carrington, What She Might Be*, ed. Salomon Grimberg (Dallas, TX: Dallas Museum of Art, 2008), 17.

11 Grateful thanks to Susan L. Aberth, who has also explained to me the crucial role that French-Canadian artist, Alan Glass, played in Carrington's acceptance of Aberth.

12 Susan L. Aberth, *Women and Magic: Hidden Territories of Women's Creative Process* (Ashfield, MA: Double Edge Theatre, 2019): https://vimeo.com/330893013 (Accessed 7 September 2019).

13 Heidi Sopinka et al., 'Resurrecting Leonora Carrington's World,' *Lenny Letter* (18 September 2018): www.lennyletter.com/story/resurrecting-leonora-carringtons-world (Accessed 25 October 2019).

14 Interview with Sopinka.

15 Maximilíano Durón, 'Paying Tribute to Leonora Carrington, 2022 Venice Biennale Takes the Title "The Milk of Dreams,"' *Art News* (9 June 2021): www.artnews.com/art-news/news/venice-biennale-2022-title-1234595242 (Accessed 29 June 2021). Via Lauren Elkin @lauren_elkin_ (9 June 2021). The

Venice Biennale poster features a painting by Chilean poet Cecilia Vicuña (1977). The flurries of press attention around this have led some journalists to ask similar questions to those in this present study, for example, Kate Dwyer, 'Why Leonora Carrington's Work Feels So of the Moment,' *W Magazine* (4 February 2022): www.wmagazine.com/culture/leonora-carrington-venice-biennale-books-history (Accessed 14 February 2022).

16 Daniel Weisz @leonoracarringtonestate (Accessed 5 February 2022).

17 Natasha Boas, 'Projects and Projections: The Leonora Carrington Effect,' *The Story of the Last Egg* (New York and San Francisco, CA: Gallery Wendi Norris, 2019), 79.

18 Michaela Carter, 'In Conversation with Wendi Norris' (6 April 2021).

19 Linda Hutcheon, *A Theory of Adaptation* (New York: Routledge, 2013), 84.

20 Mieke Bal, 'Dispersing the Image,' *Looking In, The Art of Viewing: Mieke Bal: Essays and Afterword*, ed. Norman Bryson (Amsterdam: G+B Arts International, Gordon & Breach, 2001), 68–69; see also Mieke Bal, *Quoting Caravaggio: Contemporary Art, Preposterous History* (Chicago, MI and London: University of Chicago Press, 1999), 8–9.

21 That said, Mieke Bal rightly reminds us that criticism can only ever function as a "supplement" to the artwork, *Louise Bourgeois' Spider: The Architecture of Art Writing* (Chicago, MI and London: University of Chicago Press, 2001), xii.

22 Interview with Lynn Hershman Leeson.

23 David Hopkins, 'The Politics of Equivocation: Sherrie Levine, Duchamp's "Compensation Portrait," and Surrealism in the USA 1942–45,' *Oxford Art Journal*, 26:1 (2003), 67.

24 Alyssa Harad, 'Author Panel on Leonora Carrington's *The Hearing Trumpet*: Alyssa Harad, Porochista Khakpour, Maria Dahvana Headley, Amber Sparks, and Taisia Kitaiskaia,' *Book People Events* (7 April 2021).

25 Porochista Khakpour, 'Author Panel' (2021).

26 Grateful thanks to Anna Watz, whose research demonstrates very clearly the intersection between critical, scholarly writing and surrealist creative practice, particularly in a feminist context, '"A Language Buried at the Back of Time": *The Stone Door* and Poststructuralist Feminism,' *Leonora Carrington and the International Avant-Garde*, eds J. Eburne and C. McAra (Manchester: Manchester University Press, 2017), 91–92.

27 Susan L. Aberth, *Leonora Carrington: Surrealism, Alchemy and Art* (Aldershot: Lund Humphries, 2004), 8.

28 Jonathan P. Eburne and I suggest that "Carrington's work has found such generative purchase in the artistic, literary and intellectual movements to which she contributed throughout her long career," and we were eager to emphasise how her association with a historical avant-garde informs the next generations and contemporary reinterpretations, *Leonora Carrington and the International Avant-Garde*, 4.

29 Clarissa Pinkola Estés, *Women Who Run with the Wolves* (London: Random House, 1992), 29.

30 Marina Warner, 'Leonora's Storytelling Imagination,' *Leonora Carrington: Magical Tales*, 315. On proof copies of Heidi Sopinka's novel, the "Selling Points" highlight that Carrington's "centenary has created a resurgence of interest in this leading female surrealist artist and writer" (London: Scribe, 2017), backmatter.

31 See interviews in Appendix.

32 Simphiwe Ndzube @simphiwe_ndzube (18 November 2020).

33 Stacy Klein email signature (April 2021).

34 See Yasumasa Morimura's performative photographs, *An Inner Dialogue with Frida Kahlo* (2001); and Margaret A. Lindauer, *Devouring Frida: Art History and Popular Celebrity of Frida Kahlo* (Middletown, CT: Wesleyan University Press, 1999), 173. See also Merve Emre, 'How Leonora Carrington Feminized Surrealism', *New Yorker* (21 December 2020): www.newyorker.com/magazine/2020/12/28/how-leonora-carrington-feminized-surrealism (Accessed 29 December 2020).

35 Roland Barthes, 'From Work to Text,' *Image, Music, Text*, trans. Stephen Heath (London: Fontana, 1977), 160.

36 Gabriel Weisz Carrington, 'A Celtic Window,' *Leonora Carrington* (Dublin: Irish Museum of Modern Art, 2013), 13.

37 Gabriel Weisz Carrington rightly complains about the emphasis critics place on his mother's influence: "could we call [influence] a bitch—or a dog—or a monkey?" 'In Conversation with Gabriel Weisz Carrington,' *Leonora Carrington: Living Legacies*, eds A. Cox et al. (Wilmington, DE: Vernon Press, 2020), 210.

38 Dorothea Tanning, *Between Lives: An Artist and Her World* (London and New York: W.W. Norton, 2001), 280.

39 Caroline I. Harris, 'Review: Leonora Carrington and the International Avant-Garde,' *Woman's Art Journal*, Spring/Summer (2019), 57.

40 Joanna Moorhead, *The Surreal Life of Leonora Carrington* (London: Virago, 2017), 266.

41 Catherine Grant and Kate Random Love, *Fandom as Methodology: A Sourcebook for Artists and Writers* (London: Goldsmiths Press, 2019), 3.

42 Grateful thanks to W. N. Herbert for this term.

43 Harold Bloom, *The Anxiety of Influence* (Oxford: Oxford University Press, 1997), xxiii.

44 Bal, *Louise Bourgeois' Spider*, 7.

45 Benjamin H. D. Buchloh, 'Beuys: The Twilight of the Idol,' *Neo-Avantgarde and Culture Industry: Essays on European and American Art from 1955 to 1975* (Cambridge, MA: MIT Press, 2000), 45.

46 Griselda Pollock, 'Professor Griselda Pollock: Graduation Speech' (London: Courtauld Institute of Art, 2019): https://courtauld.ac.uk/professor-griselda-pollock-graduation-speech-2019 (Accessed 25 October 2019).

47 Angela Carter, 'Notes From the Front Line,' *Shaking a Leg: Collected Journalism and Writings*, ed. Jenny Uglow (London: Penguin, 1997), 38.

48 Interview with Aleksandra Niemczyk.

49 Michael Baxandall, *Patterns of Intention: On the Historical Explanation of Pictures* (New Haven, CT: Yale University Press, 1985), 58–59.

50   Katharine Conley, *Surrealist Ghostliness* (Lincoln and London: University of Nebraska Press, 2013); 14; Lucy Skaer in *Lucy Skaer*, DVD (Edinburgh: Fruitmarket Gallery, 2008).

51   Mieke Bal analyses this dynamic of "active reworking" in *Quoting Caravaggio: Contemporary Art, Preposterous History* (London and Chicago, MI: University of Chicago Press, 1999), 1.

52   Mieke Bal, *Don Quijote: Sad Countenances* (Växjö: Trolltrumma, 2019), 6.

53   The notion of "becoming" has been widely applied, especially in gender theory, since Simone de Beauvoir's *The Second Sex* (1949), ed. and trans. H. M. Parshley (London: Vintage, 1997), 295.

54   Rachel Goodyear @rachel_goodyear (7 June 2021).

55   Josh Appignanesi cited in Jennifer Higgie,'How *Female Human Animal* Blends Documentary with Fiction,' *Frieze* (2018): https://frieze.com/article/how-female-human-animal-blends-documentary-fiction (Accessed 8 June 2020). Selena Chambers describes Carrington's art as a "survival kit," 'The Hyena's Escape Plan: Leonora Carrington's Advice on Surviving Brexit,' *The Debutante*, 1 (2020), 4.

56   Natalya Lusty, *Surrealism, Feminism, Psychoanalysis* (Aldershot: Ashgate, 2007), 10.

57   Tere Arcq and Stefan van Raay (eds), *Leonora Carrington: Magical Tales* (Mexico City: Museo de Arte Moderno, 2018).

58   Aberth, 'Animal Kingdom,' 245.

59   Homero Aridjis, *News of the Earth*, ed. and trans. Betty Ferber (Simsbury, CT: Mandel Vilar Press, 2017), 3.

60   According to Marina Warner, Carrington read Aldous Huxley's *Eyeless in Gaza* (1936) at Ascot. Warner cites Carrington in interview with Paul de Angelis (1991), 'Introduction,' *The House of Fear: Notes From Down Below* (London: Virago, 1989), 4; Marina Warner, 'Introduction,' *The Seventh Horse and Other Tales* (London: Virago, 1989), x; Aberth, *Leonora Carrington: Surrealism, Alchemy and Art*, 14–15, 79; Lusty, *Surrealism, Feminism, Psychoanalysis*, 28.

61   Jonathan P. Eburne and Catriona McAra, 'Mujeres conciencia (Women's Awareness): Leonora Carrington's Agit-prop,' *Manchester University Press Blog* (July 2019): https://manchesteruniversitypress.co.uk/articles/mujeres-conciencia-womens-awareness-leonora-carringtons-agit-prop-by-catriona-mcara-and-jonathan-p-eburne (Accessed 23 November 2020). See also Andrew Patrizio's recent call for "a dark green art history," *The Ecological Eye: Assembling an Ecocritical Art History* (Manchester: Manchester University Press, 2019), 7.

62   Natasha Boas, 'The Leonora Carrington Effect: What We Can Learn From Carrington Today,' *The Life and Influence of Leonora Carrington: A Symposium* (New York: Gallery Wendi Norris, 2019): https://vimeo.com/364355299 (Accessed 9 July 2020); "Intersectional environmentalism" has found currency via Leah Thomas @greengirlleah 28 May 2020; "Intersectionality" itself was coined by Kimberlé Williams Crenshaw, 'Demarginalizing the Intersection of Race and Sex: A Black Feminist Critique of Antidiscrimination Doctrine, Feminist Theory and Antiracist Politics,' *University of Chicago Legal Forum*, 1989:8 (1989): https://chicagounbound.uchicago.edu/uclf/vol1989/iss1/8 (Accessed 23 June 2021).

63 Intertextual theory is a form of literary analysis often assigned to the Russian theorist Mikhail Bakhtin, for whom the notion of "dialogue" was key. Bakhtin used this to argue for an inter-subjectivity, intrinsic to the inner workings of language as a system of semantic production. Michael Holquist terms Bakhtin's intellectual project "dialogism" and claims dialogue to be the "master key" to his whole endeavour, *Dialogism: Bakhtin and His World* (London and New York: Routledge, 1990), 15.

64 Julia Kristeva, 'Word, Dialogue, Novel,' *Desire in Language: A Semiotic Approach to Literature and Art*, trans. Leon S. Roudiez (New York: Columbia University Press, 1982), 64.

65 Hal Foster, *Compulsive Beauty* (Cambridge, MA: MIT Press, 1995) 7–8; 36.

66 Watz, '"A Language Buried at the Back of Time,"' 91–92.

67 Hélène Cixous, 'The Laugh of the Medusa,' *Signs*, 1:4 (1976): 875–893.

68 Suleiman, *Subversive Intent*, 173; 142; Cixous, 'The Laugh of the Medusa,' 885.

69 In June 2018, I asked Suleiman about her current thinking on Carrington's next-generation responses during a keynote address at the University of Cambridge. Suleiman said that, although she had not followed the recent responses, she had stayed in touch with the artist until her death in 2011.

70 Mieke Bal and Michelle Williams Gamaker, 'Mrs B: The film analysis of a novel,' *Flaubert [Online], Translations/ Adaptations* (2012), http://flaubert.revues.org/1837 (Accessed 2 November 2019).

71 Patricia Allmer, 'Feminist Interventions: Revising the Canon,' *A Companion to Dada and Surrealism*, ed. David Hopkins (Chichester: Wiley Blackwell, 2016), 366–381. See also, Gloria Orenstein, 'Art History and the Case for the Women of Surrealism,' *Journal of General Education* 27:1 (Spring 1975): 31–54; and Whitney Chadwick, *Women Artists and the Surrealist Movement* (London: Thames & Hudson, 1985).

72 For more on "feminist-surrealism," see Anna Watz, *Angela Carter and Surrealism: 'A Feminist Libertarian Aesthetic'* (New York: Routledge, 2017), 4; 163. The term has also become the political masthead for *The Debutante*, eds Rachel Ashenden and Molly Gilroy (January 2020). Thanks to Penny Slinger for explaining her use of the term, which she has been using to define her practice since participating in Patricia Allmer's *Angels of Anarchy* (2009).

73 Suleiman, *Subversive Intent*, 162.

74 Stephen Benson, 'Angela Carter and the Literary Märchen,' *Angela Carter and the Fairy Tale*, Danielle M. Roemer and Cristina Bacchilega (eds) (Detroit, MI: Wayne State University Press, 2001), 30. There have been a steady increase of women working on doctoral dissertations about Carrington, including Rachael Grew (University of Glasgow, 2010), Alessia Zinnari (University of Glasgow, 2020), and Tifaine Bachet (Tours, 2016), as well as long established examples including Janice Helland (University of Victoria, 1984), Julia Salmerón Cabañas (University of Hull, 1997), and Susan L. Aberth (City University of New York, 2003), among others. Karissa Adams (2021) and Elizabeth Hobbs (2022) won prizes on Carrington.

75 Marina Warner, 'Back from Below,' *The Independent* (22 July 1989), 42. Carter and Carrington were brought together in an exhibition curated by Marie Mulvey-Roberts and Fiona Robinson, *Strange Worlds: The Vision of Angela Carter* (Bristol: Samson, 2016) where three works by Carrington appeared in the historical section.
76 Amelia Jones, 'The Return of Feminism(s) and the Visual Arts, 1970–2009,' *Feminisms is Still Our Name: Seven Essays on Historiography and Curatorial Practices*, eds Malin Hedlin Hayden and Jessica Sjöholm Skrubbe (Newcastle upon Tyne: Cambridge Scholars, 2010), 15.
77 Leonora Carrington cited in Joanna Moorhead, *Leonora Carrington—Britain's Lost Surrealist TateShots* (2015): www.youtube.com/watch?v=lqXePrSE1R0 (Accessed 1 April 2020).
78 Scott Fox, 'Swimming Under Cemeteries.'
79 Jonathan P. Eburne, 'Preface,' *The Invisible Painting* (Manchester: Manchester University Press, 2021), x.
80 Pinkola Estés, *Women Who Run with the Wolves*, 25.
81 Grateful thanks to Natalya Lusty. See *Surrealism, Feminism, Psychoanalysis*, 7.
82 Mieke Bal, 'Autotopography: Louise Bourgeois as Builder,' *Biography*, 25:1 (Winter 2002), 185.

1

Archaeology

I too have been drawn to people who offer something different.
—Chloe Aridjis (2018)[1]

Leonora took everything she knew and everything she couldn't, and shaped
it—into layers of egg tempera and hand-ground pigments, words, and political
posters—and it became something else, something truthful and unsettlingly
alive. Something immortal.
—Heidi Sopinka (2018)[2]

This is not a book about egg tempera painting or gold leaf as media.
Rather it is a study of how Carrington herself has become a medium for
new generations of creative thinkers. Over time, she and her work have
become many things to many people, and the perennial question of her
ever-increasing fan base is what her impact on the contemporary arts has
been. As we will see, the name "Leonora Carrington" has become both a
conduit for ideas and a conceptual framework that enables the reincarna-
tion of artefacts, practices, and activisms. Yet without her raw materials,
her detailed iconography, her visionary imagination and sheer skillset, the
exponential interest in her work would not exist. Indeed, her manipulation
of media and epic, labour-intensive techniques are necessary to unearth
archaeologically from the outset. In Linda Hutcheon's words, we may need
to acquire a certain "media literacy" or "knowing" in order to best access
Carrington's creative interpretations, which the rest of this book will consider.[3]
To understand Carrington's reception at multiple historical moments, and
demystify how she has come to operate as a cultural icon, we must first
explore her own recurrent themes and preoccupations, as well as flag the
expanding historiography and her exhibition histories.[4] I believe there are
previously unchartered connections to be drawn between the scholarly/
curatorial industry and the creative responses to her work.

Moreover, this brief introduction to her art and literature seeks to clarify
the multiple meanings of the "mediumistic" in the context of Carrington,
proposing that her personal variation of this lively subculture is not only
an intrinsic aspect of her iconographical universe but a metaphor for ongoing

dialogues with her. By departing from some of the existing biographical literature on Carrington, which tends to commence in her childhood Lancashire in the 1920s and terminate or unravel upon her arrival in Mexico in 1943, this chapter is deliberately non-chronological. It will not provide yet another linear history that privileges her very brief encounter with surrealism. Rather I opt for something "archaeological" in dimension as Michel Foucault might put it, more concerned with Carrington as an epistemology or "theory of knowledge," mining her iconography and getting to grips with her unique vocabulary.[5] She arguably appeals to new generations precisely because of her stark refusal to fit neatly into pre-existing taxonomies as well as for the extreme longevity of her creative career, working into the first decade of the twenty-first century.

Modern shamanism

The name Leonora Carrington conjures a distinctive, anachronistic and maximal aesthetic that borrows from a curious blend of countercultures. Such arts encompass shamanism, mysticism, astrology, spirit mediums, tarot,

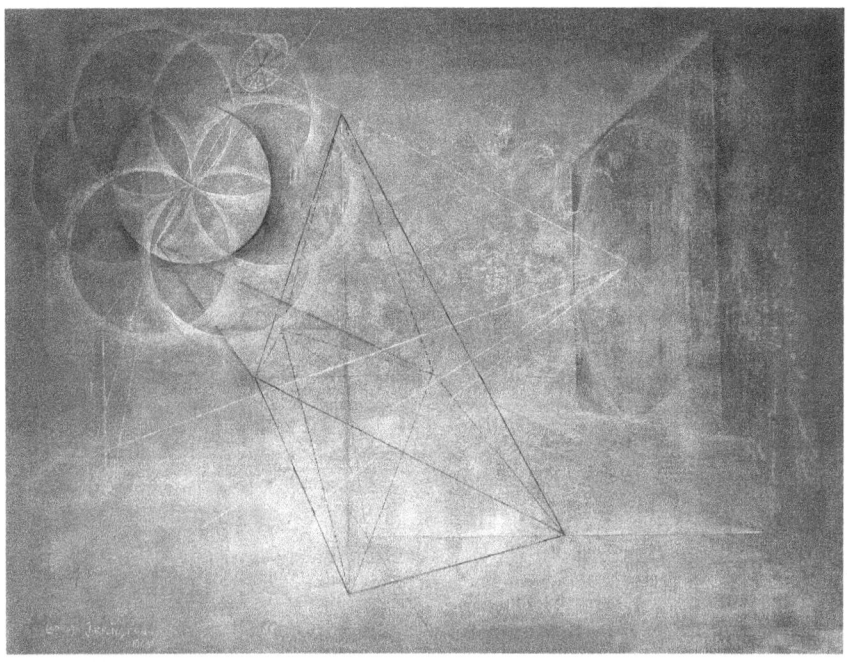

5 Leonora Carrington, *Hod's Polyèdre*, 1965

alchemy, pseudo-science, and other forms of natural magic such as witchcraft (from the Pendle witch trials of Lancaster in 1612, to the Mexican *curanderos*, or folk healers). Far from wishing to collapse such facets into a singular revival, the long-term connectivity of some of these ideas and visual cultures is important to note. For instance, Laetitia Barbier emphasises the archetypal meanings and "free association" that occur between fifteenth-century tarot iconography and alchemical imagery.[6] Meanwhile, Lisa Morton reminds us that words like "medium" and "séance" were used "interchangeably" during the early days of spiritualism in the nineteenth century.[7] A range of intersecting, alternative art histories become apparent. Lorna Scott Fox notes that "Carrington happily cherry-picked from every religion ... We know she read Robert Graves's *The White Goddess* in 1948, which lent archaeological as well as mythological shape to her exploration of prehistoric female wisdom."[8] Carrington's dreamscapes tap eclectically into a range of visual languages from Egyptian hieroglyphics to the elaborate sea monsters on medieval maps and Renaissance globes. She was also drawn beyond western traditions, finding infinite potential in eastern belief systems and Nordic indigenous cultures. Grotesque gargoyles, therefore, mingle in her work with netsuke-like zodiac creatures, suggesting Carrington developed an advanced, multicultural use of the surrealist technique of the exquisite corpse (or game of consequences). Moreover, as Serenity Young tells us: "Shamanism is not a textual religion ... Instead, it is an incredibly rich oral tradition of storytelling, mythmaking, and ritual, all of a highly complex and somewhat flexible nature."[9] An appreciation of such complexity and agility is integral to understanding Carrington's own narratives and variety of source materials.

Gabriel Weisz Carrington, has been hesitant to reveal his mother's reading lists and personal library, rightly concerned that it turns scholars into a tedious breed of "anecdote-hunters," yet he hints that there are subcultural activities to be found within her work, part of a repertoire which she termed her "psychic kitchen."[10] Weisz unpacks his paradoxical appreciation of Carrington's touchstones as follows:

> I set aside a place in my library for special interest books—texts that evidence Leonora's interest in the Celtic and Irish traditions, alchemy and magic, and even oneiric transmutation ... However, there is little point in asking how this material may or may not have influenced her work. She never became what she read. She sailed, for instance, through works on Zen and Tibetan Buddhism, but it was all incorporated into her active experience, becoming part of a quest to familiarise herself with any instrument that might help her navigate her inner world ... I don't deny that she was interested in alchemy, magic, and many other related subjects. But people tend to overlay their own stories on to her identity.[11]

Such overlaying of stories on to Carrington's identity is arguably at play in this present study. As Heidi Sopinka reminds us, we may have "mythologized her too quickly." [12] The writings of George Gurdjieff and his disciple, P. D. Ouspensky, certainly pervaded Carrington's imagination from the late 1940s onwards, likely responsible for the image of the enneagram and other, Venn-like geometries that tend to occur in her pictures such as *Litany of Philosophers* (1959), *Burning of Giordano Bruno* (1964), and *Hod's Polyèdre* (1965) (Figure 5). [13] Weisz Carrington further reminds us of the importance of politically radical feminist texts to his mother's research of the 1960s and 1970s, such as Simone de Beauvoir's *The Second Sex* (1949) and Germaine Greer's *The Female Eunuch* (1970). [14] Rosemary Sullivan adds that Carrington "claimed Margaret Atwood as one of her favourite writers." [15] Carrington was also known to have enjoyed crime writing and popular novels by the likes of Agatha Christie, while Jonathan Swift's *Gulliver's Travels* (1726) and James Stephens's *The Crock of Gold* (1912) held sway over the range of floating islands and Sidhe imagery that appear in her paintings. [16] Such wide-ranging interests, eclecticism, and intellectual curiosity contribute to Carrington's enduring success and reasons behind her extensive audience base. Her sense of mystery and unknowability are further factors.

The question of how to "explain" a Carrington picture or story to those that may not be so familiar or initiated with her extensive and varied output has been pitched frequently throughout the scholarship. The artist herself was often quick to refute or even shut down interpretation as a pointless activity and is known to have fudged any such attempts by art historians. [17] That said, Whitney Chadwick, who has tirelessly championed Carrington since at least the 1980s, tells us that "recent paintings depend on a vibrant metalanguage to overcome the limitations of linear space and time." [18] They speak using a genuinely alternative visual lexicon. Long-term ur-scholar, Susan L. Aberth, has also attempted to demystify Carrington's universe, describing her work as follows:

> One of the characteristics of Carrington's paintings is that they teem with activity: figures are moving all around, there's water, there's land, there's sky, there're different elements, there're animals, there're different climates, and a great narrative is implied but it is never *clarified*. So great things are happening that are very mysterious, there are ritual gestures and it is such a magical landscape and so unique. [19]

The suggestion that "narrative is implied but ... never *clarified*" encapsulates accurately the sheer sense of elasticity for interpretation presented by a Carrington picture or story. Her stories can be taken in multiple directions and are often non-linear and inconclusive. Her grandson, Daniel Weisz, has suggested to me that her artworks might be understood more like games, a ludics of enchantment. [20]

Carrington's lively topographies entice an archaeological approach to their comprehension; her landscapes frequently depict the underworld as an underground layer at the lower edge of her picture planes. In an early art-historical text on Carrington, Gloria Orenstein suggests that the picture *Nine Nine Nine* (1948) involves tertiary layers and "incarnates an image of three worlds—the corporeal, the intellectual, and the spiritual."[21] Indeed, Carrington's philosophical, hermetic view of universal mysteries even propose the possibility of the afterlife. Marina Warner adds that Carrington was badger-like when it came to arranging her surroundings, a creature who created by burrowing.[22] Such visual thinking already occurs in works like *Green Tea* (*La Dame Ovale*, 1942) (Figure 6), with nocturnal bats and corpses inhabiting the ground beneath the lush green meadow. Such underground layers recur in her mural commission, *El Mundo mágico de los Mayas* (*The Magical World of the Mayas*, 1963), for the Museo Nacional de Antropología. In this intricate cultural landscape, Mexican archaeology and museum artefacts undeniably infiltrated her approach.

The primeval universality and diverse range of hermetic archaeologies that Carrington drew from are echoed in Clarissa Pinkola Estés's Jungian-feminist study, *Women Who Run with the Wolves* (1992). Similar to prevailing

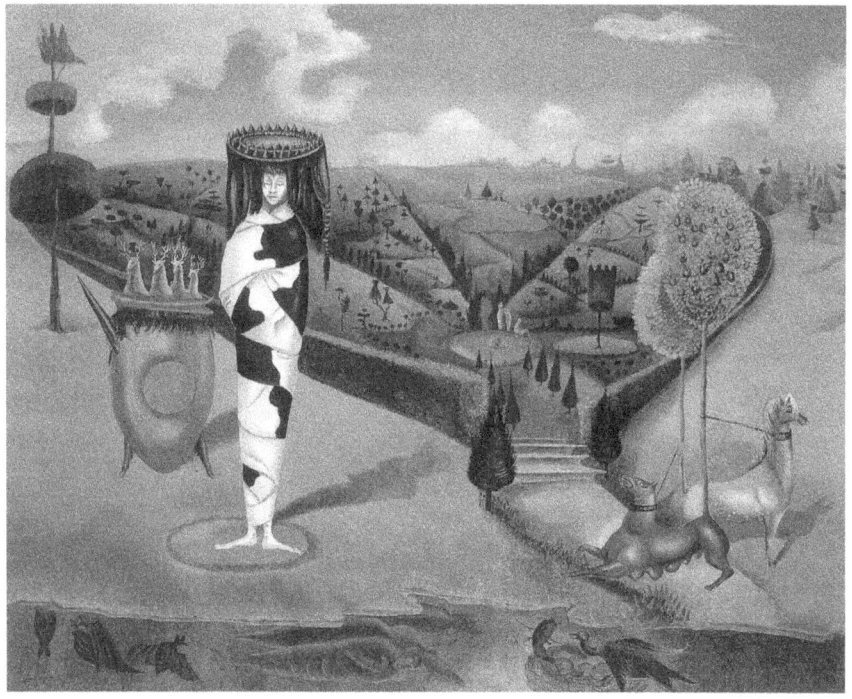

6 Leonora Carrington, *Green Tea*, 1942

perceptions of Carrington's work and persona, Pinkola Estés's book is frequently understood or categorised as a form of popular esotericism. However, in *Outsider Theory* (2018), Jonathan P. Eburne presents a model in which such writers and thinkers might be productively discussed alongside the goddess hypotheses and fantasy archaeologies inherited from New Age thinking of the 1960s and 1970s.[23] Eburne reminds us to be careful of dismissing such eco-feminist texts as essentialist or insincere, and indeed makes the case that seemingly fringe or marginal intellectual histories present parallels with the historical avant-garde, many of which have come to be institutionally recognised but were not always. A further parallel could be said to exist with women in the history of art, those who were in fact highly celebrated and curated within certain subcultures but have (somewhat conveniently for patriarchy) come to be dismissed as somehow forgotten. Patricia Allmer is rightly critical of this so-called "rediscovery" narrative and traces an illuminating and unbroken critical context for the women of surrealism.[24] Carrington herself was disinterested in any hype around reclamation narratives. Lynn Hershman Leeson further reveals that she "met Carrington mid-1980 and asked her if she felt disappointed to be overlooked historically, and she said the only thing that was important was continuing to do her work."[25] Pinkola Estés is useful here, significantly revising the archetype of the "wild woman" (like Carrington) into an active, de-civilising force that maintains the Jungian principle: "women's flagging vitality can be restored by extensive 'psychic-archaeological' digs into the ruins of the female underworld."[26] In capitalised, urbanised societies, there is something attractive and politically viable in seeking the conditions of wilderness, and in getting back in touch with instincts that may have been obliterated by our industrialised lifestyles. This is certainly something which can be seen in Carrington's trajectory, and is echoed in a letter from the surrealist artist and patron, Roland Penrose, to Carrington in which he describes "the fertile fantasy" of her paintings.[27]

Post-posh

Carrington's self-mythos and eccentric status no doubt have their roots in her class rebellion. Indeed, it is striking how many avant-gardists came from relatively wealthy, bourgeois backgrounds (André Breton, Marcel Duchamp, and Max Ernst, among others), forming paradoxical, Oedipal relationships with their family lineages, both a reliance on and relinquishing of such economic ties. The theme of rebellion is explored in Carrington's best-known and most widely anthologised short story 'The Debutante' (1937), described by Warner as a "classic modern fairy tale," in which a hyena takes the place of the young woman at a coming-out ball by chewing off the face of the maid to wear as a mask.[28] Natalya Lusty has perceptively analysed how this story "records the cross-class commodification" of the era, and critiques surrealism's own limitations on gender politics.[29] Carrington exemplified "the bright young people" generation as parodied in literary works like Evelyn Waugh's *Vile Bodies* (1930), but was critical of the limitations she observed within this social class. As Joanna Moorhead writes: "She has tasted the London season, and she can see it for all it is, for all its snobbery, narrowness and conventionality."[30] And yet, such traditional, "posh" expectations and preferences (literally "port out, starboard home" for first-class cabins on ships) were about to collapse as the Second World War profoundly altered existing social classifications.

Like most wealthy girls of the time from aspirational backgrounds, Carrington was sent to an elite boarding school (where she was later expelled) followed by Miss Penrose's Academy in Italy. At the latter, Carrington was able to observe Florentine predella panels and Renaissance frescoes first-hand, art-historical lessons which would have a long-term impact on her own painterly techniques. Despite her rebellion, finishing school was intrinsically tied to her understanding of medium and artistic self-discipline in this way. Later, during the Second World War, she would encounter the visions of Bosch in the Museo Nacional del Prado, and his example would further prompt her unusual sense of perspective and keen eye for detail, with giant birds, fish, and homunculi that comingle with human figures in a seemingly infinite range of imaginative scenarios. In her fictional biography of Carrington, Elena Poniatowska imagines visiting an art museum with the artist in her later years. Here, "Carrington" is disappointed to find contemporary installation art in place of older artefacts:

> Leonora, who had only caught the word "museum," anticipates visions of sixteenth-century Flemish paintings: the temptations of St Anthony, and the gardens of delight; triptychs by Hans Memling and Roger van der Weyden, Hieronymus Van Aken or Hieronymus Bosch, only to find herself suddenly blinded by green, amber and red traffic lights flashing on and off and criss-crossing the space like flashes of lightening [*sic*]. The noise magnified through a massive sound system is infernal.
> "What is this?"
> "An installation. Do you like it?"
> "It is horrible," Leonora cringes.[31]

Her younger companion tries to justify the exhibit, claiming that surrealist activities were previously dismissed this way, but Poniatowska's memory or version of Carrington remains dubious to the merits of installation art. A conservative aesthetic preference for the historical over the experimental and the contemporary may initially strike one as the stereotypical viewpoint of an older audience, but this would be to overlook the quieter transgressiveness Carrington herself no doubt observed in the content and technique of Flemish and Netherlandish painting. Carrington's own highly representational, miniaturist narrative art often appears deliberately at variance with modernist aesthetic developments, suggesting a longing for anachronism and a rejection of the status quo. Such reclaiming of the self through small acts of defiance, coupled with intelligent study of artistic precursors, was a combination of characteristics that continued throughout her career, an attitude that shaped much of her art and literature. Today it is perhaps difficult for some to appreciate just how daring and unconventional Carrington's artistic quest to London and Paris, then on to Spain, America, and finally Mexico would have seemed to her conservative relatives.[32] Her rebellion would significantly shape her output, from her materials to her iconography, and has become interpreted by many as a nascent mode of feminist liberation. For younger scholars, artists, and writers interested in avant-garde culture and its genuine ability to challenge establishment norms, Carrington emerges as a remarkable heroine of her time.

Carrington's literary leanings were already embedded since her bourgeois nursery, and tended towards the grotesque and macabre, especially Gothic and nonsense traditions—Lewis Carroll and Edward Lear—tastes and genres which would be enthusiastically encouraged and accommodated by her youthful association with the surrealist movement. Again, Lusty shows us how "Carrington's satire on the English upper-class debutante ritual resembles Carroll's own lampooning of Victorian manners ... nowhere better illustrated than in his satirical rendering of the 'madness' of the tea party ceremony."[33] In Carrington's literary corpus, fairy tales are regularly twisted beyond their familiar order of things: for example, Goldilocks becomes an enchanted "miraldalocks" plant in 'Little Francis' (1937–38).[34] Later, in Carrington's novel, *The Hearing Trumpet* (1974), Hans Christian Andersen's 'The Snow Queen' (1844) is used as part of her rewriting strategy alongside the Holy Grail legend. Eburne described this as a "significant intertext" and an example of what Susan Rubin Suleiman has termed "feminist intertextuality."[35] Indeed, *The Hearing Trumpet* has frequently been lauded by feminist scholars and readers (including Lusty and Sopinka) for its rare ability to feature a radical, elderly female protagonist.[36] Marian Leatherby has since become a literary icon. This is true also of works like *The Magdalens* (1986), where Carrington highlights the revolutionary potential of the modern contraceptive pill, positioning it within the tradition of the wise-women herbalists as a feminist potion.[37] In striking ways, Carrington can be seen to have prophesised her own nonagenarian status and acknowledges old age for woman as a gesture of feminist reclamation. Novelist Ali Smith praises Carrington's writing for its pragmaticism: "I loved this writer who sees through the conventional forced and false structures of things to the real thing."[38] Carrington would also pen an illustrated book of black humour for children, entitled *Leche del Sueño* (*Milk of Dreams*, *c*.1955–62), featuring scatological tales of characters called "Headless John" and "Lolita Stomach."[39] Weisz Carrington notes a reverse pedagogical purpose of *Leche del Sueño*: "we learn how to disobey the predictable well behaved traits of most narratives," surely a summary of Carrington's entire endeavour as an artist.[40] How interesting that such playfulness should come to shape Cecilia Alemani's curatorial direction for an international contemporary art festival in 2022.[41] In an international, blockbuster exhibition context celebrating the achievements of women, the overarching title "milk of dreams" emphasises a fluid, collective feminine endeavour that owes allegiance to the dreamscapes of uncompromising surrealist foremothers.

Another childhood aesthetic that recurs throughout Carrington's mature *œuvre* is the ubiquitous and often unruly character of the carousel pony or rocking horse. The horse was a regular companion throughout Carrington's equestrian childhood, and became a deeply symbolic, magical animal, often interpreted as her alter ego. The theme is reminiscent of a popular nursery rhyme of eighteenth-century England, which the Opies tell us means to straddle a toy horse:

> Ride a cock-horse to Banbury Cross,
> To see a fine lady upon a white horse;
> With rings on her fingers and bells on her toes,
> She shall have music wherever she goes.[42]

Such a bejewelled rider and her milk-white mare were depicted vividly in *Diana* (1932), one of Carrington's early *Sisters of the Moon* watercolour series. On a domestic level, rocking horses are a common feature of the bourgeois child's nursery, but, in Carrington's literary and artistic universe, they are usually broken or in some state of petrification, emblematic of a break with her family past.[43] In her short story 'The Oval Lady' (1937), the rocking-horse character, Tartar, is burnt by the father as a punishment for his daughter Lucretia's game of make-believe within their aristocratic mansion. It is a tale which invites comparison with Carrington's own youthful rebellion, and disinheritance by her father as a consequence. In her novel *The Stone Door* (1976), a fictionalisation of her husband, the Hungarian photographer Chiki Weisz, the author makes a cameo appearance as a little girl riding her real-life childhood pony, Black Bess. The rocking horse recurs in several of Carrington's paintings, prints, and drawings, especially throughout the 1930s and 1940s, suggesting both an immersion and escape from childhood nostalgia.[44] Again, Carrington provides a useful precursor for those interested in the potential of children's picture-book illustration, her growing reputation defending such material against being misread as purely whimsical or insincerely fey.

During the Second World War, flying machines and floating islands served as further vehicles of escapism for Carrington's visual imagination. In her fictional biography, *Leonora in the Morning Light* (2021), Michaela Carter imagines Carrington's crossing of the Atlantic, watching as Max Ernst, Peggy Guggenheim, and Guggenheim's family fly past Carrington's ship in a large clipper: "West. This is how it feels to travel west, toward freedom … High above, a huge plane floats past. The Clipper. It has to be. Following the plane into the bright sky, her eyes fill. For all her insistence on separation, Max and she are leaving for America in tandem. The horse on the water and the bird in the air."[45] Such synchronicity was very much a symptom of the historical avant-garde at the time, narrative crossovers in times of crisis that fascinate contemporary artists and writers.

An equivalent artwork that overlaps with Carrington's surrealist period is Marcel Duchamp's conceptual *Boîte-en-valise* (*Box in a Suitcase*, 1936–42), which contained model versions and facsimiles of his famous readymades. David Hopkins describes how such miniatures "could easily take their place in a (masculinised) doll's house."[46] Duchamp's suitcase can be read as a pivotal metaphor for surrealism's transatlantic transition during the Second World War, when many artists were fleeing persecution as dissidents— Duchamp allegedly posed as a cheesemonger in order to get through checkpoints and customs.[47] His *Boîte-en-valise* served as both vanity case and creative first-aid kit, a microcosmic synecdoche for the artist himself. Carrington's own suitcase was appropriately personalised with the word "REVELATION," though she had to leave many of her possessions behind in Saint-Martin d'Ardèche.[48] Later, Carrington would depict herself as *The Artist Travelling Incognito* (1949) (Figure 10), another encapsulation of the sense of upheaval, altered identities, and creative displacement during this period.[49] Duchamp's *Boîte-en-valise* offers an example of the traveller's classification of comfort, the "deluxe" versions representing an exclusive guest list including patrons and close friends. For example, Peggy Guggenheim, the wealthy heiress who supported Carrington and many other artists during this period, would have typically travelled first class, as we imagine Duchamp, and certainly Max Ernst, did under her patronage.[50] Laid on its side as it would have been in a luggage hold, one can observe that Duchamp's artworks were arranged geographically from the *Ampoule of 50cc Paris Air* (1919) to *Fountain* (1917), which was realised initially in New York. Carrington likewise depicts such epic journeys in her Laputa-like picture *Artes 110* (1942), a self-portrait in which the landscape has ruptured into an airborne archipelago and Carrington shows herself flying in between like a witch with a wand and dog familiar.[51] A giant porcupine or echidna serves as a majestic carrier of isles, an idea which Carrington possibly adapted from Hindu mythology, namely Akupara, the tortoise avatar of the god, Vishnu, who carries the world on its shell. Such use of diverse belief systems as allegories for real-world politics further evidences her intellectual depths.

The medium enters

Much of Carrington's output has tended to be canonised as surrealist, a movement whose main publishing activities and political clout occurred historically in the period 1924–1968. Some scholars and makers would argue for a continuity of surrealism beyond those dates, Penelope Rosemont being a very worthy exemplar of someone who was intergenerationally connected to primary surrealists and has continued to carry a torch for the movement, especially the women, through anthologising and writing on Carrington, among others.[52] Surrealism certainly coincided with Carrington's emergence as an artist and writer, and its investigations into the marvellous and the otherworldly (the French *sur* being literally "above" or "upon" reality) deserve consideration in terms of what she would go on to become.

Katharine Conley points out that: "surrealism was a haunted movement from the beginning," and that automatic writing grew out of dream transcriptions and séance-like channellings of the unconscious, as discussed in early surrealists texts such as André Breton's 'Entrée des mediums' ('The Mediums Enter,' 1922).[53] In this formative essay, Breton named Robert Desnos, René Crevel, and Benjamin Péret as those capable of "hypnotic slumbers," and used the metaphor of the "see-saw" for psychic automatism and correlative dream states.[54] Spiritualist intrigue had already been capturing the imagination as a distraction mechanism since the moment of Carrington's birth during the First World War—given the exponential loss of (predominantly male) life, family relatives had an incentivised cause to make contact with the dead. As Morton tells us:

> The original form of the séance ... before it was haunted by the spectre of mass entertainment—was a very different creature ... Spiritualism, a movement born as a counter to the rapid progressions in science, industry and urbanization in the nineteenth century, presented itself as the first religion that allowed its followers to routinely witness proof of their belief in survival after death.[55]

Surrealism had a complicated relationship with spiritualism and the related theosophy movement, with Breton initially describing the practice of the séance as an "imbecilic formality."[56] Tessel M. Bauduin rightly notes that Breton sought to distance his surrealist use of the term "psychic automatism" from the spiritualist understanding, from those psychics who claimed to foretell the future or commune with the dead.[57] Yet, a keen interest in unconscious thought-forms and a celebration of the outmoded can certainly be perceived in both lines of inquiry. Writing with Victoria Ferentinou and Daniel Zamani, Bauduin also reveals that "Ultimately, the surrealist recourse to the marvellous benefitted from the term's vague definition, exploiting its association with occultism, superstition and a sense of estrangement from the real."[58] Both surrealism and spiritualism can be further positioned against the grain of capitalist progressivism as counter-modernisms, with their innate uses of alternative, ancient, and emergent knowledges as lifestyle choices.[59]

Such overlaying of realities, attitudes, and techniques would later enthral Carrington. Following her mother's infamous gifting of Herbert Read's book *Surrealism* (1936), Carrington became acquainted with the movement during its mid-1930s spell in England with shows such as the major *International Surrealist Exhibition* at the New Burlington Galleries (1936). It was an aesthetic she recognised intimately, a feeling many contemporary artists today have, in turn, admitted to experiencing via Carrington's own output. Many years later she famously described to Warner her initial response to Max Ernst's painted assemblage, *Two Children Are Threatened by a Nightingale* (1924): "like a burning inside; you know how when something really touches you, it feels like burning."[60] Long before Ernst, Carrington had already developed a strong visual language of her own courtesy of

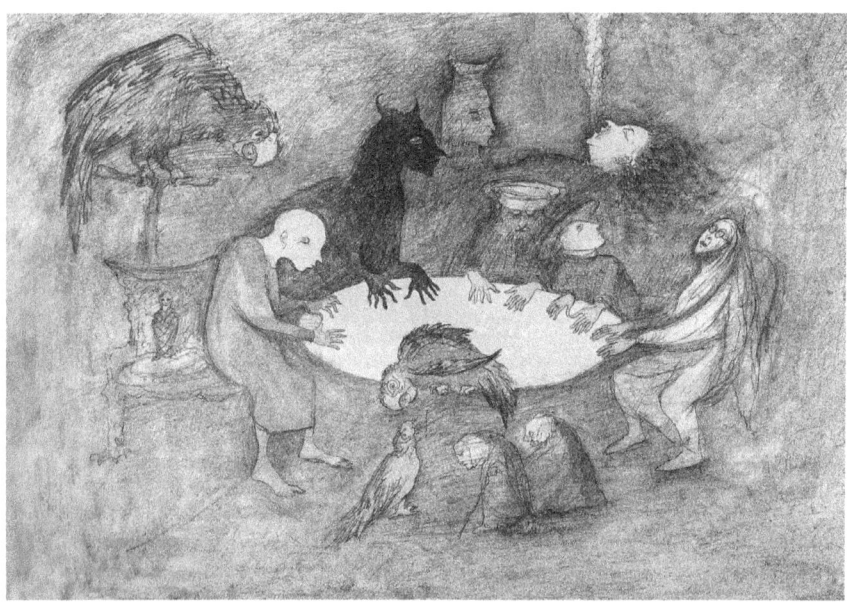

7 Leonora Carrington, *Séance*, 1998

the so-called Golden Age of children's picture-book illustrations by Arthur Rackham and Beatrix Potter, among others.[61] Carrington's *Sisters of the Moon* experiment with the visual language of fairy tales, including depictions of princesses and enchantresses that are in cahoots with a range of fantasy creatures.[62] By the mid-1930s, her visual and literary application of surrealism had sharpened her existing veristic modes of inquiry, conjuring figurative imagery and narratives (rather than deploying automatic methods which tended to yield more abstract results). Aberth and Tere Arcq nuance this artistic transformation: "It was during this time that she turned from fairy tales and ghost stories to more serious esoteric subjects directly related to art-making," suggesting a gradual professionalisation and honing of her craft as she spent more time immersed in the avant-garde with access to a wider array of source texts.[63] Yet these tendencies in her *œuvre* to date were also readily adopted by surrealism. For the first issue of *VVV* magazine (1942), Carrington contributed to a surrealist questionnaire, ranking the unicorn as her favourite mythological creature.[64] Horses and hyenas would become her most privileged, expressive vehicles as if she were invoking a medieval bestiary or borrowing from the absurd and often macabre juxtapositions of a nursery rhyme. Surrealist interests in magic (Remedios Varo and Kurt Seligmann), mythology (André Breton, Pablo Picasso, and Georges Bataille), and fairy tales (Leonor Fini and Max Ernst) would only deepen Carrington's own existing intrigue in such subjects. Moreover, surrealism's use of collage and juxtaposition offered welcome alternative narratives to the avant-gardism she had been studying to date, namely that of Amédée Ozenfant at his London academy whose purist (masculine) pedagogy insisted she draw the same apple, day after day, as still life. Carrington would then carry the mediumistic dimension of surrealism through her long-term *œuvre*, another chief reason why the contemporary arts find her work so thrilling.

Despite the fact that Carrington's feminist approach to surrealism is undoubtedly what has attracted the majority of her respondents today, her association with the primary movement was, in reality, a relatively brief membership given the longevity of the rest of her career. Her contributions to surrealist publications and exhibitions occurred in earnest in 1937–44, a significant but short moment compared to her seven decades as an artist and writer. Later in life, Carrington frequently downplayed her involvement in the movement, claiming that French surrealism was only ("at least") a little more interesting than the convent of her schooldays.[65] Her relationship with surrealism can certainly be understood as ambiguous. Her traumatic episode at the sanatorium in Santander (1940–41) undoubtedly went some way to demythologising and readjusting surrealism's celebration of madness and is documented luridly in *Down Below* (1944) and in the mummified, straitjacket restraints of *Green Tea* (1942). Recently, many contemporary artists and writers have found solace and empathy in Carrington's experiences of mental illness, and in her frank confessional account of what happened to her.[66] However, it is often erroneously claimed that the male surrealists overshadowed or took advantage of the women associated with the movement, but the evidence suggests this was not always the case—Breton, for one, held a deep respect for Carrington as a professional peer, anthologising her writing in *Anthologie de l'humour noir* (*Anthology of Black Humour*, 1940).[67] Moreover, Hermann Landshoff's famous *Exiles* (1942) group photograph of avant-gardists in Guggenheim's New York apartment includes Carrington, shoulder-to-shoulder with architect Frederick Kiesler, at the centre of surrealist activities prior to her departure to Mexico. Although she would continue to contribute remotely to surrealist exhibitions (for instance a solo show at Pierre Matisse Gallery in 1948, and *l'Exposition inteRnatiOnale du Sur-réalisme* (*EROS*) group show in 1959), it could be suggested that her association with the original French wing of the surrealist movement began to decline in the post-war era after her move to Mexico City. Here, she would find a new cohort of creative *émigrés*, many of whom (such as Varo) had also participated previously in continental surrealist activities. Eburne terms this Mexico-based network of exiles coupled with Carrington's own brand of "mythopoetic[ism]" part of an "esoteric avant-garde," with intertextuality functioning as "a principal medium of intellectual exchange."[68] Mexico (from the winter of 1942–43 onwards) offered fertile ground as a kind of critical afterlife, a chance for a new start and a safe space with which to experiment and extend her existing interests into alternative knowledge banks. Many biographies will often terminate or disperse at this point, unsure of how to work through Carrington's "exoticisation" or "middle age" beyond the strictures of surrealist classification and the cult of youth. The contemporary arts demonstrate a wider cultural import of Carrington's later works; surrealism was important, yes, but it was only ever the beginning of her creative adventure.

Dollhouse architecture

Carrington's articulation of the feminine life cycle is frequently highlighted, especially her ability to reorient, reverse, and revise traditional understandings of age brackets such as the child-woman and the crone. In my view, absorbing and unique as Carrington's life adventure was, an overemphasis on biography has frequently held women back from being appreciated as makers.[69] That said, the work inevitably comes from a specific socio-economic context that needs to be understood in order to more fully rebel against conventional narratives of limitation and bring such languages into the present as a mode of feminist revisionary history. Griselda Pollock makes a compelling case for domestic space in rethinking how creative women experienced modernity.[70] On one level, Carrington's diminutive night-nursery paintings of the mid-1940s celebrate the unique dwell time of early parenthood; but, on another, they can be seen to speak to a growing concern around emotional labour, specifically the need to balance childcare with a creative practice, the maintenance of which brings about a sense of self-identity. (Carrington boldly claimed she held the baby in one hand and the paintbrush in the other).[71] I would suggest this aspect of Carrington has been an empowering draw for younger generations of artists and writers, especially women and gender non-binaries, regardless of whether or not they choose or are able to bear children. Many in the contemporary arts have revealed that Carrington gives them licence to explore and reclaim a feminine imagery which may previously have been considered lowbrow or insincere by senior establishment figures.[72] Moreover, Lynn Hershman Leeson reminds us that "multi-disciplinarity was frowned on and 'authorities' said it meant that the artist was not serious."[73] For modernist art critics like Clement Greenberg, "literary art" was certainly a point of contention in the 1940s, viewed as an aca-demicisation which held the avant-garde back as well as a bastardisation of media.[74] Indeed, Greenberg increasingly disparaged any breaching of media boundaries, while Carrington, having departed the New York art scene, increasingly experimented with tapestry and theatre in Mexico.[75] Jenna C. Ashton suggests that "living artists are also kicking back against a certain 'contemporary art' aesthetic snobbery that has shown disdain for the sensuous, colourful, intricate and detailed figurative."[76] Carrington's refusal to conform to expectations of what a creative woman should be and how she should behave suggests a feminism that was instinctual, innate, and half a century ahead of its time.

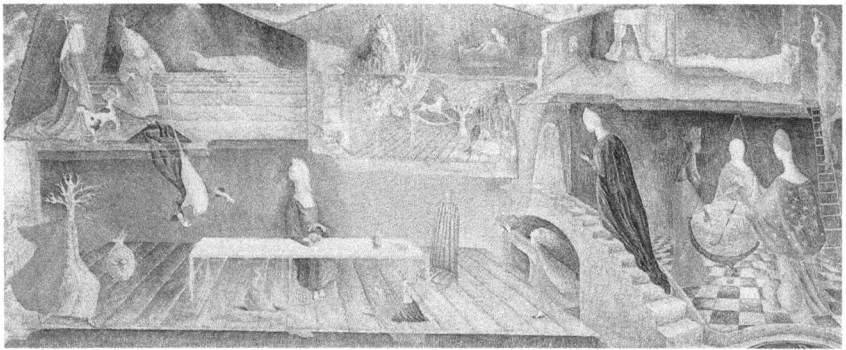

8 Leonora Carrington, *The House Opposite*, 1945

One metaphor that encapsulates Carrington's nascent feminist approach is surely the dollhouse. Among the chief theoreticians of dollhouses is the poet and cultural historian Susan Stewart who reminds us that the dollhouse is "the most consummate of miniatures," and that it "has two dominant motifs: wealth and nostalgia," both values associated with the bourgeoisie.[77] For conflicted reasons, Carrington would return, albeit imaginatively, to the dollhouse architecture of her wealthy Lancastrian childhood homes of Crookhey and Hazelwood Halls throughout her creative career. Claire Dean and the House of Opposites collective have made innovative exhibits that relate to the feminist interiority of Carrington's output, especially during the immediate post-war era when she was simultaneously working and parenting. Dean, a mother of sons who is also based in Carrington's native Lancashire, created her "hybrid story object," *House Book* (2019), to unravel a conventional reliance on linear narratives, and to unpack the illuminating aspects of Carrington's narrativity as a mode of endless rearrangement. Dean explains:

> In my stories, extraordinary things tend to happen in very mundane Northern English settings. I'm always playing with wonder and trying to see how far I can push the fantastic in a story without the need to explain it. Explaining kills the magic but carrying readers with you when the setting is a contemporary one can be tricky. Leonora Carrington is an expert guide in how to do this. There are no explanations for the bizarre and wondrous in her artworks or her fiction.[78]

Meanwhile, House of Opposites, who are also based in northern England, have utilised an innovative, collaborative skillset of puppetry, illustration, textiles, curation, and heritage studies to further rethink Carrington as a baseline for collective memory and "women's creative relationships."[79] For House of Opposites, Carrington's painting of the same title offers an inquisitive mode of exhibition-making which again can be rearranged site-specifically.

Carrington's compartmentalised painting, *The House Opposite* (1945) (Figure 8), depicts lively nocturnal activities through a series of chambers. This was swiftly followed by further interior paintings like *Night Nursery Everything* (Figure 3) and *Neighbourly Advice* (both 1947).[80] Writing on *The House Opposite*, Dawn Adès notices that "the façade has been removed, like a doll's house or theatre set. None of the rooms is a conventional living space."[81] As Janet Lyon echoes, Carrington's eccentric use of scale becomes a levelling factor, obliterating normative power relations.[82] I would further suggest the scale of these paintings are strikingly reminiscent of Victorian dollhouses and the micronarratives of children's picture-book illustration, an inversion of pre-existing structures. Parenthood in the faraway land of Mexico City may have taken Carrington back imaginatively to the comforting aesthetics of her own English nursery.[83] Moreover, Margaret Wise Brown's popular American children's book, *Goodnight Moon*, was published the same year as many of Carrington's night-nursery paintings (1947). Without necessarily suggesting that Carrington read her children this particular book, the diminutive scale and night-nursery compositions found in Clement Hurd's detailed and colourful illustrations for *Goodnight Moon* chime with the contents of Carrington's own visual narratives like *Neighbourly Advice*, such as the rocking chair and tiny domesticated animals playing on the floor. The contemporaneity of such imagery demonstrates a broader cultural fascination with the post-war lullaby, preparing the child for sleep within the safe confines of a soothing dollhouse world. Carrington's friend, Chloe Aridjis, later read *Goodnight Moon* as a young girl growing up in Mexico City in the 1970s, describing it as "a kind of phenomenology of night."[84] Thus, such imagery and narratives provide an intergenerational focus, a recurrence of past times and hand-me-downs.

Dollhouse architecture might be a useful feminist lens for Carrington studies, and we might view such pictures now as self-critical tools to readjust the historical oversight of creative women by patriarchy. Arcq interestingly points out that *The House Opposite* depicts "a house inhabited only by

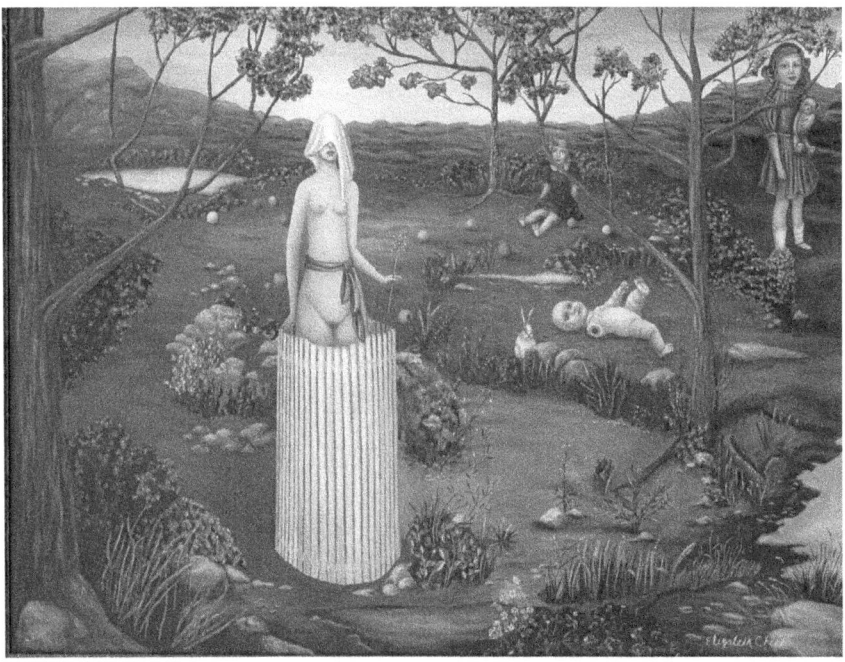

9 Elizabeth Cheche, *What We Saw When No One Was Looking*, 2018

women."[85] This is a significant fact for Carrington's broader *œuvre*, which departed from the dominant, abstract machismo of the period, and makes *The House Opposite* operate as a concentrated microcosm or synecdoche in this regard. As Aberth elaborates, by setting the viewer in those domestic spaces historically and socially inhabited by women, and by endowing the kitchen and the nursery with such emphasis, Carrington actually reappropriates and relocates the power dynamics by bringing these traditionally marginal spaces to the centre of critical attention.[86] Elizabeth Cheche's *What We Saw When No One Was Looking* (2018) (Figure 9) and Rose Moon's *A Place to Dream Up a Storm* (2019) are two contemporary examples of diminutive visual narratives that draw from Carrington's meticulous approach and iconography as found in her night-nursery paintings in order to present new possibilities for artists who are women. Cheche's painting presents an exquisite critique of motherhood, depicting a nude female figure trapped inside a white picket fence with a shroud across her eyes. The inclusion of a white rabbit and a broken doll within a bucolic scene brings to mind the ambiguous atmosphere of Carrington's *Garden Bedroom* (1941) or the revelatory mood of *And Then We Saw the Daughter of the Minotaur* (1953) (Figure 12). Moon also borrows from Carrington's lullaby imagery with a bed, as the site of dreams, cradled within the branches of a tree, and decorated with dinky objects including a tiny guitar, a windchime, and a teddy bear. Both Moon and Cheche cite Carrington as principal among their touchstones.[87]

Carrington's later work presents a different facet to her maternal politics—the need to protect her sons from the police violence associated with youth-cultural uprisings, namely the international student revolutions of 1968 while her sons were studying at university.[88] Her painting *A Warning to a Mother* (1973) offers a powerful example of her maternal instinct to protect her adult offspring from the police and governmental backlash. Here, a ghostly blue and distinctly masculine entity threatens the domestic arrangement of miniature creatures and ornaments, matryoshka dolls, and small domestic pets (a shamrock-patterned cat and a tiny jester). The scene is supervised by a maternal cooking stove, no doubt a metaphor for the culinary artist herself. Unlike the prevailing perspective of the second-wave generation, Carrington did not feel the need to separate her feminism from the kitchen but rather embraced it as a site of collaboration. Again, Carrington has become a role model for those with politics who like to bake—she demonstrates such practices need not be mutually exclusive in a feminist framework. The dominant red colour of this scene recurs in *Grandmother Moorhead's Aromatic Kitchen* (1975), another kitchen picture, this time featuring a giant goose as the matriarchal authority figure, one that Warner reminds us represents the fairy-tale preparations, gossip, and yarn-telling long associated with groups of women.[89] Again, Carrington's uncompromising feminism becomes intrinsic to understanding her work and world-view that has, in turn, shaped so many others.

To conclude this archaeology of the salient features of Carrington's work and career, her *œuvre* might be interpreted as the outcome of extensive research and curiosity into esotericism, comprising a cosmic vocabulary at the level of archetypal introspection. Surrealism was foundational as an apprenticeship which helped shape some of her existing visual language and hone her storytelling abilities, but it was one approach among many in a varied and lengthy artistic career. We must begin to see her work beyond surrealism through a contemporary lens. Mexico's mega-diverse cultures would prove just as vital, if not more so that bohemian Paris and urbane New York, as would the Women's Liberation movement of the 1970s. A radical counter-cultural attitude was the result of working through some of these eras and spaces as well as close study of the history of occult and spiritualist practices. Yet, as we will see, Carrington-as-medium is far from a passive vessel or receiver of knowledge. Rather she presents us with a critical haunting within the contemporary arts which I will now explore through the Carrington-directed themes of the performative, the conceptual, hibernation, menagerie, and edgework.

Notes

1 Chloe Aridjis cited in Josh Appignanesi, *Female Human Animal* (London: Minotaur Film, 2018).

2 Heidi Sopinka, 'Hey Necromancer!' *Paris Review* (18 September 2018): https://theparisreview.org/blog/2018/09/18/hey-necromancer (Accessed 11 February 2020). Grateful thanks to Claire Dean for highlighting this passage @claireddean (20 September 2018).

3 Linda Hutcheon, *A Theory of Adaptation* (Abingdon: Routledge, 2013), 126; 120.

4 By "historiography," I mean the history of the critical literature, cataloguing and curatorial approaches, the history of how she has been represented.

5 Michel Foucault, *The Order of Things: An Archaeology of the Human Sciences* (New York: Routledge, 2002), xii. Thanks to Jonathan P. Eburne.

6 Laetitia Barbier, 'Death and Resurrection as Muse' (6 March 2021).

7 Lisa Morton, *Calling the Spirits: A History of Seances* (London: Reaktion Books, 2020), 16.

8 Lorna Scott Fox, 'Swimming Under Cemeteries,' *Times Literary Supplement* (May 2017), www.the-tls.co.uk/articles/public/leonora-carrington (Accessed 6 April 2021). For more on Carrington's use of *The White Goddess*, see Chloe Aridjis, whose mother, Betty Aridjis, connects the painting *Pig Rush* (1960) to a passage from Graves, 'Leonora Carrington and the Secret of the Sacred

Feminine,' *Frieze* (18 June 2019): www.frieze.com/article/leonora-carrington-and-secret-sacred-feminine (Accessed 10 July 2021).

9 Serenity Young, *Women Who Fly: Goddesses, Witches, Mystics and Other Airborne Females* (Oxford: Oxford University Press, 2018), 178–179.

10 Gabriel Weisz Carrington, 'A Celtic Window,' *Leonora Carrington*, ed. Seán Kissane (Dublin: Irish Museum of Modern Art), 12; Leonora Carrington cited in Gabriel Weisz Carrington, *The Invisible Painting: My Memoir of Leonora Carrington* (Manchester: Manchester University Press, 2021), 91.

11 Weisz Carrington, *The Invisible Painting*, 94. Writing on the occult within modern cultural production, S. Elizabeth describes Carrington as "a student of the esoteric and magical arts." *The Art of the Occult: A Visual Sourcebook for the Modern Mystic* (London: Frances Lincoln, 2020), 74.

12 Heidi Sopinka, *The Dictionary of Animal Languages* (London: Scribe, 2018), 106.

13 Jonathan P. Eburne, 'Poetic Wisdom: Leonora Carrington and the Esoteric Avant-Garde,' *Leonora Carrington and the International Avant-Garde*, eds J. P. Eburne and C. McAra (Manchester: Manchester University Press, 2017), 145–146.

14 Weisz Carrington, *The Invisible Painting*, 82.

15 Rosemary Sullivan, 'On Leonora Carrington and P. K. Page,' *A Manner of Being: Writers on Their Mentors*, eds Annie Liontas and Jeff Parker (Amherst: University of Massachusetts Press, 2015), 137.

16 Seán Kissane, 'The Celtic Surrealist,' *Leonora Carrington*, 45, 61.

17 Leonora Carrington in conversation with Whitney Chadwick in Kim Evans, *Leonora Carrington and the House of Fear* (BBC Omnibus, 1992).

18 Whitney Chadwick, 'Painting on the Threshold,' *Leonora Carrington: Recent Works* (New York: Brewster Gallery, 1988), 2.

19 Susan L. Aberth and Stacy Klein, 'Leonora Carrington and the Theatre: Susan L. Aberth and Stacy Klein in Conversation' (7 March 2021): www.youtube.com/watch?v=gJUTP82shOY (Accessed 28 March 2021).

20 Grateful thanks to Daniel Weisz.

21 Gloria Orenstein, 'Art History and the Case for the Women of Surrealism,' *Journal of General Education* 27:1 (Spring 1975), 42–43.

22 Marina Warner, 'Leonora Carrington: Badger,' *Leonora Carrington in the Viktor Wynd Collection*, ed. Catriona McAra (Leeds: Leeds Arts University, 2016), 23–26.

23 Jonathan P. Eburne, *Outsider Theory: Intellectual Histories of Unorthodox Ideas* (London and Minneapolis: University of Minnesota Press, 2018), 164.

24 Patricia Allmer, 'Feminist Interventions: Revising the Canon,' *A Companion to Dada and Surrealism*, ed. David Hopkins (Chichester: Wiley Blackwell, 2016), 366–381.

25 Interview with Lynn Hershman Leeson.

26 Clarissa Pinkola Estés, *Women Who Run with the Wolves: Contacting the Power of the Wild Woman* (London: Random House, 1982), 3.

27 Roland Penrose, 'Letter to Leonora Carrington' (4 March 1960). Collection of the Scottish National Gallery of Modern Art, Edinburgh.

28 Marina Warner, 'Leonora Carrington's Spirit Bestiary; or the Art of Playing Make-Belief,' *Leonora Carrington: Paintings, Drawings and Sculptures 1940–1990*, ed. Andrea Schlieker (London: Serpentine Gallery, 1991), 12.

29 Natalya Lusty, *Surrealism, Feminism, Psychoanalysis* (Aldershot: Ashgate, 2007), 20–21.

30 Joanna Moorhead, *The Surreal Life of Leonora Carrington* (London: Virago, 2017), 23.

31 Elena Poniatowska, *Leonora: A Novel*, trans. Amanda Hopkinson (London: Serpent's Tail, 2015), 446.

32 This idea is explored in both Alice Allemano's play 'About Leo' (2018) and Moorhead's biography *The Surreal Life*, 32–33.

33 Lusty, *Surrealism, Feminism, Psychoanalysis*, 27.

34 Marina Warner, 'Introduction,' *The House of Fear: Notes from Down Below* (London: Virago, 1989), 12.

35 Eburne, 'Poetic Wisdom,' 153; Susan Rubin Suleiman, *Subversive Intent: Gender, Politics, and the Avant-Garde* (Cambridge, MA and London: Harvard University Press, 1990), 142; 173.

36 Lusty, *Surrealism, Feminism, Psychoanalysis*, 62.

37 Susan L. Aberth, *Leonora Carrington: Surrealism, Alchemy and Art* (Aldershot: Lund Humphries, 2004), 126.

38 Interview with Ali Smith.

39 Leonora Carrington, *The Milk of Dreams* (New York: New York Review of Books, 2013).

40 Gabriel Weisz Carrington, 'Shadow Children: Leonora as Storyteller,' *Leonora Carrington and the International Avant-Garde*, 139.

41 Cecilia Alemani will curate the Venice Biennale (2022) around *Milk of Dreams*, Lauren Elkin @lauren_elkin_ (9 June 2021).

42 Iona and Peter Opie, *The Oxford Dictionary of Nursery Rhymes* (Oxford: Oxford University Press, 1997), 77.

43 Aberth, *Leonora Carrington: Surrealism, Alchemy and Art*, 68.

44 Horses appear recurrently in Carrington's early *oeuvre*, including: *Self-Portrait* (*Inn of the Dawn Horse*, 1937), *Portrait of Max Ernst* (1939), *The Horses of Lord Candlestick* (1938), *Chambre d'Enfants à Minuit* (*Nursery at Midnight*, 1941), and *The House Opposite* (1945), as well as mid-career works such as *Habdalah Asejaledha* (1959), and *The Return of Boadicea* (1969).

45 Michaela Carter, *Leonora in the Morning Light* (New York: Avid Reader Press, 2021), 349.

46 David Hopkins, *Dark Toys: Surrealism and the Culture of Childhood* (New Haven, CT: Yale University Press, 2021), 121.

47 T. J. Demos, *The Exiles of Marcel Duchamp* (Cambridge, MA: MIT Press, 2007), 13; 21.

48 Moorhead, *The Surreal Life*, 112.

49 Marcel Duchamp also had a famous alter ego, Rrose Sélavy, whom Carrington may be playing on here.

50 Peggy Guggenheim was the first to own a *Boîte-en-valise*, labelled in gold: "I/ XX." In Ecke Bonk's inventory, a curious hierarchy becomes apparent when we

see who owned what, *The Portable Museum: The Making of the Boîte-en-valise* (London: Thames & Hudson, 1989), 166.

51   Tere Arcq, 'Leonora Carrington in Mexico: The Mirror of the Marvelous,' *Annual Stanley and Pearl Goodman Lecture on Latin American Art* (21 November 2019): www.youtube.com/watch?v=eF2PlzMfrVo (Accessed 11 May 2021). See also Susan L. Aberth, who reads *Artes 110* as "a goodbye letter," 'Animal Kingdom,' *Leonora Carrington: Magical Tales*, eds Tere Arcq and Stefan van Raay (Mexico City: Instituto Nacional de Bellas Artes, 2018), 250.

52   Penelope Rosemont, *Surrealism: Inside the Magnetic Fields* (San Francisco, CA: City Lights, 2019), 177.

53   Katharine Conley, *Surrealist Ghostliness* (Lincoln: University of Nebraska Press, 2013), 1.

54   André Breton, 'The Mediums Enter,' *Modernism: An Anthology*, ed. Lawrence Rainey, trans. Mark Polizzotti (London: Blackwell, 2005), 742. Benjamin Péret would later become a close friend to Carrington through Remedios Varo.

55   Morton, *Calling the Spirits*, 10–11.

56   Breton, 'The Mediums Enter,' 742.

57   Tessel M. Bauduin, 'The "Continuing Misfortune" of Automatism in Early Surrealism,' *communication +1*, 4:10 (September 2015), 2. Bauduin further emphasises how Breton saw spirit mediums as "instrumentalised (even captured in the actual phrase, 'medium')," 8.

58   Tessel M. Bauduin, Victoria Ferentinou and Daniel Zamani (eds), 'Introduction,' *Surrealism, Occultism and Politics: In Search of the Marvellous* (New York: Routledge, 2018), 9.

59   Hal Foster, *Compulsive Beauty* (Cambridge, MA: MIT Press, 1995), xii; xvii.

60   Leonora Carrington cited in Marina Warner, 'Introduction,' *The House of Fear*, 5.

61   Aberth, *Leonora Carrington: Surrealism, Alchemy and Art*, 14–15; Warner, 'Leonora Carrington's Spirit Bestiary,' 11–12. Potter's interests in natural history and mycology may be further paralleled with Carrington's ecological awareness.

62   Susan L. Aberth interestingly likens this series to illustrations from *The Arabian Nights* and makes a further link with potential Romany sources, '"An Allergy to Collaboration": The Early Formation of Leonora Carrington's Artistic Vision,' *Leonora Carrington and the International Avant-Garde*, 20–38.

63   Susan L. Aberth and Tere Arcq, 'As in a Mirror with Multiple Facets: Leonora Carrington and the Tarot,' *The Tarot of Leonora Carrington* (Lopen, Somerset: Fulgur Press, 2020), 68–69.

64   David Hare ed., 'Concerning the present day relative attractions of various creatures in mythology and legend,' *VVV magazine*, 1 (1942), 62.

65   Leonora Carrington cited in Evans (BBC Omnibus).

66   This is a highly sensitive area of Leonora Carrington studies, handled deftly by Marina Warner, Janet Lyon, and Alessia Zinnari, among others. Interestingly, *Down Below* (1944) is the most frequently cited of Carrington's written works in the interviews (see Appendix).

67   Lusty, *Surrealism, Feminism, Psychoanalysis,* 19–20.

68 Eburne, 'Poetic Wisdom,' 149–150.

69 Mieke Bal suggests that biography "can no longer be an alibi for criticism's intellectual laziness," 'Autotopography: Louise Bourgeois as Builder,' *Biography*, 25:1 (Winter 2002), 180.

70 Griselda Pollock, *Vision and Difference: Feminism, Femininity and the Histories of Art* (London and New York: Routledge, [1988] 2003), 78.

71 Leonora Carrington cited in Moorhead, *The Surreal Life*, 17.

72 *The House of Opposite* is the most frequently cited of Carrington's visual artworks in the interviews (see Appendix).

73 Interview with Hershman Leeson.

74 Clement Greenberg did not write about Carrington but denigrated some of her surrealist colleagues in 'Surrealist Painting,' *The Collected Essays and Criticism: Perceptions and Judgments, 1939–1944*, vol. 1, ed. John O'Brian (Chicago: University of Chicago Press, 1986), 225–231.

75 Aberth reminds us of the "misguided divisions between high art and craft" at this historical moment, 'Animal Kingdom,' 259.

76 Interview with Jenna C. Ashton.

77 Susan Stewart, *On Longing: Narratives of the Miniature, the Gigantic, the Souvenir, the Collection* (Durham, NC: Duke University Press, 1993), 61.

78 Interview with Claire Dean.

79 Interview with Ashton. See also, Alice Kettle, 'House of Opposites', *Alice Kettle* (13 May 2020): https://alicekettle.co.uk/the-house-of-opposites (Accessed 2 May 2021).

80 Carrington's *The Kitchen Garden on the Eyot* (1946) and *The Giantess* (*The Guardian of the Egg*, 1947) present exterior landscapes but are also from this period of maternal focus.

81 Dawn Adès, 'Carrington's Mysteries,' *Leonora Carrington* (Dublin: Irish Museum of Modern Art, 2013), 100.

82 Janet Lyon, 'Carrington's Sensorium,' *Leonora Carrington and the International Avant-Garde*, 168.

83 Carrington called this her "England nostalgias," cited in Moorhead, *The Surreal Life*, 202.

84 Chloe Aridjis, 'Reading with… Chloe Aridjis,' *Shelf-Awareness* (22 February 2019): www.shelf-awareness.com/issue.html?issue=3437#m43424 (Accessed 13 May 2021). Thanks to Victoria Irvine.

85 By my count there are approximately 15 female figures as well as their familiars which are predominantly domesticated animals such as birds and cats; see Tere Arcq, 'In the Land of Convulsive Beauty: Mexico,' *In Wonderland: The Surrealist Adventures of Women Artists in Mexico and the United States*, eds Ilene Susan Fort, Tere Arcq, and Terri Geis (Los Angeles and Mexico City: LACMA and Prestel, 2012), 81.

86 Aberth, *Leonora Carrington: Surrealism, Alchemy and Art*, 9.

87 Vince Fazio, *31 Women Artists* (Sedona, AZ: Sedona Arts Center, 2020), 28–31.

88 For more on this era, see Weisz Carrington, *The Invisible Painting*, 82.

89 Marina Warner, *From the Beast to the Blonde: On Fairy Tales and Their Tellers* (London: Chatto & Windus, 1994), 23; 25.

2

Another maybe

Stars are never sleeping
Dead ones and the living

—David Bowie (2013)[1]

...your adaptation deserves its own adaptation.
—aronoeL cited in Anne Walsh (2019)[2]

In 1995, Katherine Matilda ("Tilda") Swinton (b. 1960) conceived and starred in a performative installation entitled *The Maybe* (Figure 13). Eyes closed and supine, Swinton self-presented with a pair of reading glasses by her side, "asleep" in a glass case during the public hours of an exhibition at the Serpentine Gallery over the week of 4–10 September. The spare, unembellished exhibit was surrounded by an installation of inanimate objects selected by conceptual artist Cornelia Parker which some have read as intrinsic to interpreting *The Maybe*. These artefacts were objects supposedly discarded by celebrated people: Winston Churchill's cigar butt, a signed cheque by Virginia Woolf, and a camera belonging to Lee Miller, among others. Such *objets d'art*, coupled with the dreaming activity of Swinton's apparent sleep, lent the installation a marvellous edge associated with the ubiquitous surrealist legacy. With a title that is both deliberately tentative yet paradoxically definitive, *The Maybe* served as a rupture within the museological order of things. "It's called *The Maybe* because it is not about anything absolute," Swinton claimed.[3] Art critic, Caroline Lever, had the opportunity to reflect further on the contextual and intimate meanings of *The Maybe* on the occasion of the installation's reprisal for MoMA in 2013, reminding us that the 1995 rendition occurred in the wake of the death of Swinton's friend and mentor Derek Jarman, while the 2013 re-creation occurred after Swinton's mother's death. Lever describes it as "an open question, a proposal, a treasure hunt," and ultimately labels it "a never-ending maybe."[4]

Tilda Swinton is known to have a personal interest in the work of Leonora Carrington, having visited Gallery Wendi Norris's *Story of the Last Egg* exhibition in New York (2019) with long-term collaborator, Lynn Hershman

Leeson.[5] This is perhaps unsurprising—Carrington and Swinton have much in common. As with Carrington's upbringing in the North of England, Swinton is from an upper-class background in the nearby Scottish Borders and was the only girl in a family of three brothers, which no doubt enabled an assertive mode of femininity and appeal to feminism from the very beginning. Both demonstrate a deep knowledge of art history and have been immersed in avant-garde networks and thinking. Swinton's great-grandmother, Elizabeth "Elsie" Swinton, was painted by John Singer Sargent in 1897, and her cousin was the poet and critic, Edith Sitwell. Although the family has a military and political background, the arts have surprisingly flourished among the Swintons. Tilda Swinton worked with Jarman on the film *Caravaggio* (1986) and has frequently had her portrait painted by Scottish artist and playwright, John Byrne. Over the last 35 years, Swinton has emerged in the landscapes of cinema, fashion, and performance art and has come to represent an androgynous, otherworldly figure, capable of garnering a cult following while also appealing to mainstream audiences. She prefers to be known as a "film artist" or performer and artist's model rather than an actor.[6] She is described as one of Tim Walker's long-term "muses"—a term Carrington herself is known to have refuted: "I didn't have time to be anyone's muse ... I was too busy rebelling against my family and learning to be an artist."[7] However, Swinton embraces her own fashionable persona as part of the broader remit and expectations of her occupation. *W Magazine* claims that Swinton is "arguably the greatest chameleon of her generation."[8] She is often described as "sphinx-like" with a "blank-canvas of a face," a versatility which allows her to morph and shape-shift apparently effortlessly between ages, genders, and genres, from conceptual icon to queer enchantress.[9] She appears equally comfortable participating in low-budget, independent films and blockbuster studio-scale projects, and admits to finding the latter the more experimental. Swinton also reveals that she finds it much easier to perform the folkloric sorceress than the corporate lawyer.[10] Indeed, she has become typecast as the alternative magician, from the Life Extension company representative in *Vanilla Sky* (2001), who places clients into "lucid dreams," to the otherworldly fantasy figure of the White Witch in *The Chronicles of Narnia* (2005–10). This is likely due to the different registers of experience, and the idea of make-believe providing a safer space than a capitalist reality. For a thespian like Swinton, witches offer a habitual character study while the corporate suit presents an experimental challenge that tests the limits of her skillset. Carrington's frequent depiction of sorcery, transforming doctors and dictators into soothsayers and monsters, positions her within a parallel visionary spectrum to that of Swinton. As Wendi Norris rightly points out, "Leonora's work has a performative capacity."[11] Like Carrington, Swinton consolidates the ancient archetype of the outsider woman—the

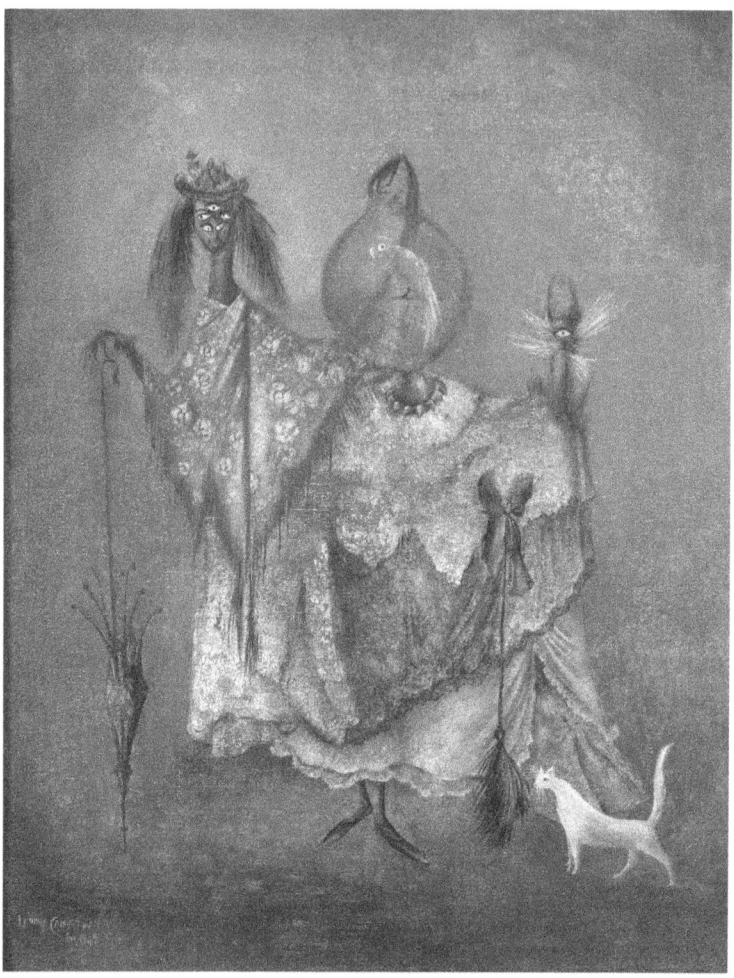

10 Leonora Carrington, *The Artist Travelling Incognito*, 1949

well-rehearsed narrative of the queer feminine as a disrupting force. This is borne out by the fact that Swinton enthusiastically embodies select characters from Carrington's paintings through the medium of the fashion story.

This chapter reconsiders Carrington in the context of late twentieth-century pop culture and the twenty-first-century fashion story as a performative medium. From a feminist perspective, I am interested in how both Swinton and Carrington have myth-busted narratives of oversight and negotiated their cult status, from high glamour to the bare bones of conceptualism. One useful model for such revisionary thinking is Mieke Bal's preposterous history: "which puts what came chronologically first ('pre-') as an aftereffect behind ('post') its later recycling."[12] As Catherine Lord and Michelle Williams Gamaker note: "[Bal] argues for an aesthetic re-visitation and re-enactment that can be flagrant and excessive."[13] This holds true for Swinton's recent performances of Carrington, and maybe even enables a preposterous reconsideration of Swinton's earlier performance installation of the mid-1990s. Here, I will reposition Swinton's notorious performance installation, *The Maybe*, within this critical framework, a conceptual dreamscape that might be used to question whether Carrington's own cult status has become encased in mythologisation.

Narrative extravagance

She could have been a character in one of her own paintings or short stories!
—Chloe Aridjis (2014)[14]

She was never a ... 'fashionable' artist so her work is outside of time and place—which is her greatness.
—Viktor Wynd (2021)[15]

Carrington's place in the visual spectrum of contemporary art has arguably been dominated in the last few years by images from Tilda Swinton and Tim Walker's two collaborative fashion stories for *W Magazine* (2013) and *i-D Magazine* (2017). Like many of my generation, I find these dream-images utterly compelling, a visual articulation of my own desires. I am fully aware they are in league with the commodification of the feminine and the queer, yet I find myself justifying and defending this appropriation of Carrington through the subcultural, alternative branding and artistic quality of such magazines, not to mention the palpable talent and unique imagination of Swinton and Walker. I am a fan.

These fashion stories follow a series of pop-cultural waves of Carrington's appropriation that continue to be laced with cult associations—a curious mixture of the highbrow and lowbrow. In order to properly contextualise them, we first need to understand Carrington's international reception as a mature artist. During the mid-twentieth-century avant-garde activities in Mexico City, Elena Poniatowska and Alejandro Jodorowsky became interested in Carrington's potential status as a guru-like figure, given her interests in tarot and world religions. Their vision of her arguably became something beyond her intended biographical persona, a possibility rather than a reality, but certainly a unique figurehead. This was followed by an another boom moment in the mid-1990s, when the cult status of Carrington began to permeate the realms of pop-music videos and fashion photography, most famously in Madonna's *Bedtime Story* (1995), directed by American filmmaker

Mark Romanek, and written by Icelandic singer-songwriter Björk, in which Madonna performs the monumental goddess from Carrington's *The Giantess* (*The Guardian of the Egg*, 1947), an iconographical gesture which is positioned in context to Latin American contemporaries such as Frida Kahlo.[16] Writing on Madonna's interest in Kahlo, Margaret Lindauer notes the mutual benefit for the publicist of pairing an artist with a celebrity—the artist gets the sales while, reciprocally, the celebrity gets to appear culturally knowledgeable and tasteful.[17] Such trends have continued in recent years. In the catalogue to the V&A blockbuster, *Frida Kahlo: Making Herself Up* (2018), Oriana Baddeley charts the continued rise of "Frida-mania" through popular, "aspirational" parodies like Beyoncé's Halloween costume of 2014, advising that such mimicry risks "obscuring the intelligence underpinning the work."[18] The repetition of a unique art-historical persona is interesting here, entailing a transition from the so-called original to the copycat or stock character. How can the contemporary arts ensure Carrington does not become cliché?

Does a comparable fandom exist for Kahlo's contemporary Carrington? Her reach may be vast in the contemporary arts but perhaps Carrington is not yet a comparable household name. The art film *Female Human Animal* (2018) features a symbolic scene where the protagonist Chloe Aridjis finds herself at a trendy art opening, repeatedly yelling in the ear of the director, Josh Appignanesi, about who she is working on: "Leonora Carrington?" Yet, such subcultural status surely lends Carrington her clout, a resistance to being kitschified. Back in 1997, Carrington appeared in an article for the *Telegraph Magazine* alongside Liam Gallagher's first solo interview since his split from indie rock band Oasis. Here, Carrington's "bizarre art" was already being co-opted, an ex-pat art star reconsidered in the context of Brit Pop: "Leonora … is today to feminist art historians what Tina Turner is to ageing rockers—something of a cult icon."[19] Such cultural appropriations are important to track because it is where we witness Carrington being plucked from her cult status and absorbed, albeit temporarily, into the pop-cultural mainstream. Although Carrington herself was far removed from the music industry, she offers a credible yet uncompromising, persona for women working in this field. For instance, English musician Alison Goldfrapp recently claimed Carrington as an "ethereal" and "intuitive" touchstone, someone whose artworks suggest "something magical [is] about to happen."[20] Imagery from Goldfrapp's lyrics and music videos, such as 'Ride a White Horse' (2006), is likely indebted to feminist-surrealist stylistics. Björk further cites Carrington's novel, *The Hearing Trumpet*, as a chief inspiration: "This book is so inspiring! You English should be proud of her. The book seems destined to be a movie. Free-flowing, spiky imagination. I love its freedom, its humour and how it invents its own laws. What specifically do I take from her? Her wig."[21] Here, Björk mischievously toys with the surprise elements of surrealist thinking in order to conjure her own version of the marvellous. The reference to Carrington's "wig" operates as a deliberate non-sequitur that denies straightforward traditions of influence. In the history of *i-D Magazine*, both Swinton and Björk are listed as iconic figures who have graced the cover with the famous wink, suggesting an equivalence of these androgynous, alternative performers.[22] Their mutual interests in and borrowing from the fancy-dress box of Carrington's art history further support such equivalence. Corresponding with poet and novelist Maggie Nelson in *AnOther* magazine, Björk explains Carrington's personal meaning:

> for me sometimes the female
> surrealists like leonora carrington (her
> "hearing trumpet" is divine!!) remedies
> varo, méret Oppenheim also offer hope.
> i felt they took over the often over-
> conceptual ideological surrealism of the
> twenties and in the next generation gave
> it flesh, nature, mythology, emotions.[23]

As one of several women working through surrealism in a technically accomplished manner, Carrington emerged as a worthy precursor for 1990s performers and stylists interested in conveying empowering messages inherited from a second-wave feminism. One could argue that this pop-cultural awareness of Carrington and her feminist-surrealist contemporaries was in no small part due to the growing literature around women's contributions to surrealism—an opportunity for "feminist intertextuality" that we know Susan Rubin Suleiman understood as a "double allegiance"—the interest in engaging with surrealist aesthetics and technique but troubled by a dominance of masculine precedents.[24]

This is true also for male icons like David Bowie, who sought out Swinton for his music video 'The Stars (Are Out Tonight)' (2013). DJ and music journalist Mary Anne Hobbs recently drew a convincing connection between Bowie and Carrington's shared use of the character Lazarus—suggesting Bowie may have read Carrington's short story, 'White Rabbits' (1941), and been inspired to write his song 'Lazarus' (2015) in response.[25] Natasha Khan, the dream pop and folktronica singer-songwriter of Bat for Lashes, emphasises the transition from subcultural to mainstream: "Bowie would take some really obscure avant-garde things and make them accessible to people. That's all part of the healing of society and how we all intricately connect to each other."[26] Swinton could be said to operate along similar lines in terms of how she works through Carrington's legacy. We are now living through an era in which auteurs are invited to curate exhibitions and guest-edit art magazines with a regularity that conforms to a trend currency.

Although one might at first assume such practices to be completely out of sync with those of a mature and geographically remote artist like Carrington, it is important to remember that the latter part of her lifespan coincided with the development of such cultural phenomena. Chadwick tells us that Carrington was "as much a follower of the physicist Stephen Hawking as of Lilith," which not only demonstrates Carrington's range of cultural touchstones but also her own awareness of popular culture.[27]

In *The Hearing Trumpet*, Carrington's character Marian laments the popularisation of surrealism: "Surrealism is no longer considered modern today and almost every village rectory and girl's school have surrealist pictures hanging on their walls" (66.) Swinton is perhaps one such former schoolgirl, revealing that she had posters of Salvador Dalí on her walls at boarding school, suggesting both her early attraction to surrealist vistas, and her awareness of the movement's iconic status and its concurrent com-mercialisation.[28] Similarly, in an interview with Tim Walker, Swinton notes that "Surrealism is liberating ... especially if you discover Surrealism in your early teens, as I did ... it's the perfect moment because it's about freedom. Your own unconscious is validated."[29] In the same interview, Swinton reveals that she and Walker had been "thinking about Leonora Carrington."[30]

Evocations of Carrington, that rub up against the pop-cultural mainstream, continue in more recent creative responses. In Anne Walsh's experimental adaptation, *Hello Leonora* (2019), Swinton is listed as part of Walsh's imaginary "cast of my movie" alongside well-known feminist practitioners (artists, writers, film directors, choreographers, and tennis players) such as Billie Jean King, Yoko Ono, Doris Lessing, Agnès Varga, and Yvonne Rainer.[31] In doing so, Walsh repositions Carrington alongside these twentieth-century icons of the contemporary imagination. Another of Walsh's strategies involved a dance workshop where participants sang 'Let it Go' from Disney's CGI feature film, *Frozen* (2013). In the context of Carrington, the song's lionising of creative isolation is, on one level, empowering. However, Walsh reminds us that the white, blonde, hourglass image of the diva-princess, Ailsa, is also restrictive and therefore not fully consistent with Carrington's overarching message of feminist liberation. This strategy of evoking popular culture recurs in the fourth chapter of Susanne Christensen's nonconformist book *Leonora's Journey* (2019) where she reimagines Carrington as Rey from *Star Wars: The Force Awakens* (2015). Specifically, Christensen rewrites the iconic scene of Rey seizing the lightsaber from Kylo Ren. By recasting Carrington in Rey's position, Christensen suggests Carrington is appropriat-ing the symbolic baton of the mysterious and powerful "force" from the fascist New Order.[32] Interestingly, both the above examples use Carrington as an opportunity to question and explore supposedly feminist scenes in millennial movies. Swinton and Walker offer the reverse strategy, the use of a famous performer to reinterpret the cult Carrington. Fashion has a long history of appropriating the historical avant-garde in order to align itself with underground pursuits. Recent examples of fashion collections that are based on or have taken inspiration from Carrington include Czech designer Tereza Rosalie Kladosova's *Muses* (2020), Canadian duo Heidi Sopinka and Claudia Dey's Horses Atelier, and *Le Mythe Dior*, a fairy-tale fashion film designed by Maria Grazia Chiuri and directed by Matteo Garrone (2020), featuring garments inspired by Carrington, among other women of surrealism.[33] Millennial model and "influencer," Kendall Jenner, even allegedly cited Carrington's collected writings on her Instagram stories reading list.[34] Like Madonna, Jenner attempts to align herself with an intellectual literary crowd as a gesture of validation. Any scepticism of bringing someone cult like Carrington into the mainstream should be weighed alongside the urgent need demonstrated recurrently in the scholarly literature to bring more creative women's achievements to the centre of critical attention. Swinton has arguably managed her own eclectic career in order to strike such a balance.

I now turn to Swinton's recent fashion stories with Walker that explicitly evoke Carrington as their mood board. As a collaborative duo, Walker and Swinton mutually complement one another. Known for his Carrollian-inspired wonderlands and eccentric English tea parties, and having photographed Kate Bush and Björk, as well as Swinton as her own ancestor Edith Sitwell (2018), Walker makes the ideal co-investigator for a fashion project on Carrington. In *W Magazine* (May 2013), Swinton appears on the cover in a hooded outfit with gloves and billowing sleeves, a surrealist fairy-tale heroine under the title 'Modern Beauty: Tilda Swinton's Surreal Fashion Fantasy.' The story includes 15 photographs of Swinton performing characters from Carrington and other surrealist artworks. Entitled 'Stranger Than Paradise,' the story begins in the mysterious domain of the Mexican jungle, with Swinton-as-Carrington haunting the gardens of Las Pozas (1949), an installation by Carrington's patron, Edward James. Las Pozas is an intricate, architectural complex of concrete columns, stairwells, pavilions, and passageways—a deliberate attempt to fuse surrealism with the archaeological imagination of Mexico. Based in the municipality of Xilitla, the location is described within the fashion story by Alice Rawthorn as a "Surrealist Xanadu."[35] Positioned within this surrealist architecture, Swinton's doll-like body becomes a focal point, as if she were a natural successor to the legacies of surrealism or a ghost of its ruins. The first magazine image recycles the architectural features from Carrington's painting, *The House Opposite* (1945) (Figure 8), namely "the double *Staircase to Nowhere*" which Carrington designed for James.[36] Swinton performs the cloaked figure from the painting. In the accompanying text, Diane Solway informs us: "[i]n Walker's dreamscapes, Swinton is the enigmatic beauty—perfectly at home in James's madcap universe."[37] The James/Carrington dialogue is updated through the Swinton/Walker collaboration. The ubiquitous "sky-blue gloves" from André Breton's surrealist novel *Nadja* (1928) have been re-created by designer Cornelia James, and become a recurrent motif throughout the tale of 'Stranger Than Paradise.'[38] The fashion story seems purpose-made for the inquisitive surrealist scholar.

Following Las Pozas, the story continues with a series of full-length portraits of Swinton often holding a prop of some kind, for example a flower or mask. Again, Swinton is rigid and doll-like in many of these images, her hair standing on end as per numerous surrealist fantasies of hysterics. The look is, at times, also reminiscent of her costume-film portrayal of *Orlando* (1992), as if harking back to her own aesthetic past. In the second image, she wears a peach-coloured dress and transparent jacket by Rick Owens and is accompanied by various props: a conch shell, a butterfly net, and a caged green parrot as in Carrington's painting *The Artist Travelling Incognito* (1949) (Figure 10). Indeed, the story has been crafted carefully into a theatrical endeavour, with set designs by Jerry Stafford and Rhea Thierstein. No doubt they are nodding to Carrington's own work for theatre via scrupulous visual and textual research. In the next image, Swinton's hair has been cropped to her "natural" (but likely enhanced) ginger colour. She is surrounded by pink roses and wears a frilly, blue Francesco Scognamiglio dress reminiscent of that worn by Carroll's literary character Alice—a favourite of Carrington's. On the following page, a monochromatic chequerboard dress and tights by Louis Vuitton match the floor, another detail from *The House Opposite*. In the background is a Carrington wall relief of a fox and iguana, perhaps the most explicit reference to her artworks in this story. Next, a banshee-like Swinton in Haider Ackerman is the first image to be accompanied by a subtitle which details Swinton's own thoughts: "Mexico's phantasmagoria ... with its innate magical realism, infuses the work of Leonora Carrington, who painted at Las Pozas. This portrait evokes one of her figures halfway transmuted into a plant, a flame, and an unknown beast."[39] Swinton makes a direct connection between an image by Carrington and one of her by Walker, and details her awareness of the hybridity so typical of the former. But this particular fashion story is not exclusively about Carrington. The surrealist techniques of photomontage, collage, and exquisite corpse are touched upon, more broadly, in an androgynous, mime-like image of Swinton wearing two black jackets, one by Balmain and the other by Max Mara. This time the gloves are different, Olivier Saillard, with lettering on the fingertips. Another surrealistic fashion detail appears on the next page—Schiaparelli-inspired pumps by Céline depict the red toenails on the outside of the shoe. Here, Swinton uses this space to comment on another exemplar of feminist-surrealism, namely Carrington's close friend, Remedios Varo: "'In works by Remedios Varo, mystical creatures, suspended in a landscape as if without gravity, create a sense of transport and vertigo,' Swinton says of the painter who 'inspired the interiors constructed for these pictures.'"[40] Elsewhere, another mouth has been collaged into Swinton's own, creating a Picasso-like grimace while she models a golden Vera Wang ballgown. For the final image of this story, giant millipedes feature on a black veil accompanied by a René Magritte quote: "ceci n'est pas une moustache," reaffirming a kitschy surrealist conundrum.[41] Overall, the poses and compositions are loyal enough to identify their sources yet detached enough to be intriguing and innovative. A classic rethink.

Swinton and Walker continued their adaptation of Carrington imagery in another fashion story four years later. This time, Swinton and Walker's collaboration for *i-D Magazine* (2017) was dedicated to Carrington's centenary. The fashion story is a chapter entitled 'To Create' within a broader guest-edit by Walker, 'The Creativity Issue,' where he reportedly photographed "135 people over 33 days."[42] This time, supermodel and activist Adwoa Aboah features on the front cover, while the Swinton/Carrington chapter is nestled within the queer English youth scene. Once again, Swinton and Walker used Carrington as a site or gauge for the contemporary *Zeitgeist* by enlisting a collaborative matrix of creative types and famous faces. Styling was again provided by Jacob K., with costumes by Spencer Horne and set design by Shona Heath, with their overall effects reminiscent of Carrington's paintings. The specific paintings re-created include: *Ab Eo Quod* (1956), *The Temptation of St Anthony* (1945), the medieval jester from *Darvault* (1950), and the horned creature in *And Then We Saw the Daughter of the Minotaur* (1953) (Figure 12). Again, a sense of intertextual elasticity allows for the possibility of details from Carrington's broader iconography to be discerned such as the headdress from *Samain* (1950), the glowing rose in *The Chair, Daghda na Tuatha dé Danann* (1955), or the dogs from *Pastoral* (1950) (Figure 20). The story becomes a detective game for the Carrington aficionado. In these vibrant, colourful, and sumptuously upholstered scenes with their exaggerated perspectives, Swinton inhabits the irrational corners of the imagination, embodying the characters of Carrington and borrowing from her distinctive iconography. The overall effect is what Bal would term "preposterous," a highly convincing, staged adaptation with a conceptual undercurrent that casts a cult film star as the queer demigod at the heart of Carrington's universe, as if this had always been her intention.[43] The fashion story has been forensically researched and carefully reframed, evidencing that Swinton and Walker have a deep, collaborative affinity with Carrington's alternative realities.

Thus, mid-twentieth-century Carrington is juxtaposed with a twenty-first-century cast list of stylists, art students, and trend-setters in fancy dress. Millner, James Merry, a long-term, former assistant and now collaborator of Björk, introduces this section by self-presenting as a "fertility god." With

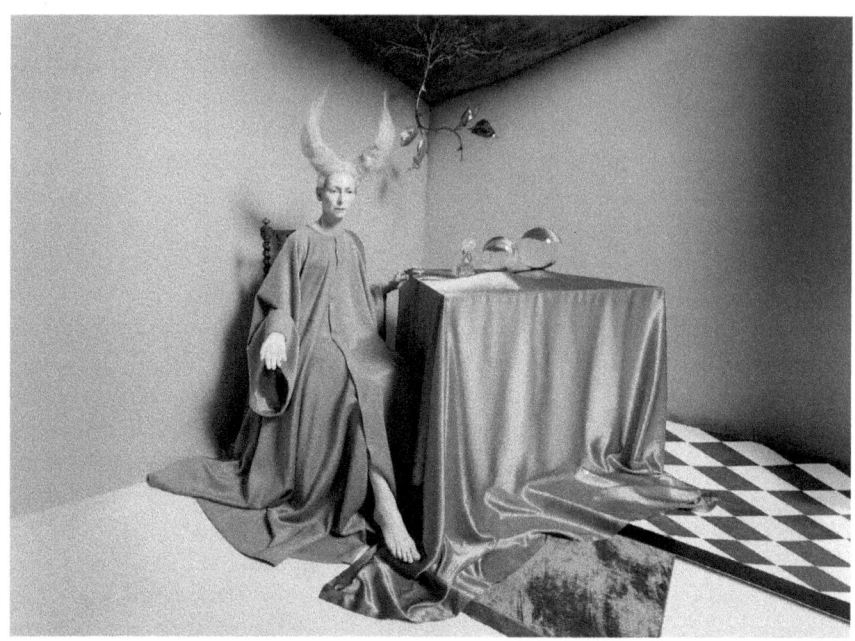

11 Tim Walker, *To Create*, 2017

ginger pigtails and an elaborate pearl headdress of his own design, the accompanying text explains that his look mimics the Fini-like moth mask which Merry has designed for the Icelandic musician while performing in surrealist guise during her *Vulnicura Tour* (2015–17). Again, one can discern an interesting parallel between Björk and Swinton, performers who have successfully navigated any perceived pop/cult divide, garnering an intergenerational following. Björk and Swinton could both be said to don Carrington's "mantle" in this regard, absorbing her powers. Here, Björk is represented by proxy; Merry is attached to her through his practice but is depicted confrontationally minotaur-like on a solo mission of creative worship. His portrait by Walker appears in the centrefold between an image of the Nike logo sprouting embroidered greenery, and a turquoise and gold-leaf re-creation of the vanitas iconography from Carrington's *Ab Eo Quod*. Merry's eco-political statement echoes Carrington: "We need to start thinking creatively about the environment and politics in order to survive. So much damage is being done by people suffering from a massive lack of imagination."[44] The melting rose seems to visually replicate this sense of climate anxiety and memento mori, while the inclusion of the Mother Goose-like golden egg heralds the beginning of a Walker-esque fairy tale where fashionista becomes activist.

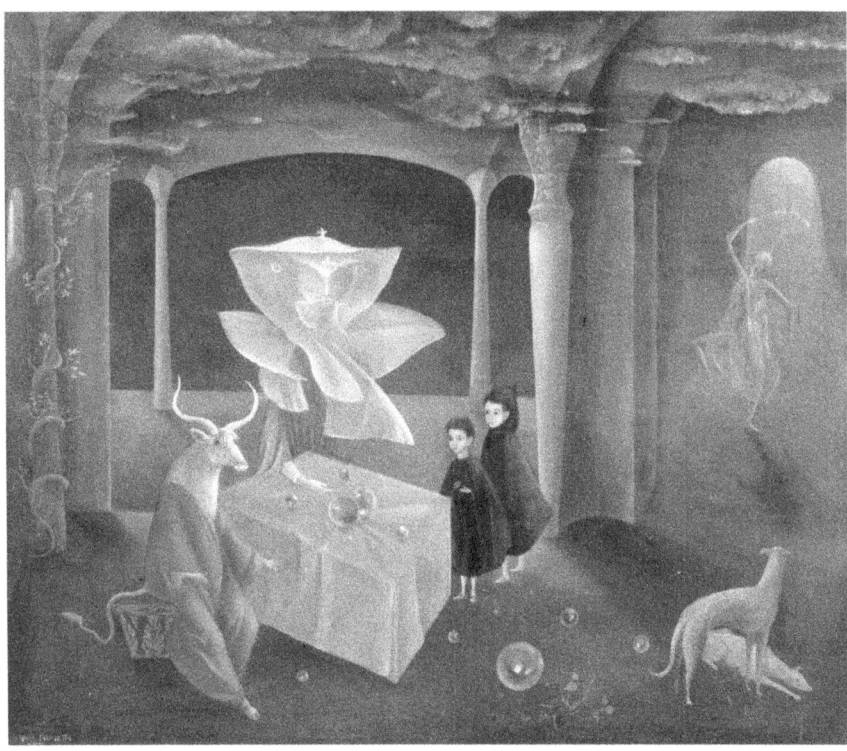

12 Leonora Carrington, *And Then We Saw the Daughter of the Minotaur*, 1953

One might say that the *i-D* spread is characteristically Carrington in terms of its maximal use of *mise-en-scène*. Her dollhouse architecture has been borrowed to build the compartmentalised narrative scenes: the jester from *Darvault* gestures the reader into the story and is juxtaposed next to another portrait of Swinton in a red dress, continuing the chequerboard flooring and turquoise-blue feature colour of the previous pages. A glimpse of *And Then We Saw the Daughter of the Minotaur* (Figure 11) beckons the reader onto the next centrefold. The source painting itself has been described as a "family portrait," with Carrington's two sons dressed in black cloaks.[45] The titular daughter meanwhile suggests a rewriting of the Minotaur myth.[46] For the realm of *i-D*, Swinton's androgynous, horned deity is flanked by two portraits of M. J. Harper, a gender-fluid dancer wearing little except spectacles and a large, gleaming trochus shell attached with a red velvet ribbon. He clutches a bouquet of red lilies and appears to be performing for Swinton like the dancing wood sprite in background of *Daughter of the Minotaur*. As with Merry, Harper is profiled biographically and his creative statement is highlighted: "Right now it's absolutely necessary for creatives to dig, dive and investigate—whether you need to scream or speak quietly."[47] Meanwhile, Swinton's contributions are entirely visual, her interest in Carrington left to speak for itself. The artist is performed as a character, the underlying visual message suggesting that 'To Create' is to be artistic and to surround yourself with non-normative, experimental, creative beings as an avant-garde culture. This sequence is concluded with another two, elongated portraits of Harper followed by a climactic vision of Swinton surrounded by plastic sheets and black curly hair, an exaggeration of Carrington's own self-presentation in her *Inn of the Dawn Horse* (1937), and, more explicitly, a miniature figure proffering a magical device plucked from the central group in *The Temptation of St Anthony* (1945).[48]

Swinton's Carrington pages are then followed by a voyeuristic, fish-eye-lensed, double spread of fine-art students Ollie Pins Azarmi and Karim Boumjimar, cavorting in a homoerotic tableau with crushed fruit, that continues some of the content of Carrington's vanitas iconography found in *Ab Eo Quod*. Readers learn that Azarmi hopes to become a dermatologist while Boumjimar had their own nipples and navel surgically removed then sold them as art objects.[49] This gesture of extreme body modification nods to the queer conceptualism of Carrington's colleague, Marcel Duchamp, and the surrealist game of the exquisite corpse. Again Swinton-as-Carrington is repositioned betwixt and between early twenty-first-century Generation Z and the so-called "bright young people" of Carrington's early career of the 1930s (an equivalent social "set" made famous by Evelyn Waugh's novel, *Vile Bodies* (1930), which we know Carrington read).[50] Both social milieus can be considered relatively London-centric, elite trend cultures as well as avant-garde in attitude. Dawn Adès reminds us that, although from elite backgrounds, both Carrington and Edward James enjoyed "satiriz[ing] the conventions and absurdities of the debutantes' ball, the gentleman's club."[51] Carrington's youth cultural status within the English surrealist milieu provides something of a poster girl for subsequent generations in this respect. Swinton and Walker's visual and eco-critical connections between Carrington and current subcultural dynamics are also worth reiterating. Interestingly, the majority of their source paintings were made when Carrington was a young mother in Mexico City rather than during her so-called "reluctant debutante" era in London, perhaps in keeping with Swinton's own sense of the queer maternal.[52] Yet, Walker and Swinton refreshingly maintain a vision of Carrington that is intergenerational, loyal to, aligned with, indeed enveloped within, queer, intersectional London subculture. Moreover, the magazine's mission statement of "originate—don't imitate" is arguably carried through in this collaborative, performative adaptation of Carrington's pictures; what Swinton and Walker achieve here is far more than simple imitation, rather a completely new visual argument for Carrington's imaginative possibilities.[53]

Before I return to Swinton's conceptual fantasy, *The Maybe*, it is worth considering one more magazine feature, this time a guest-edited issue of *Aperture* on the theme of Virginia Woolf's novel, *Orlando* (1928), and its filmic adaptation by Sally Potter (1992), in which Swinton famously starred.[54] Linda Hutcheon uses Potter's film as a chief exemplar in her *Theory of Adaptation* (2006), and proposes Potter had an "ideological motivation" for reconsidering Woolf's novel as a film, related to class and colonial critique as well as gender.[55] Swinton may have very similar reasons for adapting Carrington. The androgyny of *Orlando* might be compared with the androgyny of Carrington's early self-portrait, *The Inn of the Dawn Horse*, suggesting Carrington and Swinton share a mutual interest in gender play and in assuming different points of view. In her introduction to this special issue, Swinton writes that "[t]his book, this slender plaything of an excursion, is, perhaps, the most transgressive experiment [Woolf] ever made."[56] Like Swinton and Carrington, Woolf came from a mixed lineage, "some famous, some obscure," so there is a fitting sense of overlap and identification.[57] Placing Swinton between Jarman and Woolf, B. Ruby Rich writes: "both were conjuring new aesthetics and vernaculars that discomforted their own ages. Both were operating outside the normative rules and regulations of their craft."[58] By extension, it could be said that Woolf/Potter appear to have provided the groundwork, showing Swinton what could be done with a costumed drama when it came to her treatment of Carrington.

Sleep of reason

Orlando is the book to put under your pillow and rest upon.
—Tilda Swinton (2012)[59]

In Chloe Aridjis's novel, *Sea Monsters* (2019), the protagonist, Luisa, ponders the fate of herself and her friend Julian: "as we wandered side by side through a landscape of perhaps. Perhaps he would become a sculptor, or a rock musician. Perhaps I would become an astronomer or an archaeologist."[60] There is a poetics to such daydreaming, a perpetual "maybeing," we might term it, a glimpse into a crystal ball. The metaphor of the aquarium recurs throughout the novel: "a slice of sea in a corner of my father's study … Someone once said that the dream is the aquarium of the night, but to my mind night was the aquarium of the dream, with our visions framed within it."[61] Swinton has frequently noted her own creative reliance on the frame.[62] This is an important aspect of Carrington's narratives too—what to dream up within the picture plane or page—a series of possibilities whose meanings perpetually shape-shift. Like an aquarium, the conceptual framing of *The Maybe* (Figure 13) relies on its glass container. In Carol Mavor's *Aurelia* (2017), glass plays a significant role, particularly in terms of epiphany—the act of showing. As a substance typical of the fairy-tale genre, Mavor traces its transformative qualities, from the ubiquitous (if mistranslated) Cinderella slipper to the glass stomachs and intestines in artworks by Kiki Smith and Asta Gröting. Snow White's translucent coffin is cunningly overlaid by Mavor with the glass-plate photographic negatives of the Victorian era as *memento mori*.[63] Writing on the spare minimalism of the fairy-tale narrative form and its "normalised magic," Kate Bernheimer points out: "if you look back at traditional fairy tales you will also find a very limited use of color and a heavy reliance on things that are metallic or glass ... The images in a fairy tale are very isolated, very specific. So precise. So deceptively simple."[64] Thus, we may think of Tilda Swinton's *The Maybe* as a fairy tale, stripped back to its bare essence. Such an idea echoes Carrington's literary reminder: "Houses are really bodies. We connect ourselves with walls, roofs, and objects just as we hang on to our livers, skeletons, flesh and blood stream."[65] In reconsidering *The Maybe*, an emphasis on conceptual narrativity is important, especially in relation to Carrington, whose own work is suffuse with storytelling. Without suggesting Swinton was necessarily aware of the artworks Carrington was making around the mid-1990s when *The Maybe* was first performed, it is interesting to note that Carrington was in fact making starker, more pared-down representations such as *The Memory Tower* (1995) around this time.

The Maybe pre-dates Swinton's explicit work on Carrington, but I would suggest its conceptual architecture presents a blueprint for the subsequent fashion stories. Like Goya, who Carrington admired, *The Maybe* offers a contemporary version of his *Sleep of Reason Produces Monsters* (1799) in that dreaming alludes to invisible and irrational ideas. Another iconographical precedent for *The Maybe* might include Henry Fuseli's *The Nightmare* (1781), a picture which was surely also of high importance to Carrington, given the presence of the white mare and incubus.[66] Hans Christian Andersen's 'The Princess and the Pea' (1835) comes to mind, a fairy tale about extreme feminine sensitivity that was illustrated by many of Carrington's childhood nursery favourites—Arthur Rackham and Edmund Dulac, among others.[67] Surrealist precedents also appear to lurk compositionally in *The Maybe*, for example Claude Cahun's photographic *Self-Portrait* (1932) where the artist self-presents as impossibly tiny, as if asleep inside an antique chest of drawers. Cahun has recently received her own feminist-surrealist re-enactment through the work of contemporary artist Gillian Wearing (2017), exploring the active/passive dichotomy of appropriation and self-portraiture, and what Wearing terms her "spiritual camaraderie" with Cahun.[68] Another example

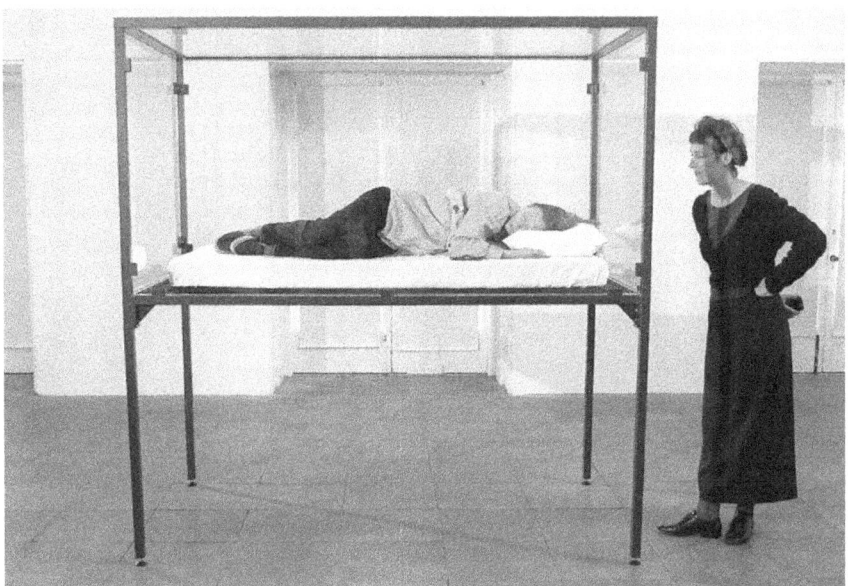

13 Tilda Swinton, *The Maybe*, 1995

is Francesca Woodman's hauntings of dilapidated furniture such as *Untitled, Providence, Rhode Island* (*c*.1975), where Woodman depicts herself tumbling out of a display cabinet containing taxidermic specimens of a racoon, a fox, and several birds.[69] Amelia Jones and Jason Farago remind us of further performance-art precursors to *The Maybe*, such as Chris Burden's *White Light White Heat* (1975) and *Bed Piece* (1972).[70] One might extend such thoughts to encompass successors such as Samantha Sweeting's performance installation, *He Loved Her, and Sometimes She Loved Him Too* (2011), featuring a bed as the performative site for storytelling.

The Maybe is frequently, albeit inaccurately, assumed to have been the idea of conceptual artist Cornelia Parker. In an interview with Lisa Tickner (2002), the piece is variously described as a collaboration, or as "a performance conceived and performed by Tilda Swinton within an installation by Parker at the Serpentine Gallery 1995." During the interview, Parker claims:

> Tilda had an idea to do a performance where she slept as a Snow White character—a fictional character—but through our collaboration it changed to her sleeping as herself. The label on her case read 'Matilda Swinton (1960–)'. Some people thought she was an imposter or a waxwork but she was really 'there,' as a non-performing performer, a sort of absent presence.[71]

The idea that Swinton would appear costumed as Snow White (one assumes Disney's ubiquitous yellow, blue, and red frock of 1937) was quickly abandoned prior to the performance in favour of casual clothing and a pair of reading glasses as a prop in her hands. It was as if Swinton had fallen asleep after reading some narrative of enchantment and assumed the role of a Sleeping Beauty instead. Tickner's reading of *The Maybe* is as follows:

> Tilda's living presence enhanced the pathos and frailty of the objects. Perhaps she dreamed them, or dreamed the narratives of the past in which they'd had a functioning place. It was very unsettling looking at her. You couldn't look at her as an exhibit; she was a human being. But you couldn't look at her as a human without feeling guilty. This was an art gallery. We were licensed to look. But she couldn't look back and sleeping is private ... Some visitors were apparently incensed that the 'star' of the show was not performing, was doing nothing, but sleeping is not really doing nothing.[72]

In Tickner's account, there is a suggestion that Swinton is somehow inaccessible, untouchable, while paradoxically still very present. Swinton was playing herself asleep, but her cult celebrity distinguished the meaning of her containment. This was not an anonymous figure that was sleeping but someone known from the medium of film. However, Farago reminds us of Swinton's "modest celebrity" in 1995 (as compared with the fame she had achieved by the 2013 rendition) and that this fact was crucial to its meaning.[73] The inverse may be applied to understandings of Carrington; Carrington was being appropriated by Madonna in 1995 but by much more DIY, experimental, and conceptual undercurrents by 2013. In the history of *The Maybe*, Swinton's mythologisation and demythologisation occur simultaneously, much like the surrealist marvellous within the everyday. The glass case not only emphasised her status as precious but provided a simple measure that both apotheosised her celebrity while offering a necessary vision of rest and creative hibernation.[74] One might make further allusions to the preservation of Lenin in his tomb, suggesting an accessible, political dimension to interpretations of *The Maybe*. In Walter Benjamin's opinion: "film responds to the shrivelling of the aura with an artificial build-up of the 'personality' outside the studio. The cult of the movie star, fostered by the money of the film industry, preserves not the unique aura of the person but the 'spell of the personality.'"[75] In an article about artists who have devised and performed within their own artworks, Deborah Cherry writes that the success of *The Maybe* lies in its "confounding museological exclusions of the animate," adding that "Swinton's compelling performance unsettled the looking of disinterested aesthetics and provoked disturbing questions about voyeurism." In Cherry's view, *The Maybe* is thus "confounding," "unsettling," and "disturbing," with its success as an exhibit located in what she terms a "troubling presence." [76]

Cherry's notion of a "troubling presence" and Parker's notion of "absent presence" may suggest the mechanics of metaphor enabling the performance to function as both a transgressive encounter and as a visual analogy or set of coordinates for something else. Yet, absence has arguably come to dominate and outweigh understandings of this particular installation, for as Amelia Jones and Joanna Scanlan have more recently argued, Swinton's labour was effectively erased by the way in which this artwork was subsequently written about.[77] Echoes of Carrington's critical erasure or suppression should be kept in mind at this point, a touchy subject given the sustained emphasis on the oversight narrative, which has arguably perpetuated such erasure (surely we should be championing her presence rather than bemoaning her absence). Scanlan points out that the nature of Swinton's performance prevented her from answering press calls, which we might compare with the fact that Carrington's location in Mexico for much of her career reduced her availability to English-language scholarship.[78] Swinton and Carrington's status as women has no doubt further contributed to their supposedly "sphinx-like" personas, although one could argue that these are partially self-induced, be it Carrington's refusal to interpret her work or Swinton's rightful guarding of her private life. Importantly, Scanlan brings the performative dynamics of *The Maybe* back to a sense of embodiment by emphasising the toll the performance took on Swinton's body (especially her kidneys, given she could not urinate for 8 hours a day) as a form of endurance art.[79] Carrington's labour and prolific output could also be understood in terms of endurance, especially her well-documented corporeal and psychological trials and tribulations during the Second World War (her induced vomiting and subjection to Cardiazol). Where Carrington was incarcerated, Swinton's containment was voluntary, yet both can be seen to explore the notion of the safe space as a feminist concept.

To secure the link between the screen and the canvas, Swinton's even earlier collaboration with Jarman must be brought back into the frame (one might recall that she was initially prompted to make *The Maybe* in the wake of Jarman's death).[80] *Caravaggio* explores the story of the seventeenth-century baroque painter, often through anachronistic *mise-en-scène*, including a motorbike, a typewriter, and a calculator. Swinton plays the role of Caravaggio's favourite model, Lena, a prostitute turned courtesan who models for his *Penitent Magdalene* (*Mary Magdalene*, 1594). Aaron Hicklin reminds us: "Not everyone appreciated his films—one critic described *Caravaggio* as 'less a movie than an act of vandalism'—but they were devoutly independent and agreeably homoerotic. It was the perfect foil for Swinton's dissident tendency."[81] Such content chimes with Swinton and Walker's *i-D Magazine* fashion story almost thirty years later. As with *Caravaggio* (1986), *The Maybe* is also told through tableau or living picture. Bal's interest in "the '*Caravaggisti*' of our time" offers a useful model for such intertextuality, be it Jarman/Caravaggio or Swinton/Carrington, especially in terms of their preferred medium, film/painting.[82] Interestingly,

Bal deliberately omitted Jarman's project from her study, as she felt she needed to "avoid a conception of quotation that might be misconstrued as too literal."[83] Swinton, meanwhile, draws on her own association with the avant-garde in her quotation of history. One way of uniting Swinton's fashion stories with her performance installation in the arena of Carrington studies may be in terms of an esoteric conceptualism, one that was offered by a primary surrealism associated with Marcel Duchamp but subsequently revised and developed by more recent generations. To further understand Swinton's treatment of Carrington through this lens, we now journey further into the world of contemporary art, to the practice of Turner-prize nominee Lucy Skaer and her *Leonora* cycle.

Notes

During the Covid-19 pandemic, I began to read images of *The Maybe* retrospectively as a visual metaphor for quarantine as well as a statement on the privacy and democracy of dreaming, and the rights to rest and hibernation.

1 David Bowie, 'The Stars (Are Out Tonight),' *The Next Day* (2013).
2 Anne Walsh, *Hello Leonora, Soy Anne Walsh* (Cambridge, MA: MIT Press, 2019), 222.
3 Tilda Swinton in *Creative Camera* (August–September 1995), 50.
4 Caroline Lever, 'Tilda Swinton's The Maybe,' *AnOther* (17 April 2013): www.anothermag.com/art-photography/2664/tilda-swintons-the-maybe (Accessed 12 May 2020).
5 Personal correspondence with Lynn Hershman Leeson (12 May 2021). Natasha Boas also tells us that Swinton visited the 2019 *Story of the Last Egg* exhibition at Gallery Wendi Norris in New York as part of Swinton's ongoing research, 'The Leonora Carrington Effect: What We Can Learn From Carrington Today' in *The Life and Influence of Leonora Carrington: A Symposium* (New York: Gallery Wendi Norris, 2019): https://vimeo.com/364355299 (Accessed 9 July 2020).
6 Aaron Hicklin, 'We'd Sit at Church Looking Down on Children From the Village,' *Herald Magazine* (2008), 9.
7 Leonora Carrington cited in Whitney Chadwick, *Woman Artists and the Surrealist Movement* (London: Thames & Hudson, 1985), 66.
8 Jenny Comita, 'Tilda Swinton Transforms Again, Into the Legendary Eccentric Edith Sitwell,' *W Magazine* (2018): www.wmagazine.com/story/tilda-swinton-tim-walker-fashion-photos-edith-sitwell (Accessed 14 May 2020).
9 Hicklin, 'We'd Sit at Church', 7–9.
10 Mark Kermode, 'In Conversation with Tilda Swinton', British Film Institute (March 2020): www.youtube.com/watch?v=PfaETIdhgcA (Accessed 13 May 2020).
11 Wendi Norris, 'An Endlessly Unfolding Gift,' *The Story of the Last Egg* (New York and San Francisco: Gallery Wendi Norris, 2019), 9.

12 Mieke Bal, *Quoting Caravaggio: Contemporary Art, Preposterous History* (London and Chicago: University Chicago Press, 1999), 7.

13 Catherine Lord with Michelle Williams Gamaker, 'House of Preposterous Women: Michelle Williams Gamaker re-auditions Kanchi,' *OAR: The Oxford Artistic and Practice Based Research Platform*, 3 (2018): www.oarplatform.com/house-of-preposterous-women-michelle-williams-gamaker-re-auditions-kanchi (Accessed 5 June 2020).

14 Interview with Chloe Aridjis.

15 Interview with Viktor Wynd.

16 Susan L. Aberth also notes Madonna's interest, *Leonora Carrington: Surrealism, Alchemy and Art* (Aldershot: Lund Humphries, 2004), 8.

17 Margaret A. Lindauer, *Devouring Frida: Art History and Popular Celebrity of Frida Kahlo* (Middletown, CT: Wesleyan University Press, 1999), 173.

18 Oriana Baddeley, 'Frida Redressed,' *Frida Kahlo: Making Herself Up* (London: V&A, 2018), 186. The actor Helena Bonham Carter also dressed as Kahlo for a photoshoot by Lorenzo Aguis in 2015.

19 Caroline Cass, 'The Mistress of Surrealism,' *Telegraph Magazine* (16 August 1997): 28.

20 Jennifer Higgie, 'Alison Goldfrapp on Leonora Carrington,' *Bow Down: Women in Art History* (September 2020) [podcast]).

21 Björk cited in Rebecca Nicholson, 'Björk: what inspires me,' *Guardian* (2012): www.theguardian.com/music/2012/may/03/bjork-what-inspires-me (Accessed 18 May 2020).

22 'About Us,' *i-D Magazine* (2020): https://i-d.vice.com/en_uk/page/i-d-about-us-en-uk (Accessed 4 July 2020).

23 Björk, 'Björk Guest-Edit: In Conversation with Maggie Nelson,' *AnOther* (Spring/Summer 2019): www.anothermag.com/design-living/11554/bjork-guest-edit-in-conversation-with-maggie-nelson (Accessed 3 June 2020).

24 Susan Rubin Suleiman, *Subversive Intent: Gender, Politics, and the Avant-Garde* (Cambridge, MA and London: Harvard University Press, 1990), 162.

25 Mary Anne Hobbs @maryannehobbs (4 November 2020). Grateful thanks to Roger Shannon.

26 Natasha Khan cited in Laird Borrelli-Persson, 'Bat for Lashes's Natasha Khan is the Vampire Heroine We Need Now,' *Vogue* (2020): www.vogue.com/article/bat-for-lashes-natasha-khan-is-the-ultimate-vampire-heroine (Accessed 14 July 2020).

27 Whitney Chadwick, 'El Mundo Mágico: Leonora Carrington's Enchanted Garden,' *Leonora Carrington: The Mexican Years* (San Francisco: Mexican Museum, 1991), 14–16. Grateful thanks to Felicity Gee @fiandshoegaze (14 March 2018).

28 Tilda Swinton interviewed by Isabel Stevens, 'Smoke and Mirrors and Make-Believe,' *Sight and Sound Magazine* (April 2020), 27. The Art Story draw a brief comparison between Dalí's collaborations with Elsa Schiaparelli and Swinton's collaboration with Walker, 'Magic and Mystery, Fantasy and Fashion: Leonora Carrington in Pop Culture,' *The Art Story Blog* (n.d.): www.theartstory.org/blog/magic-and-mystery-fantasy-and-fashion-leonora-carrington-in-pop-culture (Accessed 3 June 2020).

29 Tilda Swinton cited in Tim Walker, *Tim Walker: Wonderful Things* (London: V&A, 2019), 153.

30 Swinton cited in *Tim Walker*, 153.

31 As Julia Bryan-Wilson points out, these cast lists are "overwhelmingly non-'male,'" 'Letters on Casting,' *Hello Leonora*, 79–80; 86.

32 Susanne Christensen, *Leonora's Journey*, trans. Matt Bagguley (2019), 7. Unpublished manuscript.

33 Matteo Garrone and Maria Grazia Chiuri, *Le Mythe Dior* (2020): www.youtube.com/watch?v=yxBFwqRbI8c (Accessed 9 July 2020).

34 Chelsea Hodson @chelseahodson (7 November 2019); Bianca Nieves, '10 Best Books For Teens According To Kendall Jenner,' *Teen Vogue* (17 March 2020): www.teenvogue.com/story/books-for-teens (Accessed 17 April 2021). Thanks to Daniel Weisz.

35 Alice Rawsthorn, 'Stranger Than Paradise,' *W Magazine* (May 2013), 140.

36 Edward James owned Carrington's picture *The House Opposite*; see Tere Arcq, Stefan van Raay and Joanna Moorhead, *Surreal Friends: Leonora Carrington, Remedios Varo and Kati Horna* (Chichester: Pallant House, 2010), 25.

37 Diane Solway, 'Stranger Than Paradise,' *W Magazine* (May 2013), 129.

38 This choice is apposite because Cornelia James would have been a contemporary of Carrington (they were born in the same year, 1917). Cornelia James also studied at the very same Vienna art school from which Hitler was rejected, again suggesting the power of feminine creativity in the face of fascism.

39 Tilda Swinton cited in 'Stranger Than Paradise,' 133.

40 Swinton cited in 'Stranger Than Paradise,' 138.

41 Swinton cited in 'Stranger Than Paradise,' 145.

42 Holly Shackleton, 'Editorial: The Creativity Issue,' *i-D Magazine* (Summer 2017), 34.

43 Bal, *Quoting Caravaggio*, 7.

44 James Merry cited in Frankie Dunn, 'To Create,' *i-D Magazine* (2017), 182–183.

45 Susan L. Aberth and Tere Arcq, 'Magical Reflection: The Creative Collaborations of Leonora Carrington and Remedios Varo' in *The Life and Influence of Leonora Carrington: A Symposium* (New York: Gallery Wendi Norris, 2019): https://vimeo.com/357681039 (Accessed 9 July 2020).

46 Indeed, Marina Warner has rightly compared Carrington's painting to the lonely figure of *The Minotaur* (1885) by the English symbolist painter, George Frederic Watts, Chloe Aridjis, 'Talking about Leonora Carrington (with Marina Warner and Jennifer Higgie),' *Houses Are Really Bodies* (London: Cubitt, 2017): www.cubittartists.org.uk/event/houses-are-really-bodies-public-programme (Accessed 17 July 2020).

47 M. J. Harper cited in Clementine de Pressigny, 'To Create,' *i-D Magazine*, 188.

48 Grateful thanks to Anna Watz for this detail. Interestingly, Double Edge Theatre also perform this specific detail in *Leonora's World* (2018).

49 Ollie Pins Azarmi cited in Ryan Peterson, 'Young Londoners, Straight Up,' *i-D Magazine* (2016): https://i-d.vice.com/en_uk/article/j583qp/young-londoners-straight-up (Accessed 2 July 2020); Ted Stansfield, 'Teen artist removes his nipples and sells them as art,' *Dazed* (2016): www.dazeddigital.com/artsandculture/

article/31032/1/teen-artist-removes-his-nipples-and-sells-them-as-art (Accessed 2 July 2020).

50 Later in life, Carrington read the novels of Ian McEwan. *Atonement* (2001) focuses on a similar inter-war English context, although far less sardonically than Waugh's portrayal. See Joanna Moorhead, *The Surreal Life of Leonora Carrington* (London: Virago, 2017), 244; and Chloe Aridjis, 'Talking about Leonora Carrington (with Marina Warner and Jennifer Higgie),' *Houses Are Really Bodies.*

51 Dawn Adès, 'Carrington's Mysteries,' *Leonora Carrington* (Dublin: Irish Museum of Modern Art, 2013), 100.

52 Natalya Lusty, *Surrealism, Feminism, Psychoanalysis* (Aldershot: Ashgate, 2007), 26; Tilda Swinton cited in Jeremy O. Harris, 'Playful, Fantastical, Rare: At Home With Tilda Swinton On Her Highlands Estate,' *Vogue* (14 February 2021): www.vogue.co.uk/arts-and-lifestyle/article/tilda-swinton-interview (Accessed 28 April 2021).

53 'About Us,' *i-D Magazine* (2020).

54 Tilda Swinton ed., *Aperture* 235 (Summer 2019). The headline, "Guest-edited by Tilda Swinton. Inspired by Virginia Woolf," is comparable to Chloe Aridjis and Josh Appignanesi's film credit that *Female Human Animal* is "haunted by Leonora Carrington" (2018).

55 Linda Hutcheon, *A Theory of Adaptation* (Abingdon: Routledge, 2013), 94.

56 Tilda Swinton, 'Introduction,' *Orlando* (Edinburgh: The Canons, 2012), xiv.

57 Woolf cited in Swinton, 'Introduction,' *Orlando*, xi.

58 B. Ruby Rich, 'The Time Travellers,' *Aperture*, 235 (Summer 2019), 42.

59 Swinton, 'Introduction,' *Orlando*, xvi.

60 Chloe Aridjis, *Sea Monsters* (London: Chatto & Windus, 2019), 9.

61 Aridjis, *Sea Monsters*, 11.

62 See for example Gregory Crewdson, '20 questions with Tilda Swinton and Gregory Crewdson' (14 April 2020): www.youtube.com/watch?v=q0XkPo1P360 (Accessed 10 July 2020).

63 Carol Mavor, *Aurelia: Art and Literature Through the Mouth of the Fairy Tale* (London: Reaktion Books, 2017), 121.

64 Kate Bernheimer, 'Fairy Tale is Form, Form is Fairy Tale,' *The Writer's Notebook: Craft Essays from Tin House*, eds Aimee Bender, Dorothy Allison, and Susan Bell (Portland, OR: Tin House Books, 2009): 67; 69.

65 Leonora Carrington, *The Hearing Trumpet* (London: Penguin, 2005), 13.

66 Marina Warner has previously made this visual comparison, 'Leonora Carrington's Spirit Bestiary; or the Art of Playing Make-Belief,' *Leonora Carrington: Paintings, Drawings and Sculptures 1940–1990*, ed. Andrea Schlieker (London: Serpentine Gallery, 1991), 14.

67 Tim Walker also made a version of Andersen's 'Princess and the Pea' for *Vogue* (2006).

68 Felicity Gee, 'Review: of Gillian Wearing and Claude Cahun: Behind the Mask, Another Mask,' *ASAP/J* (27 April 2017): https://asapjournal.com/a-review-of-gillian-wearing-and-claude-cahun-behind-the-mask-another-mask-felicity-gee (Accessed 12 May 2021). Grateful thanks to Anna Watz for this thought.

69 Katharine Conley discusses both Cahun and Woodman in *Surrealist Ghostliness* (Lincoln and London: University of Nebraska Press, 2013).

70 Amelia Jones and Adrian Heathfield, eds, *Perform, Repeat, Record: Live Art in History* (London: Intellect, 2012), 470; Jason Farago, 'The Real Story Behind Tilda Swinton's Performance at MoMA,' *New Republic* (28 March 2013): https://newrepublic.com/article/112782/real-story-behind-tilda-swintons-performance-moma (Accessed 11 July 2020).

71 Cornelia Parker cited in Lisa Tickner, 'A Strange Alchemy: Cornelia Parker,' *Difference and Excess in Contemporary Art: The Visibility of Women's Practice*, ed. Gill Perry (London: Blackwell, 2004), 66.

72 Tickner, 'A Strange Alchemy,' 66.

73 Farago, 'The Real Story.'

74 Tilda Swinton, 'Another Email from Tilda Swinton to Amelia Jones, 29 April 2008,' *Perform, Repeat, Record: Live Art in History*, eds Amelia Jones and Adrian Heathfield, 476 (London: Intellect, 2012).

75 Walter Benjamin, 'The Work of Art in the Age of Mechanical Reproduction,' *Illuminations*, ed. Hannah Arendt, trans. Harry Zohn (London: Pimlico, 1999), 231.

76 Deborah Cherry, 'Troubling Presence: Body, Sound and Space in Installation Art of the Mid-1990s,' *RACAR: Revue D'art Canadienne / Canadian Art Review*, 25:1/2 (1998), 23 www.jstor.org/stable/42630590 (Accessed 12 May 2020).

77 Jones and Heathfield, eds, *Perform, Repeat, Record*, 438.

78 Joanna Scanlan and Tilda Swinton, 'The Maybe: Modes of Performance and the "Live,"' *Perform, Repeat, Record: Live Art in History*, eds Amelia Jones and Adrian Heathfield (London: Intellect, 2012), 480.

79 Scanlan and Swinton, 'The Maybe', 480.

80 Swinton, 'Another Email,' 473.

81 Hicklin, 'We'd Sit at Church', 9.

82 Bal, *Quoting Caravaggio*, 2.

83 Bal, *Quoting Caravaggio*, 21.

3

Esoteric conceptualism

The ongoing practice of Surrealism seemed suddenly radical to me when thought about as current: a strategy of living by the irrational.
—Lucy Skaer (2008)[1]

Leonora Carrington and conceptual practice may strike one initially as an unlikely pairing. The excessive esotericism, fantastical landscapes, and overall maximalism that characterise her approach and mythical, otherworldly status would at first sight appear completely out of sync with the cerebral concerns and mode of thinking generated by colleagues like Marcel Duchamp. Yet, Carrington was included in *First Papers of Surrealism* exhibition and accompanying catalogue curated by Duchamp and André Breton at the Whitelaw Reid Mansion in New York (1942). As is now well known, Duchamp deployed a series of "compensation portraits" to represent the exhibiting surrealists, shoring up the sense of dislocation and the opportunity to forge a new identity during wartime commotion. For Carrington's page in the catalogue, Duchamp appropriated Walker Evans's portrait of Allie Mae Burroughs, *Sharecropper's Wife* (1936), to introduce a reproduction of Carrington's painting *La chasse* (*The Hunt*) (1942). Writing on such "compensation portraits," art historian David Hopkins makes an intriguing link with a much later art-historical context, namely conceptual artist Sherrie Levine, who also appropriated this portrait in her practice and renamed it *After Walker Evans* (1981). Given the revisionary feminist scholarship that was emerging around this period, Levine may have knowingly done this as an intellectual response, recycling the portrait as a surrealist micro-history. As a double appropriation, Hopkins argues that Levine deployed it as a "symbolic avatar" for Carrington.[2] Since then, Carrington has come to operate as an avatar for numerous other contemporary artists.

The Glasgow-based conceptual artist Lucy Skaer (b. 1975) offers one of the most insightful inversions of Carrington. For anyone familiar with Skaer's critically self-reflexive work on the nature of visuality and mixed-media approach to interrogating "the image," her interest in a visual narrator like Carrington might again initially strike one as surprising. Yet, since 2006,

Skaer has claimed Carrington as a "disassembling logic," a catalyst for being able to reconsider her own approach to art-making.[3] Stacy Boldrick effectively summarises Skaer's iconoclastic practice as follows: "In all her work, Skaer turns found images into drawings by breaking relationships between forms and meanings, abstracting and enlarging the images, and using specific techniques and materials to create new systems of representation."[4] This chapter seeks to investigate Carrington's prompt to contemporary conceptual art practices. The cerebral aspects of Duchamp are rarely compared with Carrington's elaborately narrative and painterly imagination, but I would insist they are present here. For instance, one might consider her impish collaboration and assisted readymade, *Untitled (For Juan Soriano*, 1961), comprising a gilt picture frame, shooting gallery, and accompanying toilet roll, within this context, not to mention her earlier *Untitled (The Dogs of the Sleeper)* (1942) etching (Figure 17), with its strange lozenge of space and clusters of surrealist imagery. I propose that Skaer's undoing of the image arguably enables a greater understanding of such connections. With close reference to Skaer's *Leonora* cycle, including my own curation of this exhibit in 2016, I consider how such detonation and reconfiguration has ultimately transformed Carrington into a *medium* for the early twenty-first century, one to be worked in and through.

Five years prior to her first encounter with Carrington, Skaer had arguably already been experimenting with a recalibration of the marvellous in the everyday, not as a form of surrealism *per se* but rather as a contemporary acknowledgement of a historical legacy which continues to shape conceptual practice. One of Skaer's most marvellous juxtapositions was an action she made during a residency in 2001 entitled *Scorpion/Diamond* (Figure 14), where she purchased a scorpion and a diamond, placed them together on a street in Amsterdam, and then left the scene, abandoning her objects of curiosity to their own devices. Like much of her work, this gesture or happening survives through a photograph which has been turned into an unlimited-edition poster. The choice of objects was important. Both scorpions and diamonds are rich in poetic associations, from the colonial and luxury commodity to the nocturnal, the astrological, and the dangerous. A loose diamond on a street offers a precious lost or found object, while the scorpion unpicks the very fabric of reality, completely outside its expected desert context. As the poet and cultural theorist, Susan Stewart notes: "The more disparate the domains, the stronger, the more integral, the image … The surrealist use of metaphor was a matter not only of a 'fresh cut,' but a fresh cut across a series of contradictions, a gesture of impossibility."[5] On one level, this artwork serves to interrogate how contrived some of the surrealist "chance encounters" can be—the ubiquitous image of the umbrella and sewing machine on the dissection table have arguably become a kind of cliché or

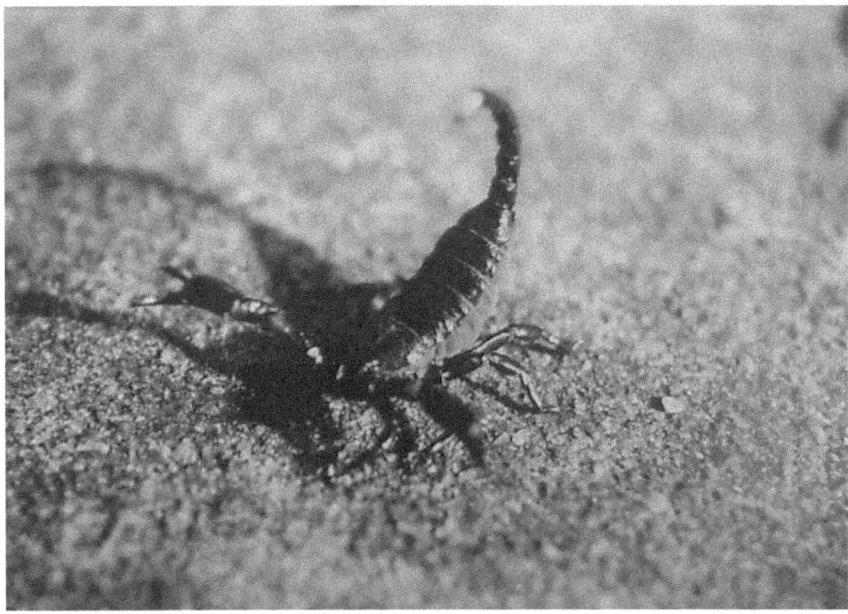

14 Lucy Skaer, *Scorpion/Diamond*, 2001

dead metaphor, a broken image. But on another level, the evocation of magic and surprise seem to tempt or, as Mieke Bal might say, "beckon" the fantastic and "once-upon-a-time-ness" on the same playing field as Carrington's visual narratives.[6]

Another poster image from the same residency is *Untitled* (2001), an eerie red-wine spill that conjures an amorphous form like a Rorschach test. The effect is what Katharine Conley might term a ghostly anamorphosis, which was "widely prevalent in surrealist art and represents the strongest evidence of surrealist ghostliness as a unifying phenomenon throughout the movement."[7] It is interesting that such ghostly forms would continue to haunt contemporary practice, with Skaer giving credence to the notion of the surrealist legacy. As with her previous action/poster, *Untitled* evokes the chance encounter, this time an abstract automatism which can neither be controlled by rational nor conscious means. Fiona Bradley observes that Skaer wanted "to bring different objects, and orders of reality, into the same image. She wanted, perhaps, to reverse her own process, and to set up a scenario that could crystallise impossibility."[8] Carrington's artworks and writing similarly seek to "crystallize impossibility" and challenge conventional logic, often in the pursuit of rewriting ethical codes and disturbing complacency. Skaer's early practice was not surrealist *per se*, but, prior to her encounter with Carrington, can already be seen to revive the surrealist technique of juxtaposition as an evocation of the marvellous.

Such thinking is underscored by Skaer's early interest in Venn diagrams as structuring devices, for example *Venn Diagram (Rorschach/Corn)* (2001). Again, Skaer's uses a slash in her title, a recurrent conjunction to juxtapose two apparently separate objects or images brought together through a speculative, artistic logic. A Venn diagram itself (named after mathematician and logician John Venn, who introduced the concept in 1880) visualises mutual points of overlap for objects or ideas with shared sets of characteristics. Such overlaps recur throughout this study—the Venn diagram becomes a means of articulating where responses to Carrington might intersect. For example, one might think of Carrington's own geometry in *Hod's Polyèdre* (1965) (Figure 5). Tilda Swinton also offers a similar analogy of the process of film direction: "in amongst this mayhem, you get this middle point, it's like the Venn diagram, you get this little, thin strand of coherence."[9] Indeed, it is this "strand of coherence" that Skaer could be said to have found when Carrington was glimpsed in her periphery.

Bearing this in mind, I will explore how Skaer offers an alternative approach to some of the key concerns of Carrington's artistic universe, and, in doing so, revisions Carrington herself as a set of topological coordinates. I propose that Skaer's practice reveals a dimension to Carrington that might be understood as a mode of esoteric conceptualism, one that combines hermetic magic with a political art logic.[10] An esoteric conceptualism might offer a useful way of bringing together Carrington's wide and varied interests in archaeology, world religions, and alternative knowledges in context to the cerebral rethinking of the nature of art-making which occurs in the avant-garde and contemporary art as a mode of challenging the establishment and the status quo. For Skaer, Carrington's esoteric conceptualism offers a medium through which to practice the marvellous and dislodge expectations.

"Late-night internet booking"

The possibility of meeting the elderly artist in the early 2000s became something of an obsession for many of the creative respondents discussed within this book. Lucy Skaer has been especially candid about how her own unique chance encounter coalesced. In an article for *Tate Etc.* (2008), Skaer explains how two drawings by Carrington vied for Skaer's attention on a visit to the Tate Collection in 2006: *Do you know my aunt Eliza?* and *I am an Amateur of Velocipedes* (both 1941) (Figure 35), inks on paper with perforated edges torn from a sketchbook; the former depicting a beast-headed hybrid, the latter featuring a nude female figurehead driving a tandem.

Given their availability in a public collection, these drawings have subsequently provided a starting point for further creative responses to Carrington. Dancers James Hewison and Michelle Man describe how these drawings provoked the concept for their choreography: "the energized lines, the intricate care and detail, and the near microscopic intensity in the cross-hatching technique ... From a choreographic perspective, we feel there is something of a controlled dance in play between these seemingly wild lines."[11] Curiously, Skaer set out with the initial intention of investigating another mysterious artwork entirely, *The Cholmondeley Ladies* (*c.*1600–10), a portrait of two women with an inscription declaring they "were born the same day, married the same day, and brought to bed the same day," astral twins who gave birth to their own children at the same time. Although she did not pursue further research on this early seventeenth-century picture in favour of the Carrington drawings, Skaer continued to ponder the conceptual premise of such happenstance, the sheer universal unlikelihood of such mysterious coincidences. She became preoccupied with the idea that Carrington was still alive at that moment, and that Skaer should coexist with this art historical, avant-garde figure: "I was struck by how the world had changed during Carrington's life, and that her internal vision had remained more constant than reality had."[12] A strange sense of intergenerational anachronism began to emerge when she thought about the idea of their coexistence, an eccentric convergence of seemingly disparate time periods and historical contexts, a juxtaposition which is very in keeping with surrealist principles and legacies; an example of a contemporary artist revisiting art history.

Shortly after the Tate visit, Skaer went on a Scottish Arts Council residency to New York. After receiving no reply to a handwritten letter (the handwriting having been provided by Skaer's roommate, Stevie Richardson), Skaer decided to embark on a more impulsive mode of encounter. Skaer writes of her spontaneous pilgrimage to meet Carrington in Mexico City as being the result of a "whim and some late-night internet booking," and explains in an interview with Isla Leaver-Yap that she "daydream[ed]" the whole idea: "I simply made what I imagined."[13] In fact, much of Skaer's account is about this prospect of being in transit and in questioning such cheap, commercial city-hopping and international lifestyle of contemporary artistic practice as "a kind of crisis point."[14] This speaks volumes, 15 years later, in an era when the carbon footprint of globalised travel is becoming an ever more conscious, ecological question mark. Skaer's gesture simultaneously serves to de-romanticise and de-exoticise Carrington's own historical exile to Mexico.[15] Skaer is careful to discuss how this epic journey occurred, as if merely by happenstance, extracting the chance encounter from the surrealist repertoire of techniques while simultaneously undermining the self-mythmaking of one of surrealism's chief auteurs. To ingratiate herself, Skaer brought tributes: homespun staples of tea from Fortnum and Mason and indigenous Chorley cakes, as icebreakers to grant safe passage through Carrington's door.[16] Her meeting with the older artist was documented anecdotally through a cycle of artworks she made in response to this visit.

"Hide the box of PG Tips!"[17]

One of the biggest surprises for visitors to Carrington's home on Chihuahua in the Colonia Roma was the strange selection of souvenir postcards pinned up on her kitchen cupboards, amid the clutter of her lived-in larder—pictures of her intrigues and elsewhere which Skaer, among others, have built into a conceptual puzzle. Indeed, Skaer entitled a resulting photograph *Leonora Carrington's Kitchen, Showing a Postcard of Tate's Painting 'The Cholmondeley Ladies'* (Figure 15) in honour of the marvellous encounter that triggered her interest in Carrington in the first place: "a document of coincidence."[18] Many of these postcards reference Carrington's English heritage and birthplace, some featuring the British royal family, especially Lady Diana and jubilee portraits of Queen Elizabeth II. In *The Hearing Trumpet,* the protagonist Marian mentions postcards of Buckingham Palace sent from her supercentenarian mother's valet, suggesting Carrington may have been re-creating fictional details from her novel in her own domestic sphere.[19] Yet, this kitchen cupboard shrine to the English monarchy seems somewhat dubious and inconsistent, given that Carrington rebelled against her wealthy *nouveau riche* background for almost all her adult life.[20] For example, she infamously denounced her presentation at court in her well-known satire 'The Debutante' (1937), where a hyena attends the ball on the protagonist's behalf, wearing the face of the maid as a disguise.[21] Moreover, Carrington's Edwardian father did not want her to go to art school and eventually disowned her; art-making became a bohemian gesture of resistance. However, her Englishness was emphasised through her status in Mexico as a British expat and political refugee amid a community of other European asylum seekers.[22] The patronage of wealthy English art collectors, Roland Penrose and Edward James, was integral to Carrington's income and recognition in England. She was later awarded an OBE but refused to travel to London to collect it.[23] Although Carrington left her English upper-class background behind, she maintained a firm sense of her cultural identity—after 60 years of living in Mexico, she certainly spoke the language and used Mexican imagery within her paintings, but remained far from fully assimilated. A sense of self-conscious foreignness is borne out in Carrington's visual imagery—*The Artist Travelling Incognito* (1949) (Figure 10), for instance, presents a somewhat inconspicuous hybrid figure in fancy dress as a faulty disguise. As Chloe Aridjis confirms in her novel *Sea Monsters* (2019), Carrington remained an eccentric "émigré" long after her arrival.[24] Other postcards mounted on Carrington's cupboards further depicted her eclectic interests: archaeological artefacts, medieval sea monsters, a map of Iceland, and reproductions of a Turner painting, *Light and Colour (Goethe's Theory): The Morning After the Deluge—Moses Writing the Book of Genesis* (1843), and, as chance would have it, *The Cholmondeley Ladies* in the Tate Collection, London. The majority of these postcards seem to have been plucked straight out of a museum gift shop. This is true also for the peacock-printed Liberty oilcloth, a souvenir that Aridjis brought Carrington from England.[25]

Surrealism scholars Katharine Conley and Jonathan P. Eburne have also been drawn to Carrington's kitchen, both likening it to Breton's archival cabinet of curiosities in Paris.[26] Rosemary Sullivan writes of being "dumbfounded by the Spartan rigor of her house" and how "[a]ll the warmth of the house was collected in the modest kitchen."[27] Sylvia Cherem further highlights the postcards as Carrington's only domestic embellishment.[28] The scholarly and artistic fixation on this relatively unassuming site is worthy of pause, yet the kitchen for Carrington is known to have been inhabited

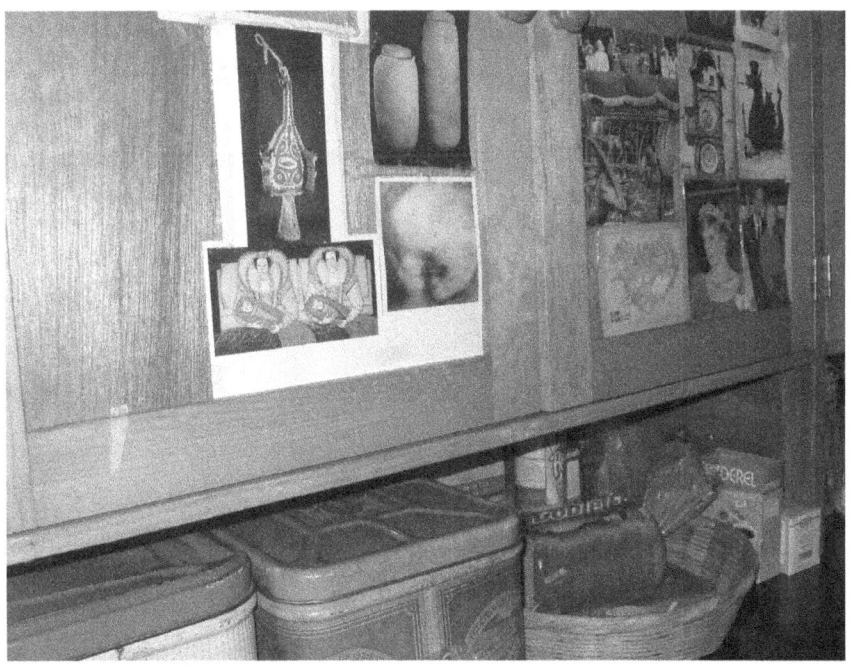

15 Lucy Skaer, *Leonora Carrington's kitchen, showing a postcard of Tate's painting The Cholmondeley Ladies*, 2006

creatively as one would a studio, as a site for cooking, social gatherings, conversation, and transformation. The authenticity of Carrington's kitchen provides a key scene in Alice Allemano's play *About Leo* (2018). Interestingly, Lee Miller's son, Antony Penrose, explains that when he visited Carrington's house, he "did not take a single photograph … To do so would have violated the magic of that place."[29] However, many, including Skaer, have since been prompted to document in order to make further work about her.

It seems significant that Skaer, Aridjis, and Anne Walsh each took candid photographs of Carrington's kitchen cupboards in 2006, 2008, and 2009, respectively, documenting them for posterity, and in doing so, drawing attention to Carrington's art-historical status as a primary artefact and authorial surrealist voice (Figure 21).[30] On one level, the photographic documentation of Carrington's postcards and tablecloth perform an intimate and de-hierarchical gesture, emphasising Carrington's lowbrow, domestic "inhibition" in contrast to the more public exhibition of the celebrated artist. Contrary to the prolific scholarly fascination in the alchemy, witchcraft, and taxonomy of Carrington's kitchen, here Skaer attempts to capture the magical in the mundane as well as the uncanny experience of being in a famous artist's space. Yet, on another level, the contemporary fascination with Carrington's kitchen, as depicted by Aridjis, Skaer, and Walsh complicates the arguments in Walter Benjamin's famous artworks essay—Carrington's throwaway possessions, even at the reproductive level, are imbued with the aura of her association.[31] As Susan Stewart points out, the postcard is one of the most "remarkable" kinds of souvenirs in terms of the transformation it goes through as a mode of the gift economy; although it is a mass reproduction, we expect a postcard to have been uniquely sent from the point of origin depicted, which lends the souvenir its authenticity.[32] Like colonial tea, postcards are usually from elsewhere and associated with leisurely rituals. The postcard can be seen as a useful conceptual device or metaphor for the intergenerational relationship between Carrington and her contemporary correspondences; distant connections made tangible as found objects.

Curatorial tarot

In the installation that I made I'd been wanting to break the logical links of my work. As you make a body of work a logic emerges that you are using and I think at some point you have to disrupt that in order to move forward or move sideways, and I needed a way of doing that, so my visit to Leonora Carrington became a kind of backbone for me being able to disassemble the logic of my own work while citing it within the historical context of her, not of her own work but of the existence of her.

—Lucy Skaer (2008)[33]

Following her meeting with the elderly Carrington, Skaer began to refer to Carrington as the "wild card" in her practice, an anomaly or force of disruption that encourages viewers to rethink their visual categories.[34] Interestingly, Donna J. Haraway describes her own subjects of study as "feminist discards from the Western deck of cards," claiming that her overarching project is "to look for the trickster figures that might turn a stacked deck into a potent set of wild cards for refiguring possible worlds."[35] A wild card is traditionally the Joker in games of canasta or rummy; it functions as a substitution card that can be used to forge connections. Broadly speaking, a wild card is also a metaphor for unpredictable behaviour or a surprising choice. In tarot, the wild card is part of the major arcana, usually the Fool or the Joker, which is considered a very powerful if ambiguous card, representing the innocent vessel, the beginning of one's life journey, as well as serving as a device which cannot be pinned down.[36] Now widely celebrated, Carrington designed her own major arcana (*c*.1955), which Susan L. Aberth and Tere Arcq have linked convincingly to many other details of her wider iconography.[37] Moreover, Carrington's silver and black design for *The Moon* card features a scorpion which, unintentionally but somewhat miraculously, evokes Skaer's aforementioned *Scorpion/Diamond*.

For Skaer, Carrington herself has come to represent this intuitive trickster card. Skaer's resulting body of "disassembled" work comprises a séance-like,

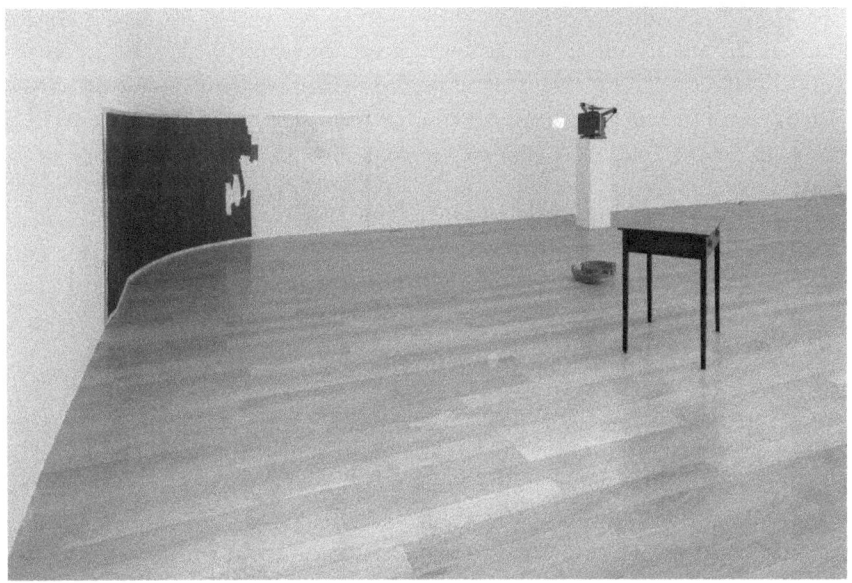

16 Lucy Skaer, *Leonora*, 2006. Installation view at The Fruitmarket Gallery, 2008

mixed-media installation: a short 16mm film, a large, curved drawing, a mahogany table inlaid with abalone shell, and a miniature cherrywood carved amphitheatre. For this first stage of her *Leonora* cycle (2006) (Figure 16), each component was titled after a card from the major arcana, *The Joker*, *The Tyrant*, *Death*, and *The Wheel*. As Lizzie Carey-Thomas explains, the tarot "introduc[es] a linguistic subsystem disconnected from but running in parallel to the objects."[38] On close inspection, the individual elements make up a kind of deconstructed shrine to the artist. Carrington's friend Alejandro Jodorowsky reminds us that the true meaning of the Fool card is dependent on its spatial arrangement.[39] In Skaer's case, the divining of a precise meaning from this arrangement or combination remains opaque; suffice to say that Skaer uses these tarot-esque titles to provoke the notion of a reading, and in doing so, toys with (or indeed confounds) the very notion of artistic interpretation. Here, I would suggest tarot performs an esoteric mode of curation for Skaer.

The installation was first shown at Galerie Elisabeth Kaufmann in Zurich (2006), subsequently at Art Statements in Basel (2006), and the Fruitmarket Gallery (2008), before finally being acquired by the Hunterian in Glasgow (2009).[40] Viewers tend to be drawn to the whirring analogue dynamics of *Leonora* (*The Joker*) (a 16mm silent loop film lasting approximately 45 seconds). *The Joker* features Carrington's hands interspersed with short clips of a washing line, paint cabinet, and the artist herself wrapped in a shawl and holding a notebook. Attention is devoted to domestic details such as the artist's hands, a digestive biscuit, and an envelope. These hands on the table poised for this artistic séance could be a direct quotation from Carrington's own iconography, for example *Séance* (1988) (Figure 7). Writing on such gestural activity, Joanna Fiduccia says that Skaer's silent film of Carrington "is less to silence the historical figure than to distil her language into an image—an image, precisely, of the artist speaking."[41] *The Joker*'s sculptural companion piece, *The Tyrant*, comprises a mahogany table that has been inlaid with mother-of-pearl claws, mirroring the wrinkled and spotted hands encountered in the film and those on the séance table. Again, the combination of factors plays on the surrealist notion of the chance encounter, here those seemingly random but marvellously destined juxtapositions that occur in the flea market. The antique English furniture possibly links to Carrington's family heritage, while Skaer has hinted, somewhat enigmatically, that the combination of table and "exotic" abalone shell "reflect[s] the tyrannical stages of early colonialism."[42] In context to Carrington this seems like a non sequitur but, as discussed in relation to her postcards and colonial tea, Skaer observed that Carrington staunchly maintained her English identity in Mexico. It presents another kind of legacy, a surrealism in the attic. Like the "joker," a "tyrant" at first appears to be a pejorative label, suggesting someone whose lofty position maintains authority long past its prime. As a piece of anthropomorphic furniture, akin to those that might appear in one of Carrington's own visual narratives, it initially ingrains Carrington as an invested art world heirloom but, on critical reflection represents, if indeed anything, a stubborn, corporeal being.

In 2016, I curated part of Skaer's *Leonora* cycle into a small, experimental research exhibition about Carrington's legacies. The title was *Leonora Carrington/Lucy Skaer*—the slash was intended to operate like the marvellous chance encounter of Skaer's *Scorpion/Diamond*, but also as a temporal fulcrum which would secure readings of Carrington's late prints and early art-school paintings through a contemporary, curatorial language and in the context of an educational environment. As Derek Horton recognised, the show's purpose was "not only to demonstrate Carrington's continued relevance, but also to reframe Carrington's career in contemporary terms."[43] Horton also placed emphasis on *The Joker*: "[Skaer's] works are not intended as portraits of Carrington, but rather a means for the artist to examine her own practice through that of another—to find herself through finding Carrington."[44] During the exhibition installation, it struck me as deeply telling that of particular interest to Skaer's thinking should be Carrington's wartime drawings and etchings made during a liminal moment in her career. One "wild card" produced during this era, and exhibited in my show, was Carrington's untitled etching for *VVV* portfolio (1942), sometimes known as *The Dogs of the Sleeper* (Figure 17), which had been part of a fundraising campaign for the surrealist magazine. Upon entering the exhibition space, I noticed that Skaer was immediately drawn to this particular etching.

The *Untitled* etching features unruly iconography and strange compositional techniques that both characterise and disrupt understandings of Carrington's New York output. For someone interested in coincidence and interrogation of the very notion of "the image," Skaer revealed to me the importance of this particular iconoclastic etching, describing its effect on her as follows: "I like that it has a physical domain, in that the elements seem like they exist (are tied together) but there is no clear orientation or purpose. In that way it seems to challenge representation, making a world that seems only just to gel into something that we can accept."[45] While the medium of etching certainly allows for this compositional structure, the irrational contents question stable understandings of representation. As Bradley reminds us, Skaer "is perpetually wary of our natural impulse towards resolution, and seeks instead a kind of resolute irresolution … of crashing different orders of reality together, of making logical drawings which disrupt the logic we use to position images in relation to reality"[46] Carrington's etching can be read as a nonsense rhyme in its own right, an incongruous, disrupting device; an image which very much operates along the lines that Skaer herself

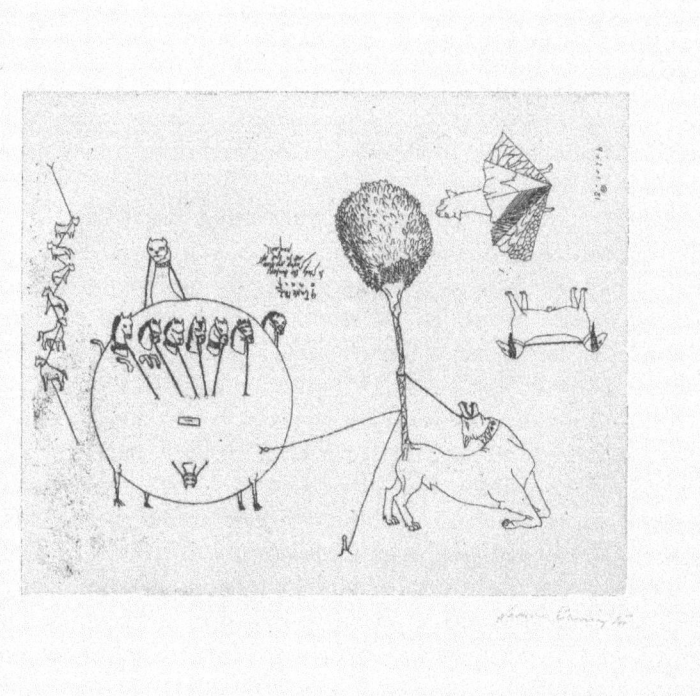

17　Leonora Carrington, *Untitled* (*The Dogs of the Sleeper*) for *VVV,* 1942

wishes to achieve—a disorientating force which dislodges the viewer into a more visionary spectrum.

Unpacking such enigmatic imagery and layout is no easy task. In Carrington's etching, upside-down mirror writing appears alongside curious patterns and clusters of canines and equestrian imagery, suggesting a sense of topsy-turvydom associated with temporary disorder (again, she made this print during wartime upheaval). Various accounts suggest that Carrington's dexterity with handwriting occurred early in her schooling, as did her strange juxtapositions of visual motifs.[47] Mirror writing offers another slanted view on reality, one that requires decoding on the part of the reader/viewer. As if to scramble a straightforward explanation of the accompanying imagery, just off-centre, the etching includes a short, almost indecipherable caption that reads: "9 June 1942, 10, 14, 16, = 7 to study the numbers seven and nine, the dogs of the sleeper."[48] The text is deliberately symbolic, and the imagery is almost hieroglyphic. One constellation presents a pregnant belly or cauldron full of wolf-horse exquisite corpses—possibly a surrealist reference to the fairy tales that troubled Freud's 'The Wolf Man' (1913), such as

'Little Red Riding Hood,' where the wolf swallows whole both the protagonist and her grandmother, and 'The Wolf and the Seven Little Goats,' where the goats in the wolf's belly are replaced with stones. Psychiatrist Salomon Grimberg further claims that this etching "is painful to look at," suggesting Carrington's wartime trauma underpinned the making of this picture.[49] Yet such psychoanalytic narratives are unlikely to be what piqued Skaer's interest. Rather, she seemed more intrigued by the seemingly unruly spatial arrangements of odd, surrealist imagery, and how each seems to confound interpretation of the next. This is further shored up by the cascading paper chain of dogs towards the left-hand side and the pair of conjoined dogs towards the right. In the centre, the guard dog tethered to a tree is the same iconography that appears in Carrington's painting *Green Tea* (1942) (Figure 6), suggesting the etching can be understood as a sketch of ideas in progress. In total, the etching presents Carrington at her most conceptual—the Carrington that most appeals to Skaer.

In a curatorial project of 2017 focusing on Carrington's writing, this etching reappeared, evidencing its ongoing significance to contemporary curatorial and conceptual practice. For *Houses Are Really Bodies* (2017) at Cubitt, curator Helen Nisbet exhibited *Untitled* very selectively as primary matter alongside *The Memory Tower* and an undated drawing of a monstrous creature. Although Skaer was not included in this particular show, a conceptual emphasis was once again apparent, with the space itself divided into two separate zones: one reading area with the three select artworks and a small critical shelf of literature, with the authentic inclusion of Angela Carter's personal copy of Carrington's novel *The Hearing Trumpet* as a primary artefact under protective perspex; and one more aurally immersive space, featuring lavender lighting based on the "violet flavoured lozenges" sucked by Carrington's literary character Carmella, and tarpaulin-protected settees where visitors could lounge and immerse themselves in the dreamy soundscapes of Carrington's short stories through recordings by a number of different voices, among them a reading of *Down Below* (1944) recited by Chloe Aridjis.[50] As with Skaer's *Leonora* cycle, *Houses are Really Bodies* similarly confirmed how Carrington has prompted an esoteric mode of curation, as well as demonstrating a conceptual dimension to posthumous interpretations.

A conceptual harlequin

The idea of Carrington as a "wild card" in Skaer's practice continued in the second chapter of her *Leonora* cycle. After Carrington's death from pneumonia in 2011, Skaer became aware that the existing installation and related documentation from their meeting had now transformed in its meaning. This sense of recalibration was true for many creative researchers of Carrington's legacies, a process of grieving that was managed particularly well by Skaer. The younger artist returned to Mexico City and took a series of photographs outside the late artist's house on Chihuahua in the Colonia Roma district with a focus on the door and nearby trees lining the street. Skaer then worked these photographs up into a series of silkscreened images comprising veiled, overlaid shapes including crescent moons and traditional harlequin diamond patterns which lent this series its definitive title, *Harlequin is as Harlequin Does* (2012).

Throughout western art history, the harlequin has traditionally been positioned as culturally "other."[51] The harlequin is one of the most recognisable and ubiquitous characters of the Italian *commedia dell'arte*; the costume a distinctive iconography, a colourful quilt of diamond shapes that is actually indicative of a patchwork poverty.[52] Writing on the history of this theatrical form, Lynne Lawner reminds us: "while we revel in its trappings, commedia itself remains mysteriously unknown, its history a jumble of shadowy patterns."[53] Such a readily familiar yet historically ungraspable genre provides a topographical coordinate at which point Carrington and Skaer converge. Carrington herself depicted jugglers and magicians, for example in *The Conjurer* (1950) and *El Juglar* (1954). Like the Fool, the harlequin and the

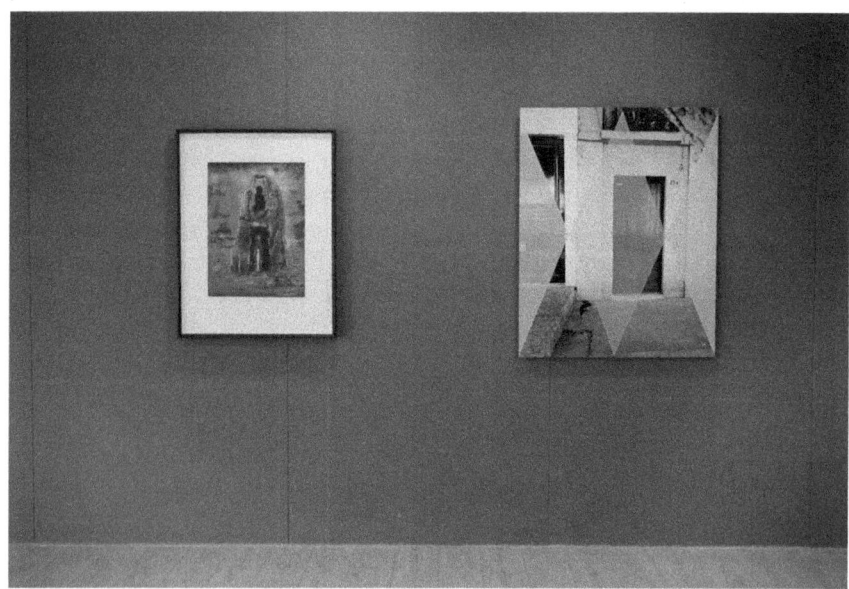

18 Installation shot featuring Lucy Skaer, *Harlequin is as Harlequin Does*, 2012; Leonora Carrington, *The Memory Tower*, 1995

court jester are granted licence to reveal the truth through comedic means. Skaer's title for her series suggests that Carrington represents an ungraspable, existential force, a site of playfulness that cannot be tamed—she will do as she likes and be whatever she wants but will ultimately speak the truth. In the *Carrington/Skaer* exhibition (2016), I positioned a Skaer *Harlequin* next to Carrington's *The Memory Tower*—two completely different types of printmaking technique, but images which are comparable in their architectural, mnemonic stance (Figure 18). Both might be said to mimic Arnold Böcklin's *Isle of the Dead* (1888), while offering a modern and contemporary updating of such *memento mori* iconography. Eburne has pointed out the trick-image of the minotaur in Carrington's *The Memory Tower* and notes how "we squint to find the living shapes" in this "portrait of Leonora's art itself."[54] The authenticity of the front door and the chambers of the imagination are once again pared back to their conceptual essences. Skaer brings Carrington's lofty, cerebral fantasy down to earth and back to the present while overlaying it with an ectoplasmic harlequin diamond veneer.

In 2018, Skaer was amused to learn that her epic installation *La Chasse* (2016–18) shared its title with a Carrington painting, *La Chasse* (1942). Skaer's idea was based on a medieval hunting manual (1785) and formed a major part of *Lucy Skaer: The Green Man*, an exhibition curated by Tessa Giblin at the Talbot Rice Gallery in Edinburgh. The evocation of the Green Man itself continues this evocation of irrational figures, this one positioned at the point of language, a magical being that spews leaves. The Green Man is also a legendary figure that represents seasonal regrowth, and for pagans, eco-critical awareness. For theatre-maker Stacy Klein, the esoteric cannot "be separated from an awareness of the world as ecological."[55] Moreover, the unconscious overlap with Carrington appealed to Skaer's ongoing interest in kismet and chance encounters. Arranged in chapters, or what Giblin termed "an allegorical set of 'sculptural sentences,'" *La Chasse* comprised a floor-based artwork, presenting scenes in abstract lozenges of bronze, copper, terracotta, ruby glass, mahogany, and other materials. At a material level, much of this was consistent with previous installations by Skaer producing a sense of intratextuality—one that self-references and mines from within her own output as well as beyond. Its layout was, once more, deeply esoteric and conceptually so. Moreover, Giblin points out: "*La Chasse* exists in an increasingly complex overlap between the wild and the cultivated," raising an ecological inquiry that my next chapter will investigate.[56]

In summary, Lucy Skaer's artistic dialogue with Carrington can be seen to channel an esoteric and cerebral marvellous via a conceptual artistic framework. Skaer's interest in Carrington culminated or crystallised in two particular moments or chapters: first, in Skaer's *Leonora* installation made in 2006 during her meeting with the older artist in Mexico City and secondly on Skaer's return pilgrimage to Carrington's front door after Carrington's death in 2011. *Leonora* can be understood as an epic cycle, a statement on the nature of conceptual practice, as well as a *Gesamtkunstwerk* in microcosm. Comprising mixed media from found objects, to a large-scale drawing and 16mm filmic micro-portrait, the cycle offers a necessary inversion of Carrington's visual narrative universe. Unlike Carrington's hectic and diminutive canvases, Skaer's work presents a cooler, sparer, possibly more agnostic view on the nature of art-making, one which curates Carrington through isolating and paring her back to her conceptual essence. So far it seems the most re-visionary reincarnations of Carrington have been by artists who work in media that is quite deliberately separate from her—Skaer, for instance, is a multidisciplinary artist but someone who tends to work in photography, screen-printing and found objects or assisted readymades. Carrington and Skaer both share an interest in bronze casting and printmaking but with different objectives—Carrington for the realisation of her characters and Skaer due to an interest in process, series, and trace. The very character of Skaer's conceptual practice constitutes an interrogation of "the image" whilst drawing on the surrealist notion of locating the marvellous within the everyday. Thus, the visionary spectrum for both is paradoxically a mode of iconoclasm as well as a mode of insight.

Notes

1 Lucy Skaer, 'The Transcendence of the Image,' *Tate Etc.*, 14 (Autumn 2008): www.tate.org.uk/context-comment/articles/transcendence-image (Accessed 11 March 2020).

2 David Hopkins, 'The Politics of Equivocation: Sherrie Levine, Duchamp's "Compensation Portrait" and Surrealism in the USA 1942–45,' *Oxford Art Journal*, 26:1 (2003), 67.

3 Lucy Skaer in *Lucy Skaer*, DVD (Edinburgh: Fruitmarket Gallery, 2008).

4 Stacy Boldrick, 'Skeletons Within,' *Lucy Skaer* (Edinburgh: Fruitmarket Gallery, 2008), 57.

5 Susan Stewart, *Nonsense: Aspects of Intertextuality in Folklore and Literature* (Baltimore, MD and London: Johns Hopkins University Press, 1979), 159–160.

6 Mieke Bal, *Louise Bourgeois' Spider: The Architecture of Art Writing* (Chicago: Chicago University Press, 2001), 29.

7 Katharine Conley, *Surrealist Ghostliness* (Lincoln and London: University of Nebraska Press, 2013), 14.

8 Fiona Bradley, 'Introduction,' *Lucy Skaer*, 11.

9 Tilda Swinton, specifically speaking about Joanna Hogg's direction; Joanna Hogg, 'Joanna Hogg, Honor Swinton Byrne and Tilda Swinton on The Souvenir,' *Film at Lincoln Center* (15 May 2019): www.youtube.com/watch?v=xzfBXkmo2Kg (Accessed 18 May 2020).

10 "Esoteric conceptualism" appears in Maja Fowkes, *The Green Bloc: Neo-Avant-Garde Art and Ecology under Socialism* (Budapest: Central European University Press, 2015), 89. Carrington's work is certainly already known and appreciated for its "esoteric feminism," a term Carrington scholars Janice Helland and Tere Arcq both use in descriptions of Carrington's work; see Susan L. Aberth and Tere Arcq, 'Magical Reflection: The Creative Collaborations of Leonora Carrington and Remedios Varo,' *The Life and Influence of Leonora Carrington: A Symposium* (New York: Gallery Wendi Norris, 2019): https://vimeo.com/357681039 (Accessed 9 July 2020).

11 James Hewison and Michelle Man, 'Imaginarium: Dancing with Carrington,' *Leonora Carrington: Living Legacies*, eds Ailsa Cox et al. (Wilmington, DE: Vernon Press, 2020), 67.

12 Lucy Skaer cited in 'The Art Fund helps Hunterian acquire work by Turner Prize-nominated artist Lucy Skaer,' *Art Fund Blog* (24 June 2009): www.artfund.org/blog/2009/06/24/the-art-fund-helps-hunterian-acquire-work-by-turner-prize-nominated-artist-lucy-skaer (Accessed 21 May 2020).

13 Skaer tells us that she had been given Carrington's Mexican address by an art collector in Texas, 'The Transcendence' (2008). Isla Leaver-Yap responds: "It's like a legacy of Surrealism—you made what you dreamt," 'Lucy Skaer: Drawing Close,' *Map Magazine*, 10 (June 2007): https://mapmagazine.co.uk/lucy-skaer-drawing-close (Accessed 21 May 2020).

14 Lucy Skaer cited in Leaver-Yap, 'Lucy Skaer.'

15 Carrington travelled across the Atlantic by ship (the *Essex*) and from New York to Mexico City by road. Even later in life, she avoided air travel, preferring the bus for longer trips to Chicago, New Orleans, and New York.

16 Chloe Aridjis advises that Fortnum and Mason tea was too lofty for Carrington, who preferred PG Tips, 'Talking about Leonora Carrington (with Marina Warner and Jennifer Higgie),' *Houses Are Really Bodies* (London: Cubitt, 2017): www.cubittartists.org.uk/event/houses-are-really-bodies-public-programme (Accessed 17 July 2020).

17 How England is perceived in Mexico is, of course, crucial here. English tea is prized above almost everything else—Chloe Aridjis tells us that Carrington kept her PG Tips on permanent lockdown as a rare, treasured possession: "Cacher la boîte de PG Tips," ("Hide the box of PG Tips") 'An A-Z of Leonora Carrington's memories, mostly in quotes, gathered over years of visits to her home,' *Leonora Carrington and the International Avant-Garde*, eds J. P. Eburne and C. McAra (Manchester: Manchester University Press, 2017), 18.

18 Skaer, 'The Transcendence' (2008).

19 Leonora Carrington, *The Hearing Trumpet* (London: Penguin, [1974] 2005), 3.

20 Carrington was partial to the guilty pleasure of royal gossip, and indeed any news from England, whilst simultaneously dismissing the entire Establishment through her painting and writing. Carrington was someone whose politics went full circle in terms of her simultaneous avant-garde abhorrence and acceptance of the monarchy for humorous ends. Thanks to Gabriel Weisz Carrington.

21 For an excellent reading of class critique in 'The Debutante,' see Natalya Lusty, *Surrealism, Feminism, Psychoanalysis* (Aldershot: Ashgate 2007), 27.

22 Many have commented that she retained a very particular "British Broadcasting" accent that is now almost entirely extinct, for example interview with Heidi Sopinka.

23 Dawn Adès explains that the ceremony had to be held in the British embassy in Mexico City after Carrington turned down the invitation to meet the queen in person in England, 'Testimonial,' *Leonora Carrington: Magical Tales*, eds Tere Arcq and Stefan van Raay (Mexico City: Instituto Nacional de Bellas Artes, 2018), 443.

24 Chloe Aridjis, *Sea Monsters* (London: Chatto & Windus, 2019), 16.

25 Thanks to Chloe Aridjis for this detail. In a testimonial included in the recent *Leonora Carrington: Magical Tales* retrospective, Norah Horna reminisces about a toy, a "golden chariot of Queen Elizabeth" that Carrington brought her back as a souvenir from a rare trip to England (2018), 408.

26 Katharine Conley reminds us that "[e]veryone who has written about visiting Leonora Carrington in Mexico describes her kitchen," 'Carrington's Kitchen,' *Papers of Surrealism*, 10 (2013): www.research.manchester.ac.uk/portal/ files/63517394/surrealism_issue_10.pdf (Accessed 22 May 2020). See also, Jonathan P. Eburne, 'Breton's Wall, Carrington's Kitchen: Surrealism and the Archive,' *Intermediality: History and Theory of the Arts, Literature and Technology*, 18 (Fall 2011), 17–43, www.erudit.org/en/journals/im/1900-v1-n1-im087/1009072ar.pdf (Accessed 22 May 2020).

27 Rosemary Sullivan, 'On Leonora Carrington and P. K. Page,' *A Manner of Being: Writers on Their Mentors*, eds Annie Liontas and Jeff Parker (Amherst: University of Massachusetts Press, 2015), 133.

28 Silvia Cherem, 'Eternally Married to the Wind: Interview with Leonora Carrington,' *Leonora Carrington, What She Might Be*, ed. Salomon Grimberg (Dallas, TX: Dallas Museum of Art, 2008), 18–19.

29 Antony Penrose, 'Testimonial,' *Leonora Carrington: Magical Tales*, 405.

30 For Anne Walsh, the kitchen is a "scene" for the interview, *Hello Leonora, Soy Anne Walsh* (Cambridge: MIT Press, 2019), 63.

31 Walter Benjamin, The Work of Art in the Age of Mechanical Reproduction,' *Illuminations*, ed. Hannah Arendt, trans. Harry Zorn (London: Pimlico, 1999), 219–253.

32 Susan Stewart, *On Longing: Narratives of the Miniature, the Gigantic, the Souvenir, the Collection* (Durham, NC and London: Duke University Press, 1993), 138.

33 Skaer, *Lucy Skaer*, DVD (2008).

34 Skaer, 'The Transcendence' (2008); Lizzie Carey-Thomas, 'Garlic and Sapphires in the Mud,' *Lucy Skaer* (Edinburgh: Fruitmarket Gallery, 2008), 33.

35 Donna J. Haraway, *Simians, Cyborgs, and Women: The Reinvention of Nature* (New York: Routledge, 1991), 4.

36 Gabriel Weisz Carrington confirms the importance of the trickster card for his mother, 'Leonora's Inner Compass,' *The Tarot of Leonora Carrington* (Lopen, Somerset: Fulgur Press, 2020), 12.

37 Susan L. Aberth and Tere Arcq, 'As in a Mirror with Multiple Facets: Leonora Carrington and the Tarot,' *The Tarot of Leonora Carrington*, 65.

38 Carey-Thomas reminds us that each title within Skaer's *Leonora* installation is taken from a particular tarot card, 'Garlic and Sapphires in the Mud,' *Lucy Skaer* (Edinburgh: Fruitmarket Gallery, 2008), 34.

39 Alejandro Jodorowsky and Marianne Costa, *The Way of Tarot: The Spiritual Teacher in the Cards* (Rochester, NY: Destiny Books, 2009), 38.

40 The work was acquired from doggerfisher, Edinburgh, for the sum of £35,997.50, with £13,000 assistance from the Art Fund (2009).

41 Joanna Fiduccia, 'Fathoming Gestures,' *Lucy Skaer: A Boat Used as a Vessel* (Basel: Kunsthalle, 2007), 31.

42 Carey-Thomas, 'Garlic and Sapphires,' 34; Skaer in Leaver-Yap, 'Lucy Skaer.'

43 Derek Horton, 'Review: Leonora Carrington/Lucy Skaer,' *Corridor 8 Magazine* (28 July 2016): https://corridor8.co.uk/article/review-leonora-carrington-lucy-skaer-leeds-college-of-art (Accessed 23 May 2020).

44 Horton, 'Review: Leonora Carrington/Lucy Skaer.'

45 Correspondence with the author (29 January 2018).

46 Bradley, 'Introduction,' 14.

47 Leslie Sills, 'Leonora Carrington,' *Visions: Stories About Women Artists* (Morton Grove, IL: Albert Whitman, 1993), 21.

48 Writing on Carrington's visionary imagination, Tere Arcq points out the kinds of Celtic sorcery associated with the numbers "3, 5, 7 and 9," claiming that "incantations repeated three, five, seven or nine times consecutively increased the creative activity between the hemispheres, which in turn could bring about the desired effects of the magical act," 'A World Made of Magic,' *Leonora Carrington*, trans. Jonathan Brennan (Dublin: IMMA, 2013), 25.

49 Salomon Grimberg, 'Travelling Toward the Unknown, Leonora Carrington Stopped in New York,' *Leonora Carrington: Magical Tales*, 61.

50 Carrington, *The Hearing Trumpet*, 55.

51 Lynne Lawner, *Harlequin on the Moon: Commedia dell'Arte and the Visual Arts* (New York: Harry N. Adams, 1998), 18.

52 'Commedia dell'arte,' The Metropolitan Museum of Art (2020): www.metmuseum.org/toah/hd/comm/hd_comm.htm (Accessed 20 May 2020). This article also explains how the commedia has infiltrated contemporary language—for example, the word "zany" comes from the commedia-based term *zanni*.

53 Lawner, *Harlequin on the Moon*, 8.

54 Jonathan P. Eburne, 'The Memory Tower,' *Leonora Carrington Centenary Symposium* (Biblioteca de México, 2017): www.youtube.com/watch?v=K8fTDkN_x8s (Accessed 16 July 2020).

55 Stacy Klein cited in '"All Artwork Is a Magical Act,"' *ASAP/J* (10 October 2019): http://asapjournal.com/all-artwork-is-a-magical-act-an-interview-with-susan-aberth-and-stacy-klein-jennifer-johnson (Accessed 16 April 2020).

56 Tessa Giblin, *Lucy Skaer: The Green Man* (2018): www.trg.ed.ac.uk/sites/default/files/2020–04/LucySkaerTheGreenMan.pdf (Accessed 16 July 2020).

4

Hibernation

We live, as we dream—alone.

—Joseph Conrad (1899)[1]

Leonora Carrington is often understood to have been a highly collaborative practitioner whose open embrace of "feminist intertextuality" enables an ongoing querying of binary thinking.[2] For instance, Susan L. Aberth and Tere Arcq have developed a convincing case for the "sisterhood" with her great friend Remedios Varo as sharing in a range of dual investigations, providing one another with mutual support, and creating a distinctly feminine space amid a predominantly macho, avant-garde, patriarchal milieu.[3] While I maintain that such dialogic thinking remains integral to studies in this area, revisionary histories seek to challenge accepted narratives, offering alternatives which may nuance our understanding. For instance, Aberth and Arcq have also recently acknowledged the importance of the Hermit card in tarot for Carrington.[4] I would therefore like to consider the question of solitude as a necessary moment within the creative process as well as a sense of critical awakening, and how this has become manifest in the practices of two distinctive writers critically invested in her legacy, Chloe Aridjis and Heidi Sopinka (both born in 1971).

For both, the *roman-à-clef* and techniques of the surrealist marvellous are harnessed and revised for contemporary purposes. A sense of introversion is paramount, as is an emphasis on alternative soundscapes (from birdsong to post-punk). Both explore the primacy of feminine subjectivity within their quest narratives and present a quiet feminist politics that grapples with the marvellous in the everyday. Carrington's own notion of the "female human animal" from her essay 'What is a Woman' (1970) becomes intrinsic to Aridjis and Sopinka's self-articulation of their second-generation eco-feminisms. Paradoxically, "solitude" for both involves communion with the non-human. Georgiana Colvile points out that "animal representation" was a "strong common denominator" for the women of surrealism.[5] Meanwhile, Whitney Chadwick reminds us that animals can be interpreted as "symbolic intermediaries," often occurring as spirit daemons or familiars for Carrington.[6]

Moreover, the character of "Carrington" presents an ambiguous, sometimes reclusive persona. Marina Warner has frequently characterised Carrington as a badger or burrowing creature from the English hedgerow, someone who preferred to live below ground.[7] Carrington is often said to have been a rebel, a black sheep, a lone wolf, a misfit, someone who had "an allergy to collaboration."[8] Meanwhile, much of her visual corpus, for example, *Pastoral* (1950) (Figure 20), or the hieroglyphic painting *Oxyrhynchus: Kingdom of Heaven as Pointed Out by Animals* (1965), suggests not so much an invasion of species but rather an instinctual need to go feral. With reference to the animal studies of Donna J. Haraway and Peter Matthiessen, among others, I will argue that Aridjis and Sopinka enable readers to look beyond the proliferation of biographical fantasies towards fictional accounts that arguably offer more accurate portraits of Carrington as a wilding force.[9]

Going feral

> when I saw the hyena, something was set in motion.
> —Heidi Sopinka (2018)[10]

The Dictionary of Animal Languages (2018) by the Canadian, second-generation Ukrainian novelist, Heidi Sopinka, offers a fictional biography,

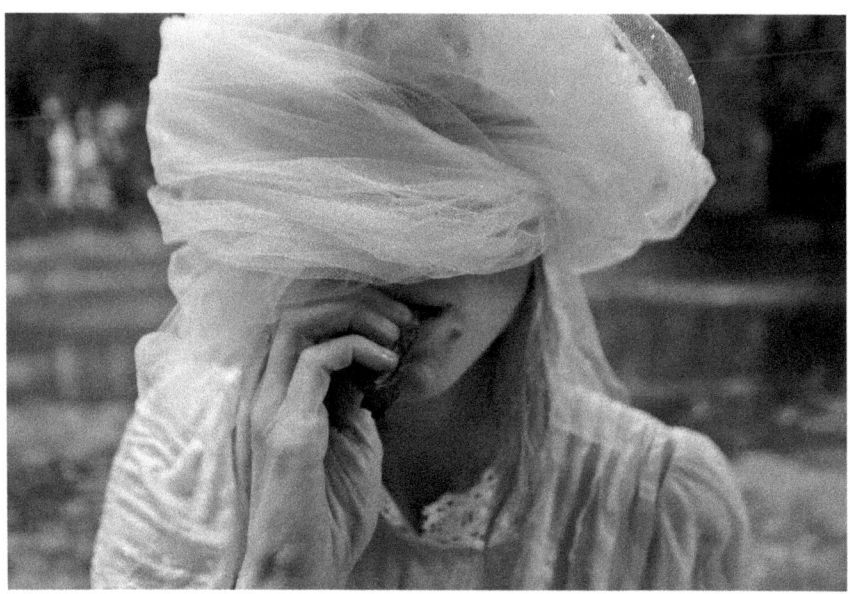

19 Heidi Sopinka, 2009. Photo by Natalie Matutschovsky

or, more precisely, what Mieke Bal and Michelle Williams Gamaker might term a "theoretical fiction" of Leonora Carrington.[11] It constitutes a major project of quotation and rewriting, a mode of embodied storytelling told in non-linear, dreamlike flashback that empathises with what being Carrington could have felt like as she moved through history. A marvellous chance encounter underpins the entire endeavour—a copy of Carrington's novel *The Hearing Trumpet* (1974) in Sopinka's local library inevitably piqued her interest when she was trying to research the very few novels which feature an elderly female protagonist.[12] Sopinka was struck by the parallels or synchronicity between Marian Leatherby and her own lead character, and even more so when she realised that Carrington was then still alive and sharing the same nonagenarian status as the emerging protagonist in her manuscript: "The ghost of her was already in the draft before I'd even known of her which is very odd. Her time period was exactly the same time period of my heroine."[13] Sopinka would go on to interview Carrington in 2009 for *The Believer Magazine* (2012), where the conversation focuses on the unknowability of death and finishes with Carrington's loaded assertion "I'm not a prophet."[14]

This follows a diverse career to date, having also written on Yoko Ono ("one of evolution's wild ones") and with a second novel forthcoming on feminist performance artists of the 1970s (including Judy Chicago, Adrian Piper, Hannah Wilke, and Ana Mendieta).[15] Sopinka is perhaps best known for her design work with Claudia Dey under the Toronto-based fashion label Horses Atelier. Founded in 2012 and named after Patti Smith's famous album, *Horses* (1975), the label is no doubt also a nod to Carrington's favourite spirit animal, which appears recurrently in many of her paintings and short stories. Horses Atelier is consciously ethical in their approach to slow fashion, using their loyal following and studio shop as an activist platform and mood board. Dey and Sopinka describe their clothing line as "jumpsuits for the matriarchy" and "feminised workwear," with garments including loose overalls and Victorian lace blouses, interestingly, the same styling as found in photographs of Carrington by Lee Miller (1939) and Hermann Landshoff (1942).[16] The observation that "[m]ovement was essential to fieldwork" (62) and an admission that "solitaries look odd" (124) are claims that run throughout Sopinka's novel, detailing women's struggles with autonomy, self-presentation, and emotional labour. The practical, minimalist design of Horses Atelier would seem tailor-made for Sopinka's intrepid character and suggests that Sopinka embeds her vision into her entire creative practice. Sopinka is also a licensed helicopter pilot and has worked as a travel writer in South-East Asia and bush cook in the Yukon, roles which have significantly shaped her views on ecology and survival in extreme environments.[17]

In *The Dictionary*, a range of spare, wintery landscapes, including Lapland, the Yukon, and fairy-tale Iceland, provide the visionary settings for her protagonist's creative solitude: "Once you are in the north there is always the myth of farther out. Nothing is ever north enough" (40). True to form, she prefers the company of animals to people, but also begins to understand significant figures in her life as animals. Sopinka's *Dictionary* offers an epistemological unpacking of what the animal kingdom meant to Carrington. It concurs with Jonathan P. Eburne's view of Carrington's "virtual collecting habits" within her eclectic iconography, and represents a lifelong, and infinite, classification project: "I don't tell her of my collections I have begun to catalogue in notebooks: leaves, nests, insects, the hollow bones of birds" (77).[18] The dictionary structure assists such meaning-making, a self-reflexive gesture where the field notes drive the narrative. Sopinka claims that F. Schuyler Matthews's *Field Book of Wild Birds and Their Music* (1904) offered a further crib or structuring device for her novel, particularly its textual interspersing of birdsong in music-note format with detailed descriptions, illustrations, and observations of species.[19] The contents are arranged in order to mimic a scientist's field notes.

In Sopinka's novel, the Leonora Carrington character is artistically rechristened Ivory Frame, an animal painter turned acoustic biologist, who researches communication and ecosystems in remote locations and hostile environments close to the Arctic circle. The idea of becoming so immersed in animal painting that the artist has turned into a biologist has a marvellous logic within this novel: "Practical theories that would lead to magical work" (62). Her discernible shift in the senses from visual (paintings and sculptures) to aural (data and sound recordings) is similarly apposite. At the age of 92, Frame's long-term fieldwork is now being threatened by funding cuts and that most "significant deadline" which she believes to be her impending death (66). In an article for *The Paris Review* (2018), Sopinka explains that after the birth of her own children, she paradoxically found herself increasingly thinking about death. Playfully entitled 'Hey necromancer,' Sopinka's article invites the posthumous Carrington to be her "death guide": "After the violence of birth, I felt joltingly alive, the distressing kind of alive that has a bit of death in it. I was in the unsettling place between human and nonhuman, being and nonbeing—that dark, debilitating nothingness that causes our last and final disappearance."[20] In her "old lady" novel, Sopinka realised she wanted to devote attention to a much older woman: "someone who was older, quite old, not just in their 70s. Someone who is contending with death."[21] Sopinka's reasons behind such a character study are feminist in attitude: seeking to make visible those whom often become invisible to society; to reclaim those whose practices exist on the fringes; and to present a case for the necessity of retreat as one part of the creative process often denied to mothers or parental figures due to societal expectations and social pressures: "We grant men a right to solitude, why can't we do the same for women?" (163).

The question of solitude lies at the very kernel of *The Dictionary*—Sopinka's writing offers a call to arms for any parent actively engaged in creative practice. She interrogates an ongoing double standard; men's creative solitude is rarely, if ever, questioned while women are regularly guilt-tripped socially for having any interests beyond their children. For Sopinka and her character Ivory Frame, the writing life has to be that of a hermit researcher—a form of creative hibernation that enables reflection and advanced thinking.[22] To go feral also enables edgework and unpredictability. Through Carrington, Sopinka encourages her feminine readership to take back their solitude, and slip under the radar in order to practice and produce new knowledge:

> I see the struggle looking at Leonora's life. She was such a radical thinker but she had to be satisfied with practicing her art in a way that she felt was symbolic of what she wanted to do ... My own personal issues were around how to balance motherhood with a creative practice ... To go deeply into work, you have to really disappear. And that doesn't exactly bode well for motherhood ... I loved the notion of getting at the heart of dedication with a woman ... How does a woman navigate love and nurture? I wanted to look at all those issues, and turn them over and examine them and persevere in them.[23]

For Sopinka, Carrington was "a solitary" her whole life, and this attitude drives and renews the need to write towards a feminist marvellous, to reimagine what the chance encounter might be. In light of existing historiographical tropes and intergenerational dialogues, we can begin to harness the draw of Carrington to contemporary feminist practices—to work within and through her.

The Dictionary begins with the once exotic, now common 'Pigeon,' where we are introduced to her research assistant, Skeet. Indeed, pigeons are of mutual interest to both Aridjis and Sopinka. The flashback tale of Skeet's destructive, under-aged mother is overlaid with the sudden, present-day disclosure that Frame has a granddaughter despite not knowingly ever having a child of her own. The information is conveyed, as one might expect, through a letter from a museum. Meanwhile, a bird throws itself relentlessly against the windowpane, and Skeet wonders if it is Frame's daughter reincarnated. Such synchronicity is threaded throughout the entire novel, the unknown child of corporeal secrecy adding a latent sense of mystery made manifest when Frame undergoes Carrington's episode at the sanatorium. In this fictional account, the suggestion is that during the wartime interlude, Frame gave birth to a daughter whom the nurses misinform her died in childbirth. Although such an idea departs from Carrington's historical record, Sopinka presents a logical outcome of such clinical confinement or time out from the public sphere. This phantom pregnancy narrative chimes with Carrington's own wartime short story 'The Seventh Horse' (1941), in which a character called Mildred claims to be pregnant. She is later found trampled to death but a "small misshapen foal" appears miraculously in the stables at the end of the tale, suggesting that an interspecies union or human-animal transformation has taken place.[24]

The second chapter of Sopinka's *Dictionary* is 'Nautilus,' in which Remedios Varo is reimagined as a Hungarian artist called Tacita. Later the reader learns that they were planning a collaborative installation of animal portraits and sound transcriptions that Frame ends up having to finish solo (the titular dictionary) following the sudden death of her beloved friend. *The Dictionary* comprises several such thinly veiled pseudonyms, and, again, many of the well-known surrealist figures from Carrington's past find their articulation as animal familiars: Varo as Tacita is an esoteric nautilus, a collector of culture and fabricator of assemblage, while the traditionally birdlike German artist Max Ernst transposes into a fairy-tale wolf, the blue-eyed, Ukrainian painter Lev Aleksandr Volkov (his relocated nationality offering a subtle, fictional tie to Sopinka's own ancestry). Surrealist darling Marie-Berthe Aurenche is similarly rewritten as a Russian ballet dancer, an elegant, if jealous, swan. Meanwhile, Marcel Duchamp is simply a readymade Duchamp, and Leonor Fini also makes a direct cameo as a party host.

In Sopinka's 'Magpie' chapter, a present-day journalist, Marisol, poaches quotations and other snippets of information while writing up her portrait of Ivory Frame. As we know, Sopinka herself interviewed Carrington, and the character, Marisol, is no doubt based on the author's real-life encounter with her subject. Moreover, in order to write the novel, Sopinka had to temporarily remove herself from her domestic reality, and retreat to "a cabin in the woods" in order to work meaningfully on her manuscript.[25] Virginia Woolf's famous dictum that a woman who writes must have "a room of one's own" (1929) suggests a long lineage of such feminist thinking. Carrington confirms this idea in a BBC documentary (1992): "The real work is done when you are alone in your studio."[26] Sopinka's *Dictionary* likewise presents a strong argument in defence of longitudinal scientific research and artistic residencies, and there are many moments where the author and her protagonist blur and mingle self-reflexively.

Unlike previous attempts at romanticising Carrington's avant-garde life, Sopinka demythologises the prevailing mystique surrounding the artist and her circle. For Sopinka, Carrington is a raw encounter: flesh and blood, scales and fur. She also refreshingly explores the more practical and economic aspects of her persona. The book's emphasis on intertextuality places the

Carrington scholar at its very core. Frame tells us: "I had to do a lot to convince my university of my animal language project" (94)—a funding predicament to which many scholars can likely relate. Carrington's literary voice is often collaged directly, whether "procuring an omelette with hair" (48), "speaking French without mistakes" (56), or the idea of being "more animal than human" (116). Carrington's notion of a "female human animal" has become integral to Sopinka as such hybridity enables interrogation of binary thinking. Kristoffer Noheden explains that "[f]or Carrington ... the categories of humanity and animality are not so much markers of species, as they are contingent upon opposing authority," again bringing to mind a feral-feminist familiar.[27] Aberth concurs that Carrington's "distinguishing characteristic ... is her breakdown of traditional boundaries between humans and animals."[28] Reflecting on animal languages still further, Sopinka says: "I love the notion that we exist in a language-less place with them, and yet we see our own humanity reflected back at us when we look at them, and [Carrington] really explored that."[29]

Turning to another real-life Ivory Frame, eco-feminist theorist Donna J. Haraway has explored the importance of touch in terms of accountability when encountering animals. For Frame, it is rather the sense of hearing that consolidates this relationship, that listening to animals will lead to

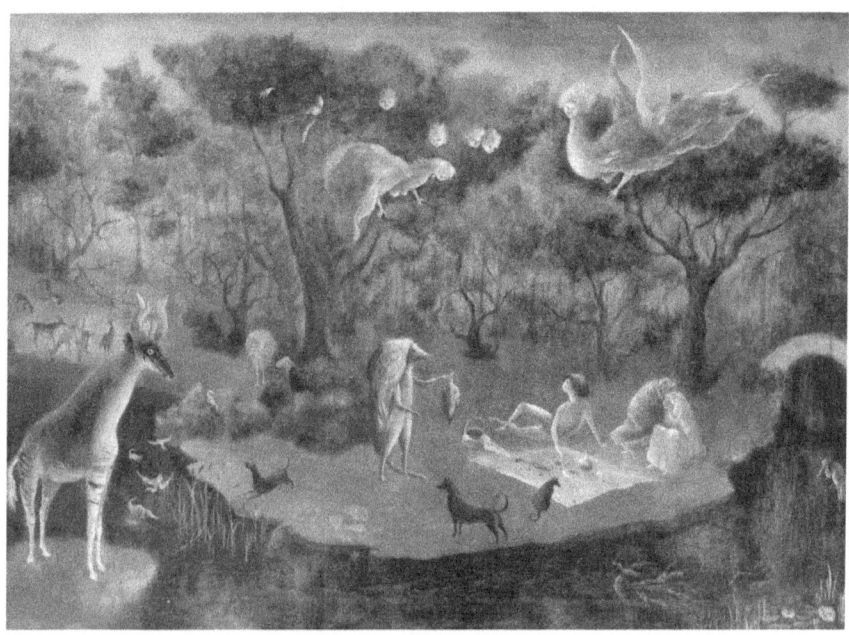

20 Leonora Carrington, *Pastoral*, 1950

communication with them. Haraway writes: "Once again we are in a knot of species coshaping one another in layers of reciprocating complexity all the way down. Response and respect are possible only in those knots with actual animals and people looking back at each other sticky with all their muddled histories … a question of cosmopolitics."[30] The sense of mutual respect is palpable—like the real-life Carrington, Frame is a vegetarian and she finds taxidermy "a revolting act" (37).[31] When Paris is under siege, Frame shows equal concern for the evacuated zoo animals as she does for the museum paintings. The hyena, of course, has a privileged position in Carrington's universe, a figure of transgression, whether lactating in her self-portrait, *Inn of the Dawn Horse* (1937), or chewing around the maid's face to wear as a mask in the short story 'The Debutante' (1937). Natalya Lusty shrewdly claims the hyena as a metaphor for transgressing gender and class relations: "In choosing the figure of the hyena for her story about social rebellion, Carrington registers the animal's mythological and zoological status as a sexually hybrid creature."[32] Marina Warner similarly notes how "Carrington's stories throw important light on the development of the beast symbol in the literature of women, for women."[33]

The genre of the fairy tale is alluded to throughout Sopinka's *Dictionary*, no doubt due to Carrington's own childhood interests in the writings of Lewis Carroll, and illustrations of Arthur Rackham and Beatrix Potter which segue into her visual narratives and short stories. For example, Sopinka writes: "Fairy tales and nursery lore are crammed with creatures. Coded reminders that we once knew animals to be on the same footing as us" (64). Again, *The Dictionary* subscribes to Carrington's mandate that we must de-civilise and reconnect with our instinctual animal selves to prevent further war and global apocalypse. Carrington writes: "If all the Women of the world decide to control the population, to refuse war, to refuse discrimination of Sex or Race and thus force men to allow life to survive on this planet, that would be a miracle indeed."[34] This statement presents Carrington as a trailblazer for the feminist cause, querying the gendering of women within an ecological context, quixotically absolving women from the violent aspects of so-called civilisation, and envisaging a matriarchal uprising. Frame similarly ponders "why extinction isn't more of a source of horror" (118), further emphasising the complacency and disavowal that perpetuates around this urgent topic. Fairy-tale editor and curator, Kate Bernheimer, concurs on how the genre contains "a deeply ecological world," and how the world of animals is "collapsed" into the world of humans, obliterating the cultural distinctions between the human and animal and revelling in their corporeal, visceral equivalencies.[35] Sopinka's loaded assertion about the pleasure/pain nexus continues such thinking: "Fairy tales grow teeth all around them" (33). Consistent with the nibbling instinct of

Carrington's hyena, there is a psychoanalytic undercurrent to this statement conjuring ambiguous feelings of desire and abhorrence.[36] The wolf that lurks within *The Dictionary* is perhaps the ultimate representation of this dynamic, and crucially the choice of animal Sopinka chooses to represent Carrington's lover, Max Ernst. Later, one of Lev's wolf paintings is sent to Ivory Frame from the past and bequeathed to the granddaughter she has never met, suggesting a genealogical inheritance through animals and art, again echoing Haraway's aforementioned "layers of reciprocating complexity all the way down."[37]

Another mode of Carrington-invested intertextuality for Sopinka is the embedding of existing visual artworks within her writing. Frame's understanding of the history of art includes Bosch, Brueghel, Vermeer, and Velázquez, whom the protagonist recognises to be undeniably good painters. Frame also observes the remarkable lack of white paint in the snowy pictures of Millet, Daubigny, and Corot (53). Audubon's bird illustrations are inevitably referenced as an aesthetic Frame tries to emulate commercially (173). But it is when her own artworks are cameoed that the ekphrasis becomes animated and starts to operate. For instance, Sopinka summons Carrington's inquisitive visual content from *Femme et Oiseau* (1937) as follows: "I have been working on an animal painting … Thick bright paint, an off-kilter feeling. When you look closer you can see that one of the creatures is a woman with an animal's face. She is like a ghost, familiar somehow, but unusual-looking" (53). Later, Sopinka describes Frame's version of Carrington's carnal painting, *The Meal of Lord Candlestick* (1938) (Figure 24), which she submits as her response to a didactic brief on the still-life genre before leaving the academy:

> The last painting I submitted was not received well. I had the usual animals, birds, horses, but the main subject was a ritualistic meal. A banquet of cannibals that Tacita thought to be a blasphemous take on the Eucharist. There is a group of gluttonous grotesque women, with heads that she described as phallic though I thought of them as equine. They sit at a table, abundant with extravagant dishes. It is all writhing and moving and somewhat alive … It was part of a series of banquets I had begun sketches for. The last being one that depicts forest animals who turn against the humans they encounter hunting boar—the prey eat the predators (106–107).

These artworks include a cautionary tale. Her tutor's prosaic inability to understand how the painting matches the still-life brief creates a feeling of isolation for Frame, yet Tacita's fictional engagement with, and interpretation of, the painting changes our reading of it. Linda Hutcheon reminds us that "context conditions meaning."[38] Many years earlier, Sopinka and two creative friends, bookbinder Alisha Piercy and photographer Natalie Matutschovsky, had already tried to channel Carrington through a series of highly aestheticised picnic performances in the heart of Mexico City in 2009 (Figure 1), photographic documentation of which appears to marvellously restage Carrington's animal meadow painting, *Pastoral* (1950). Such levels of detail demonstrate both Sopinka's familiarly with Carrington's *oeuvre* and her fine-tuned ability to collage it so seamlessly into her text while rewriting it anew.

The Dictionary invites such sensory overload; Sopinka's dedication to the sonic reveals an intermedial dimension. The novel is threaded throughout with references to famous composers, including Brahms, Dvořák, Chopin, Satie, Liszt, Clara Schumann, Debussy, and Stravinsky, as well as one of Bach's Brandenburg Concertos. Given the era under consideration, vocalists Édith Piaf and Patsy Cline are also referenced as part of the background music. An interest in early twentieth-century analogue technologies offers another persistent suggestion of the nonagenarian protagonist's historical time-span. Skeet scolds her for saying "brochure" rather than "webpage" (31), and her administrator Valentina insists on academic composure and bureaucracy. Yet Frame does have a very skilled technical awareness; she is utterly enchanted by records, phonographs, and tape recordings which she uses to capture her data: "I opened the windows to the sterling high pitches of two mockingbirds in conversation, the whistling of a train, and played it back, the sounds magically preserved in tinfoil" (63). She also cautions her research assistant about allowing her findings to be misappropriated for quasi-commercial purposes: "Please. Don't let them use the dictionary to make ring tones for European mobile phone networks, or for relaxation like that station, bird radio" (66). Again, this continues a narrative where the protagonist believes most people simply do not understand her work. Yet, in the end, it is she who comes to the realisation that much of her obsessive, and uncompromisingly lonely, research-practice has been a way of proactively working herself through the traumatic moments of her history.

"Moth, seeking leopard"[39]

> There on the very fringes of tranquillity ... should be at least one or two pacing wolves.
>
> —Chloe Aridjis (2013)[40]

Parallel literary strategies, lines of introspective inquiry, and a profound interest in animal rights occur independently in the practice of the Mexican novelist and curator, Chloe Aridjis, another conjurer of Carrington. The Aridjis family are known for their long-term commitment to environmental activism, as well as their friendship with the like-minded Carrington, an early signatory of the Group of 100 (1985) founded by the poet and diplomat, Homero Aridjis (known as "the green conscience"), and translator, Betty

Aridjis, Chloe Aridjis's parents. Chloe Aridjis herself is a member of Writers Rebel, a facet of the Extinction Rebellion movement in London: "my main activism has been environmental: I am above all interested in animal rights. If I were going to picket outside somewhere or go chanting down the street, it would be for the animals, who are completely voiceless. They matter more to me than anything."[41]

She remembers meeting Carrington in the early 1990s, being introduced through her family doctor (though her father had known her since the 1970s).[42] The family would often visit Carrington at her home in Chihuahua Street on a Sunday afternoon for tea and/or whisky, leading to a long-term friendship and like-minded creative values. Domestic details such as the peacock-patterned Liberty oilcloth Aridjis gifted Carrington from London, and Carrington's storage of her English teabags under lock and key are two of Aridjis's favourite anecdotes.[43] In matters of friendship, both Aridjis and Carrington have professed a preference for being in the company of women. As someone who grew up in a culture where women were often expected to be very reserved and devout, Carrington's command of her own self-hood and association with the feminist movement in Mexico impressed the then twenty-something Aridjis, who'd been struck by the outspoken American women she encountered as a student at Harvard University.[44] From the time she met her, Carrington became an inspiration for Aridjis, a prosperous and long-term haunting. Aridjis actively conjures such encounters through a productive mode of daydreaming, and the spirit of Carrington is positioned at the forefront of this practice, as a mechanism for displacement. Aridjis believes that she has always had a "strong affinity with her work," an idea which infiltrates her novel writing, curatorial practice, and a screenplay for a film.[45] Both covet alternative realities and subcultural forms of magic and the poetics of the surrealist marvellous. For instance, when asked how Carrington figures in her writing, Aridjis believes that they shared a system of beliefs, especially in the marvellous possibilities of the quotidian and the fantastical inhabiting the same space as well as the need for "tiny acts of rebellion."[46] They also share a commitment to animal rights and overlap in their ecological concerns through their writing and other modes of expression. Given such affinity, Aridjis has become a primary spokesperson for the artist, regularly promoting Carrington's legacy through articles for *Tate, Etc.* (2015) and *Frieze* (2017, 2018, 2019), and an 'A-Z' of Carrington (2017). She co-curated the major Tate Liverpool show *Leonora Carrington: Transgressing Discipline* (2015), which contributed a ripple effect to studies in this area, introducing new scholars and makers to Carrington's output.[47]

Aridjis has published three novels, *Book of Clouds* (2009), *Asunder* (2013), and *Sea Monsters* (2019), two of which include cameos of the artist. She has also translated the writing of her father into English as *The Child*

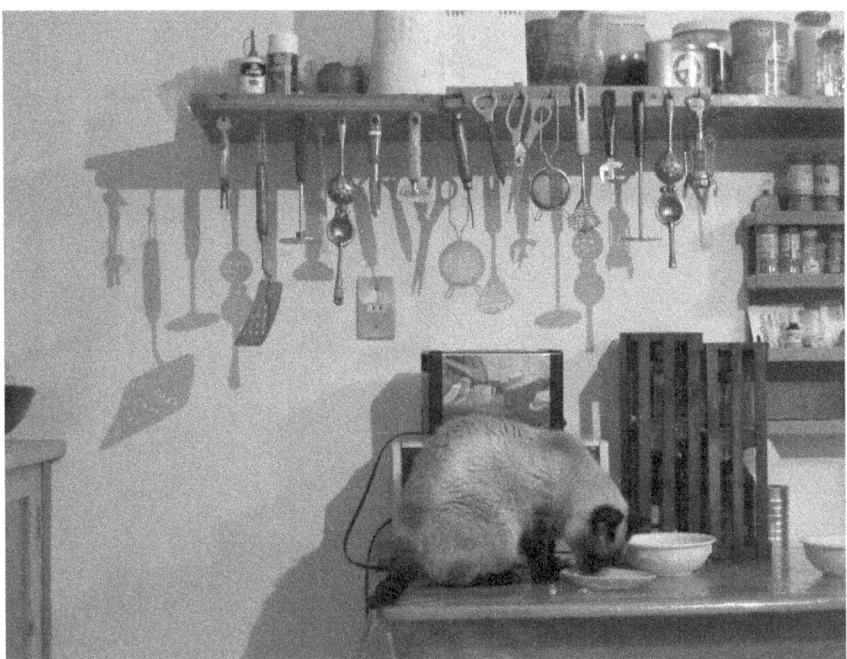

21 Chloe Aridjis, *Leonora Carrington's Kitchen, c.*1998

Poet (2016) and has co-written and starred in a documentary-style psycho-thriller *Female Human Animal* (2018), directed by Josh Appignanesi and produced by Jacqui Davies. Aridjis's literary universe is inhabited by dreamy meteorologists, marine archaeologists, gallery invigilators, historians, poets, loners, beachcombers, flea marketers, goths, and other transients or oddballs—indeed, she tends to gravitate to those that operate on the fringes of culture or margins of society. Another hallmark of Aridjis's writing is an archaeological interest in cultural landmarks or the proverbial haunted house: the underground bowling alley in *Book of Clouds* which may have been used for recreation by the Nazis or Stasi; a ruined chateau in *Asunder* where the chatelain-goth has burnt all his books and furniture; and the former apartment of William Burroughs in *Sea Monsters* where he allegedly shot his wife, Joan Vollmer. Further touristic vistas in each novel include: Alexanderplatz, Berlin in *Book of Clouds*; the National Gallery, London in *Asunder*; and Zipolite, a beach in Oaxaca, as the foreground for *Sea Monsters*. Whether real or imagined, these sites lend an authentic sense of temporal longevity in which to locate her characters.

As with Sopinka, Carrington could be said to underscore and unify many aspects of Aridjis's multidisciplinary practice, and I would suggest that a fuller reading and interpretation of Aridjis's individual outputs can be achieved through concurrent immersion in her novel writing, filmmaking, and curating, as well as within Carrington's visual imagination. A subtle sense of intra-textuality has become another of Aridjis's signature techniques. For instance, one thinks of the tenacious plastic bag in *Book of Clouds*—"the ghost of the object it once carried"—that recurs as a metamorphosing motif in *Female Human Animal*. Moreover, the alternative magic associated with Carrington looms large for Aridjis. As for Sopinka, Carrington remains something of a mirage. Here, one might consider the presence/absence metaphor of the *Snow Leopard* (1978), a travelogue and literary meditation by Peter Mat-thiessen (another of the Aridjis family supporters and signatories).[48] Throughout Matthiessen's pilgrimage, the titular snow leopard is importantly left both mystery and perpetual possibility:

> I long to see the snow leopard, yet to glimpse it by camera flash … is not to see it. If the snow leopard should manifest itself, then I am ready to see the snow leopard. If not, then somehow … I am not ready to perceive it, in the same way I am not ready to resolve my *koan*; and in the not-seeing, I am content. I think I must be disappointed, having come so far, and yet I do not feel that way. I am disappointed, and also, I am not disappointed. That the snow leopard *is*, that it is here, that its frosty eyes watch us from the mountain—that is enough.[49]

Richard Mabey further emphasises the philosophical nature of Matthiessen's *Snow Leopard*: "the very stuff of human longing … It is, I think, the animal I would most like to be eaten by … The animal is never seen, of course." [50] In this way, the snow leopard functions much like a McGuffin or the slippery white rabbit in Lewis Carroll's *Alice's Adventures in Wonderland* (1865), as a cipher for the search for knowledge.[51] The character Alice is a lone pragmatist amid the nonsensical world she finds herself in. Carrington is known to have had a deep interest in Carroll and wrote her own tale of 'White Rabbits' (1941). Although snow leopards are far from frequent in Carrington's own work, its Latin American cousin, the jaguar, appears in several of her artworks, for example as an ancient subterranean relic in the corner of *El Mundo Mágico de los Mayas* (*The Magical World of the Mayas*, 1963), and as one of a trio of animal familiars in *White People* (2005). Ocelots, too, appear in compass formation in *Summer* (1941) and have a cameo role to play in 'The Invention of Molé' (*c.*1960). Lions and cheetahs also occur in Carrington's early *oeuvre*, such as her watercolour illustration, *Erebus: Sisters of the Moon* (1932). In another early picture, a snarling blue "hell-cat" confronts a "devil-bear" in a cave (1933).[52] Arguably, Carrington herself operates in much the same way for Aridjis and Sopinka, as an elusive, glittering creature.

In *Book of Clouds*, Carrington is name-checked during a rare exchange between the protagonist, Tatiana, and her employer Doktor Weiss:

> 'I was once there, in Mexico City, many years ago. 1967. I had a good friend, a photographer from Budapest named Chiki Weisz. Ever come across him?'
> 'No.'
> 'He was married to Leonora Carrington.'
> 'I don't know them.' (2009, 41)

In this passage the real-life figures of Carrington and her husband Chiki Weisz are enrolled within the fictional domain of Aridjis's story, an authenticating gesture which endows the ageing character Doktor Weiss with greater credibility as a historian. His namesake ("Weiss" being close to "Weisz," the surname of Carrington's husband) further bears this thought as a process of translation. Mieke Bal has described such a technique as "the glamor of historical reference, the historical 'reality effect.'"[53] In cameoing Carrington, Aridjis excuses herself from direct autobiographical association with her protagonist, Tatiana—as mentioned above, the Aridjis family were, in fact, well acquainted with Carrington and Weisz in Mexico City. Here, it is also refreshing that it is Weisz who is married to the famous artist; his social status is defined in relation to her. As a creative response to the flurry of revisionist scholarship on the surrealist movement, Aridjis adopts Carrington's feminist intertextuality but uses it to re-present an avatar and alternative viewpoint. In doing so, Aridjis creates a believable historical context both linked to and displaced from her own biography. Aridjis has revealed that Carrington found it hard to reconcile that the real-life Aridjis lived in Berlin for nearly six years, given its connections to fascist history.[54] Hitler makes an appearance in both Aridjis's *Book of Clouds* and Sopinka's *The Dictionary* as another authenticating certificate in context to the wartime Europe Carrington had to flee. Aridjis hallucinates an elderly Hitler still alive and disguised as an old woman on public transport in the 1980s, while Sopinka's Carrington challenges the vegetarian hypocrisy of the dictator and chastises her assistant for his generational complacency in attitude towards the very threatening political history she survived her way through. In *Book of Clouds*, the historian, Doktor Weiss, proposes that Tatiana "experienced what one could call the Hitler syndrome," a paranoid delusion where his face can be glimpsed everywhere as a form of pareidolia (98). But later, Tatiana wonders if she spies the same historian, again on public transport, in his own form of drag. She can't be sure; there is scant evidence other than a burnt sienna lipstick in his bathroom. The novel's overarching title seems to propose that, like clouds, appearances can be deceptive, obscuring or revealing the truth, "withhold[ing] its language" (107).

This idea is further explored through some of Tatiana's interview subjects. Her first is Jonas Krantz, a meteorologist with a rich inner life, with whom she has a brief romance. But none are stranger than "the Simpleton of Alexanderplatz" (74), one of Tatiana's regular sightings, a woman in a flowered dress and plastic jewellery, with an inane smile, begging every day in front of the Deutsche Bank cash machine. Tatiana is given an assignment by the historian to "Find someone who in some way embodies the city for you" (132). However, when Tatiana attempts to interview the Simpleton, what follows is an irrational conversation of juxtapositions involving a sweater-wearing poodle, a "wheezing cat," and numerous alternative calculations about passers-by suggesting a unique and marvellous way of approaching the mundanity of her surroundings. The Simpleton becomes the resident surrealist of Berlin, leaving Tatiana to conclude: "there must have been some logic that escaped me" (137). Carrington may not operate directly as one of these curious, nebulous figures but the juxtaposition of such peculiarity and sense of metaphorical collapse common to much of Aridjis's practice suggests that Carrington may be an associate of her eccentric cast, evoked at one remove.

As with Sopinka, the figure of the non-human also piques Aridjis's literary attention. For example, when temperatures drop, Tatiana worries about the animals in the zoo (131). Another marvellous chance encounter that steers a narrative "shift" (95) is the reappearance of a black, hairless Mexican dog, a Xoloitzcuintle called Murci, which turns out to belong to her employer, providing a rare opportunity for a dialogic encounter. Again, Haraway's notion of "cosmopolitics" is interesting to ponder here—if touching animals is touching history, it seems marvellously logical that the dog should belong to a historian. Such animal ciphers are a recurrent narrative device for Aridjis, as they are for Carrington.

Although not mentioned precisely by name, in Aridjis's third novel, *Sea Monsters*, one can infer that Carrington makes a further cameo as one of two, dog-walking, "aging émigrés"—the other presumably Carrington's husband Weisz:

> I'd been on my way to the stationery store when I came upon two ageing émigrés. Our local enigmas, they had fled a Europe in ruins to live, later, among our slightly more humble ones. I'd often see them at the VIPS diner on Insurgentes bent over their coffee and *molletes*, the woman with a hand on her bag and the man with a hand on his cane, as if ready to leave at the slightest prompting. That day they were accompanied by their ancient dog, whom they'd take on walks around the neighbourhood, the man in his black beret—the street kids called him Manolete—and the woman in grey with her hair swept into an irreverent bun. Yet it seemed that this trio, dignified and decrepit, had run into trouble, for they'd come to a standstill and the dog lay with his hind legs splayed behind him (2019, 16).

Contrary to *Book of Clouds*, this time Aridjis openly acknowledges her friendship with Carrington and Weisz. Their guest appearance occurs relatively early in the narrative, and they are referred to two more times as part of the background of La Roma. In typically marvellous terms, their first appearance coincides with a significant moment for the adolescent protagonist, Luisa; a seemingly quotidian congregation with an "ancient dog" on a street corner ends up serving as a catalyst for the rest of this quest narrative. Luisa soon embarks on a self-initiated pilgrimage with her fair-weather love-interest, Tomás, to a coastal beach in Oaxaca in the hope of finding "[t]welve Ukrainian dwarfs ... on the run from a Soviet circus ... touring Mexico" (2019, 61), a curious headline she chances upon in a day-old newspaper, a "story that ... set[s] everything in motion" (108). The extraordinary premise itself suggests connections to a surrealist poetics of the marvellous. This is further underpinned by the choice of book Luisa takes with her, a foundational text for the surrealist movement and blueprint for the notion of the chance encounter, Comte de Lautréamont's *Les Chants de Maldoror* (1868–69).

We know from Whitney Chadwick that Carrington herself went on a bus trip to Oaxaca while researching for her large mural *El Mundo Mágico de los Mayas* (1963).[55] Carrington also infamously ran away from her English childhood home, when not that much older than the fictional Luisa, to pursue her association with the French avant-garde, yet she was adamant that "I always did my running away alone."[56] Aridjis wanted to use her novel as a space to explore *why* people run away, having previously done just that as a 16-year-old herself and always knowing that she would write about this episode.[57] As a coming-of-age novel through the running-away-from-home narrative cycle, one might also be reminded of Carrington's own brave desire to shed her wealthy English family background and prospects in favour of association with the more bohemian, French avant-garde. But this story is not as romantic as many have reported, and too often tends to be turned into hagiography. Aridjis rather seeks to demythologise such a journey. Living on a tropical beach may sound appealing, even typifying the exotic with acclimatised characters who insist on "tropicalization" as a form of assimilation (117), but the reality is a strange void, and the majority of the mysterious "sea monsters" Luisa encounters turn out to be empty layabouts. Tanks and aquariums containing lizards and fish are positioned throughout the novel. When she encounters a wild iguana in Oaxaca, the implicit suggestion is that the beach itself is a macrocosmic trap. Elsewhere, she likens this artificial version of nature to the electric blue of her cocktail or to a naïve drawing on a paper tablecloth which is easily torn. Moreover, as with Matthiessen's snow leopard or the elusive Carrington herself, Luisa never finds the circus performers. Occasionally, she wonders if she has glimpsed them in her peripheral vision, whizzing past in a vehicle or dreamlike visions of small figures contemplating the moon at night (a vision inspired by Aridjis's interest in a painting by Caspar David Friedrich). However, their existence is merely a ruse or mirage to justify her odyssey: "shipwreck or no shipwreck, most voyages end in failure" (172). As with other anticlimactic pilgrimages, her running-away-from-home turns out to be narrative process, not a destination.

Sea Monsters is set in 1988 in the wake of the devastating earthquake of 19 September 1985. This natural disaster had a particularly detrimental effect on Carrington's real-life street, Chihuahua, the ubiquitous "house opposite" becoming a ruin that the local government failed to restore. Reflecting on this crisis 30 years later (2015), Homero Aridjis laments the government's perpetual inability to act: "Other streets in the city have never recovered, such as Chihuahua, home to the painter Leonora Carrington … Across the street from her house, the remains of a ten-story [sic] building, ostensibly a solid mass, have been colonised by squatters. 'It's a monument to incompetence,' her husband would say."[58] According to Chloe Aridjis, Carrington called this damaged site a "garden of scorpions" with many "mysterious inhabitants" and hints of the relentless weeds emerging through the cracks.[59] Jonathan P. Eburne likens this site and its living organisms to Carrington's *The Memory Tower* (1995) (Figure 18) in terms of its "nobility of ruin."[60] In *Sea Monsters*, the site is further described as "a living archive of the disaster" and "a menagerie of strays" (15). The novel touches on the squatting and trespassing that occurred in such abandoned properties, an idea that is collapsed onto the poetics of corrosion on underwater shipwrecks by macroorganisms (28). "Ribbon[s] of foam" offer an explicit mode of "rewrit[ing]" (122), while the metaphor of marine archaeology recurs throughout the novel, underscoring the local ruins of their landlocked city, suggesting that traces of the historical surrealist marvellous can still be found lurking between the fissures.

Her second novel *Asunder* can be read similarly as a chain of poetic associations.[61] Indeed, Aridjis has spoken about her writing process as a series of distillations: "I distil, I distil, I distil, until it's down to what I feel is essential in the language and imagery."[62] Carrington does not appear directly in this second novel but the profile of the introvert, the lone animal lover, and the marvellous textures of "craquelure" are present throughout. Here, the protagonist is a gallery invigilator called Marie who, like Sopinka's character Ivory, is "content to carry out life at a low volume" (2013, 14) but itches under the surface with more violent instincts. Moths have an important role to play in *Asunder*, part of the "ecosystem" of Marie's domestic reality (23), the only inhabitants of the delicate landscapes which she crafts out of eggshells and later smashes in frustration. The novel is, in the author's words, "haunted" by a feminist narrative of suffragette icono-clasm, namely Mary Richardson's real-life, political gesture of 1914, where she vandalised Velázquez's *Rokeby Venus* (1647–51).[63] Marie's great-grandfather, Ted, is imagined as the guard on duty at the time, again creating a conflation between history and fiction, and throwing the spotlight onto the characters around the edges. Richardson's cleaver fascinates Marie, particularly the angles at which it is struck and how it renders the female nude as meat. For Ted, suffragettes and comets become "equated" (59), and this segues into Marie's own burgeoning understanding of "craquelure," which she encounters through eavesdropping on an art restorer's site visit with a group of students in the gallery and quotes from a famous conservator: "Forged craquelure is arbitrary, monotonous and pedantic—whereas natural craquelure throbs with rich variety" (61). The idea serves as a catalyst for what follows. When a tour guide in the National Gallery enrages Marie by contrasting the drab uniform of the gallery assistants with the beauty of the mythological nudes, she experiences the wildness of silent wrath building up inside her: "[an] animal was awakening, cracking its joints and flexing its claws" (67). As the narrative unfurls, Marie meets a chatelain in a broken-down palace outside Paris, and such cracking becomes further associated with animal scratching—she later tells her flatmate she was "scratched by a feral cat" (175).

Where birds constitute the majority of Sopinka's literary allusions, Aridjis is drawn to a frequency of canine and feline metaphors. In *Asunder*, Marie yearns to stroke the fur of stray dogs but disciplines herself not to. A briefcase is likened to a "small, obedient dog" (145), and she frets about the fate of the lion in paintings of St Jerome. Her friend Daniel, also a museum invigilator but really an aspiring poet, offers a curious position within this narrative, and Marie often observes him or peeks at his notebooks. She is perturbed by his voyeuristic fascination in the hysterics of the Salpêtrière, so celebrated by the (male) surrealists. Marie is naïve to, but perhaps necessarily critical of, their avant-garde associations. One further slither of the surrealist marvellous can be found in the scraps of poetry Daniel writes: "On a torn piece of paper: *Verbs locked away/ The snow leopard's winter hoard.*" (51). Again, this rarely sighted animal becomes a secret code or hint of surrealist techniques. Marie and Daniel later take a trip to the surrealist capital of Paris, and visit one of the oldest menageries in the world, the Jardin des Plantes, where the snow leopard is, of course, the central exhibit:

> As if in answer to this sudden burst of quotation, we arrived at the snow leopard. Judging from the enraptured crowds circling the enclosure this animal was the zoo's main attraction. People held up their children, murmured and exclaimed, snapped dozens of pictures. The metallic light at that hour, a bluish silver, made the cat look even more powerful and mysterious, and before long I too succumbed to its spell, transfixed by the glacial green eyes flecked with

sparks of boredom and irritation, pride and captivity impossible partners, and the fluid, elegant movements of the large spotted paws. It was the only creature that day that looked straight back at us, silently hissing—ears pinned back and jaws sprung open—and for a heart-stopping second I forgot there was a pane of glass between us (141).

While the she-hyena provided aforementioned intrigue for Carrington, especially during her youthful visits to the zoological garden in Blackpool, Aridjis chooses the snow leopard as her animal guide, a hinge or "boundary creature" between reality and what lies beyond.[64] The quotation above draws parallels between the features of the gallery exhibit and that of the zoo, both behind glass, the latter animated. However, the suggestion throughout *Asunder* is that gallery pictures are similarly alive and responsive to viewer interaction, both in their physical membranes as well as their visual contents. Carrington is evoked vicariously through the emphasis on paintings as well as through Aridjis's personal devotion to the animal kingdom.

Elusive felines continue to feature prominently as a surrealist-related motif in Aridjis's film with Josh Appignanesi, *Female Human Animal* (2018). The film at first appears to be a documentary-style pseudo-fiction, set against a backdrop of Aridjis's real-life co-curation of the Tate Liverpool exhibition (2015), and the finalising of her *Sea Monsters* manuscript. Imagery from her earlier novels is also collaged into the film, once again the ubiquitous plastic bag in *Book of Clouds*.[65] Shot on antique video, the credits also acknowledge that the film is "haunted by Leonora Carrington." Here, Aridjis's own domestic pet or "companion species," a magnificent, green-eyed, Russian Blue called Ludwig, stars as the metaphorical snow leopard.[66] The inclusion of the cat prolongs Carrington's interest in dæmons and witch familiars. Aridjis knew both Carrington's fluffy Siamese cats, Ramona and Monsieur, one of whom appears in her photographs of Carrington's kitchen next to silhouettes of cutlery and the rest of her domestic toolkit (Figure 21). This visionary perspective continues in *Multigraph 006* (*Chloe Aridjis*, 2018), an experimental portrait of Aridjis with her Carrington cat maquette, by photographers Iain Forsyth and Jane Pollard. Here, the multigraph format with its séance-like composition offers the possibility of an uncanny dop-pelgänger. For both Aridjis and Carrington, the figure of the cat represents an uncanny or marvellous presence, domesticated in their habits yet wild and unpredictable in their instincts—a snow leopard within the everyday reality. Aridjis explains in the film that Carrington "was expelled for behavioural problems" and "identified with feral spirits." Moreover, like Carrington, Aridjis claims that she also identifies as a "female, human, animal but not necessarily in that order." Elsewhere Aridjis says that "Leonora's work teemed with hybrids—a bestiary of human-animal composites and extravagant cross-breeds where even human figures seem feral" (2018). Found interview footage of Carrington appears to discipline her intermittently as a ghostly super-ego: "You are trying to intellectualise something desperately and you are wasting your time!"[67]

After its release to wide critical acclaim in 2018, *Female Human Animal* became seen as strikingly topical for its contemporaneity with the #MeToo campaign.[68] While some of the gender politics of the film are fictional, it touches on the difficulties Carrington likely experienced in the predominantly masculine surrealist movement. As the director notes, the film can be seen as a "queering of heterosexuality" as well as a form of "social surrealism."[69] Aridjis's protagonist is teased as a "romantic" with "high hopes" by art-world characters played by her real-life friends and writers, Juliet Jacques and Devorah Baum. Aridjis soon falls for a peculiar masculine presence straight out of one of her novels.[70] Importantly, Aridjis's protagonists, Marie, Tatiana, Luisa, and even the version of herself whom she plays in *Female Human Animal*, are all introverts well-versed in social distancing. Inquisitive and, at times, verging on socially awkward, Aridjis's protagonists prefer to inhabit their imaginations and the security of their domestic environments, whilst daydreaming and longing for true and equal communication with another member of their species. Tellingly, both Aridjis and Sopinka's protagonists struggle with playground relationships. In *The Dictionary*, the schoolgirls dislike the young Ivory Frame "the way a fox hates a dog" (2018, 13), while in *Sea Monsters*, Luisa "tend[s] to avoid the girls; in one way or another, the friendships were all-consuming but quickly consumed" (2019, 25). For Aridjis's protagonists, relationships with men recurrently come about through curiosity yet are often fleeting or unrequited. Like Carrington, her desires go beyond a heteronormative union.

A sense of solitude, introspection, and, at times, ennui, is integral to the mood of Aridjis's practice. In *Sea Monsters*, she notes the solitude of an atheistic perspective (123), while in *Book of Clouds*, she emphasises "There's solitude and then there's loneliness" (16), a philosophical idea which she expands upon in interview: "I believe solitude is more likely to be self-imposed. You can create your own solitude, but loneliness isn't something that is necessarily chosen."[71] Elsewhere, she points out the practical and emotional necessity of such solitude for the writing life: "Most of us writers lead fairly quiet, low-key lives … You write and write, apart from the world, in a certain solitude and in your mental sanctuary. An award serves as a reminder that you are part of a community that sometimes feels abstract, and that all that loneliness may have served some purpose."[72] Again, this viewpoint concurs with Sopinka's bare necessity of "a cabin in the woods."[73] One might further suggest that contrary to a pack mentality, solitude is a condition of being animal, of commanding one's own space or territory.[74] Aridjis inherits not only Carrington's eccentric status but also her father, Homero

Aridjis's notion of "the solitary enchanter," a short story which starts with a game of tag.[75] Luisa, a supporting character in this short story, is likely to have provided the initial profile for the protagonist of the same name in *Sea Monsters*, thus operating as a subtle homage to her father's writing.[76] Indeed, *Sea Monsters* offers a complex relationship between the father and the daughter who do not fully understand each other but try to find common ground in their mutual interest in shipwrecks and corrosion studies. Carrington had to run away from her father, Harold, but, unlike the Aridjis family, there was no reconciliation. Homero Aridjis's *The Child Poet*, a Proustian recollection from his childhood, is described by his daughter as "a succession of interconnected vignettes."[77] Chloe Aridjis further reminds us that "the very act of transforming dreams into text is in itself a form of translation, and at best an approximation of the original."[78] One may ponder the same for all these quotations of Carrington. Yet, as I have tried to show here, Carrington's message is reactivated through compelling literary curation and feminist intertextuality by two authors who both knew Carrington and continue to practice through her eco-criticism.

Group of 100

the doves fluttered up and resettled into new configurations.
—Chloe Aridjis (2019)[79]

I love history that lives in the dirt and cracks and stains of things.
—Heidi Sopinka (2018)[80]

In Homero Aridjis's compendium of environmental activist writings, *News of the Earth*, a photograph of him with Carrington and one of her cats is included (Figure 22). Carrington is presented as a proud member of the Group of 100, and the image is accompanied by the following caption: "There are many animals I like. Human beings are not top of the list. In fact, they are lowest in my preferences. Humans are terrible beings who commit murder and I'm very sad to think I am one of that species."[81] The thoughtful protagonists of *Book of Clouds*, *Asunder*, *Sea Monsters*, and *The Dictionary of Animal Languages* would likely echo such sentiments.

The literary worlds of Aridjis and Sopinka merge with their broader practices of curating, fashion designing (in Sopinka's case), and filmmaking (in Aridjis's) in their investigations into the surrealist marvellous as lifestyle choice, looking between the cracks in the veneer of reality, or complacency. For Carrington, the marvellous was importantly extended into her eco-political awareness, an approach which still has much currency today. Aridjis and Sopinka recycle Carrington as a representative of the complex interplay of solitude, feminist activism, and animal rights. Posthumously, Carrington

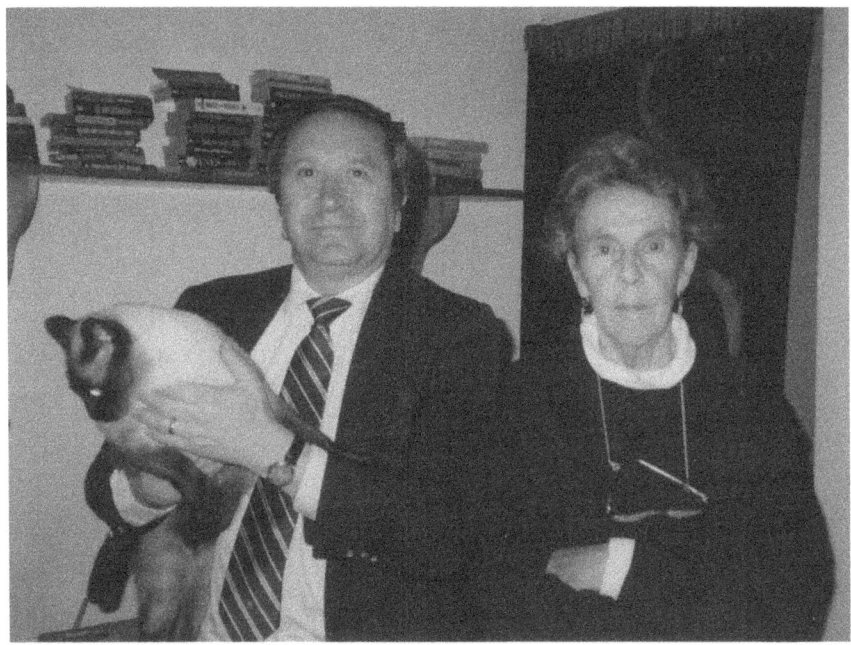

22 Homero Aridjis and Leonora Carrington, *c.*1994

has come to represent a palimpsest, an imaginative bestiary of feminist politics, and Aridjis and Sopinka, in London and Toronto, have emerged as chief promoters in this campaign. In doing so, both novelists offer next-generation replies to Carrington's perceptive notion of the hybrid "female human animal." Their literary curating in the early twenty-first century insists that during these anxious political times when the world is being threatened by climate change and a mass pandemic, we must use what time remains to re-embrace the marvellous, re-embody our inner creature, reconnect with our instincts, de-civilise, de-mythologise, rewild.

Notes

At the time of writing this chapter, I was seeking the conditions of creative hibernation through a remote residency in the Westfjords, Iceland. The worldwide Covid-19 pandemic brought rapid, new meaning to the notion of solitude, with terms like "social distancing" and "self-isolation" swiftly becoming common parlance.

1 Joseph Conrad, *Heart of Darkness* (London: Penguin, [1899] 1994), 39.

2 Susan Rubin Suleiman, *Subversive Intent: Gender, Politics, and the Avant-Garde* (Cambridge, MA: Harvard University Press, 1990), 171.

3 Susan L. Aberth and Tere Arcq, 'Cauldrons and Curanderas: The Magical Collaborations of Remedios Varo and Leonora Carrington,' *The Story of the Last*

Egg, ed. Wendi Norris (New York and San Francisco: Gallery Wendi Norris, 2019), 75–77.

4 Susan L. Aberth and Tere Arcq, 'As in a Mirror with Multiple Facets: Leonora Carrington and the Tarot,' *The Tarot of Leonora Carrington* (Lopen, Somerset: Fulgur Press, 2020), 70; 85.

5 Georgiana M. M. Colvile, 'Women Artists, Surrealism and Animal Representation,' *Angels of Anarchy: Women Artists and Surrealism*, ed. Patricia Allmer (New York: Prestel, 2009), 64.

6 Whitney Chadwick, 'El Mundo Mágico: Leonora Carrington's Enchanted Garden,' *Leonora Carrington: The Mexican Years* (San Francisco: Mexican Museum, 1991), 11.

7 Marina Warner, 'From high society to surrealism: in praise of Leonora Carrington—100 years on,' *Guardian* (6 April 2017): www.theguardian.com/books/2017/apr/06/leonora-carrington-from-high-society-to-surrealism-in-praise-of-100-years-on (Accessed 15 April 2020); Marina Warner, 'Leonora Carrington: Badger,' *Leonora Carrington in the Viktor Wynd Collection*, ed. Catriona McAra (Leeds: Leeds Arts University, 2016), 23–26.

8 Susan L. Aberth, '"An Allergy to Collaboration": The Early Formation of Leonora Carrington's Artistic Vision,' *Leonora Carrington and the International Avant-Garde*, eds J. P. Eburne and C. McAra (Manchester: Manchester University Press, 2017), 27. As ever, Carrington was notoriously fickle and inscrutable about her own feelings on this subject—in *The Stone Door*, Carrington writes: "Return ghost, animal or man. I cannot bear this loneliness, I am sick of being alone with myself" (New York: St Martin's Press, [1976] 1977), 14–15.

9 Wendi Norris makes a similar point about the poetic accuracy of Michaela Carter's interpretation of Carrington in *Leonora in the Morning Light* (2021), 'Michaela Carter in Conversation with Art Expert Wendi Norris' (6 April 2021), www.youtube.com/watch?v=obywWxBprkY (Accessed 13 April 2022).

10 Heidi Sopinka, *The Dictionary of Animal Languages* (London: Scribe, 2018), 85.

11 Mieke Bal and Michelle Williams Gamaker, 'Mrs B: The film analysis of a novel,' *Flaubert [Online], Translations/Adaptations* (2012): http://flaubert.revues.org/1837 (Accessed 2 November 2019).

12 Heidi Sopinka went on to read all of Carrington's published writing, followed by Susan L. Aberth's accessible 2004 monograph and a few other accounts.

13 Interview with Heidi Sopinka.

14 Heidi Sopinka, 'Interview with Leonora Carrington,' *The Believer*, 94 (November/December 2012), 86.

15 Heidi Sopinka, 'Master Pieces,' *Brick*, 102 (January 2019): https://brickmag.com/master-pieces (Accessed 29 April 2020).

16 Claudia Dey and Heidi Sopinka, *About Horses Atelier* (2020): www.horsesatelier.com/pages/about (Accessed 9 February 2020).

17 Courtney Toderash, 'An Intimate Discussion with Claudia Dey and Heidi Sopinka: Designer-Novelists, and the Duo Behind Horses Atelier' (18 December 2018): www.kobo.com/blog/claudia-dey-and-heidi-sopinka-horses-atelier (Accessed 9 February 2020).

18 Jonathan P. Eburne, 'Breton's Wall, Carrington's Kitchen: Surrealism and the Archive,' *Intermediality: History and Theory of the Arts, Literature and Technology*, 18 (2012): 31; 33.
19 Interview with Heidi Sopinka.
20 Heidi Sopinka, 'Hey Necromancer!' *Paris Review* (18 September 2018): https://theparisreview.org/blog/2018/09/18/hey-necromancer (Accessed 11 February 2020).
21 Interview with Sopinka.
22 Aberth and Arcq,'As in a Mirror with Multiple Facets,' 85.
23 Interview with Sopinka.
24 Leonora Carrington, 'The Seventh Horse,' *The Debutante and Other Stories* (London: Silver Press, 2017), 87; the tale was written in 1941 and first published in *VVV* magazine, 2–3 (March 1943). For a close reading of 'The Seventh Horse,' see Annette Shandler Levitt, 'The Bestial Fictions of Leonora Carrington,' *Journal of Modern Literature*, 20:1 (Summer, 1996), 74.
25 Sopinka cited in Toderash, 'An Intimate Discussion.'
26 Leonora Carrington cited in Kim Evans, *Leonora Carrington and the House of Fear* (BBC Omnibus, 1992).
27 Kristoffer Noheden, 'The Grail and the Bees: Leonora Carrington's Quest for Human-Animal Coexistence,' *Beyond Given Knowledge: Investigation, Quest and Exploration in Modernism and the Avant-Gardes*, eds H. Veivo et al. (Berlin: De Gruyter, 2018), 250.
28 Susan L. Aberth, 'Animal Kingdom,' *Leonora Carrington: Magical Tales*, eds Tere Arcq and Stefan van Raay (Mexico City: Instituto Nacional de Bellas Artes, 2018), 245.
29 Interview with Sopinka.
30 Donna J. Haraway, *When Species Meet* (London and Minneapolis: University of Minnesota Press, 2008), 42.
31 In an interview with Anne Walsh, Leonora Carrington says "I prefer not to eat meat," *Hello Leonora, Soy Anne Walsh* (Cambridge: MIT Press, 2019), 67.
32 Natalya Lusty, *Surrealism, Feminism, Psychoanalysis* (Aldershot: Ashgate 2007), 40.
33 Marina Warner, *From the Beast to the Blonde: On Fairy Tales and Their Tellers* (London: Chatto & Windus, 1994), 384.
34 Leonora Carrington, 'What is a Woman,' *Surrealist Women: An International Anthology*, ed. Penelope Rosemont (London: Athlone Press, [1970] 1998), 374; 'Female Human Animal,' *Leonora Carrington: What She Might Be*, ed. Salomon Grimberg (Dallas, TX: Dallas Museum of Art, 2008), 12–13.
35 Kate Bernheimer, 'Editor's Note,' *Fairy Tale Review: The Green Issue* (Detroit, MI: Wayne State University Press, 2006), 140.
36 Sigmund Freud's *Civilization and its Discontents* (1930) is not far away here, and his work on the disavowal model of 'Fetishism' (1905) also comes to mind, *Civilization and Its Discontents*, trans. David McLintock (London: Penguin, 2002); 'Fetishism,' *Standard Edition of the Complete Psychological Works of Sigmund Freud*, ed. James Strachey (London: Hogarth Press and Institute of Psychoanalysis, 1961), 152–157.
37 Haraway, *When Species Meet*, 42.

38 Linda Hutcheon, *A Theory of Adaptation* (Abingdon: Routledge, 2013), 145.
39 Leonora Carrington, 'For Alain,' *Alan Glass* (New York: Claude Bernard Gallery, 1971/1991), 5.
40 Chloe Aridjis, *Asunder* (London: Chatto & Windus, 2013), 82.
41 Interview with Chloe Aridjis.
42 Interview with Chloe Aridjis.
43 Chloe Aridjis, 'An A-Z of Leonora Carrington Memories, Mostly in Quotes, Gathered Over Years of Visits to Her Home,' *Leonora Carrington and the International Avant-Garde*, eds J. P. Eburne and C. McAra (Manchester: Manchester University Press, 2017),18; Interview with Aridjis.
44 Interview with Aridjis.
45 Chloe Aridjis in conversation with Marina Warner, *London Review of Books* (4 April 2017).
46 Chloe Aridjis, 'Leonora Carrington at Home in the Colonia Roma and the Mexican Underworld,' Centre for Mexican Studies, King's College London (3 June 2019).
47 Interview with Claire Dean.
48 Peter Matthiessen signed 'A Milkweed-Butterfly Recovery Alliance' (2014); see Homero Aridjis, *News of the Earth*, ed. and trans. Betty Ferber (Simsbury, CT: Mandel Vilar Press, 2017), 382.
49 Peter Matthiessen, *The Snow Leopard* (London: Vintage, 2010), 221.
50 Robert Mabey, 'Introduction,' *The Snow Leopard* (London: Vintage, 2010), viii, xiv.
51 Laura Mulvey, 'Pandora's Box: Topographies of Curiosity,' *Fetishism and Curiosity* (Bloomington and Indianapolis: Indiana University Press, 1996), 59. See also Anne Walsh, who describes the myth of the Holy Grail in *The Hearing Trumpet* as a "MacGuffin," *Hello Leonora*, 150.
52 *Prim: A Nursery Story* [unpublished Carrington family catalogue]. Thanks to Roger Shannon.
53 Mieke Bal, *Quoting Caravaggio: Contemporary Art, Preposterous History* (London and Chicago: Chicago University Press, 1999), 15.
54 Aridjis, 'Leonora Carrington at Home in the Colonia Roma.'
55 Chadwick, 'El Mundo Mágico,' 23.
56 Leonora Carrington cited in interview with Paul de Angelis, *Leonora Carrington: The Mexican Years* (San Francisco: Mexican Museum, 1991), 36.
57 Chloe Aridjis in conversation with Juliet Jacques, *London Review of Books Podcast* (2019): www.lrb.co.uk/podcasts-and-videos/podcasts/at-the-bookshop/chloe-aridjis-and-juliet-jacques-sea-monsters (Accessed 8 May 2020).
58 Homero Aridjis, 'Mexico's 1985 Earthquake Awoke a Social Earthquake that is Still Roiling,' *News of the Earth*, 307–308.
59 Aridjis, 'Leonora Carrington at Home in the Colonia Roma.' The "garden of scorpions" reminds me of Lucy Skaer's *Scorpion/Diamond* (2001).
60 Jonathan P. Eburne, 'The Memory Tower,' *Leonora Carrington Centenary Symposium* (Mexico City: Biblioteca de México, 2017): www.youtube.com/watch?v=K8fTDkN_x8s (Accessed 16 July 2020).

61 One might compare the poetic chains of *Asunder* to Roland Barthes's reading of Georges Bataille's *Histoire de l'Oeil* (1928), 'The Metaphor of the Eye,' *Story of the Eye* (London: Penguin, 1979), 121.

62 Chloe Aridjis cited in Devorah Baum and Josh Appignanesi, 'Fluidity, Indeterminacy, Interdependence: A Conversation with Chloe Aridjis,' *Wasafiri*, 36:2 (2021): https://doi.org/10.1080/02690055.2021.1879477 (Accessed 23 July 2021).

63 Interview with Aridjis.

64 Donna J. Haraway, *Simians, Cyborgs, and Women: The Reinvention of Nature* (New York: Routledge, 1991), 2.

65 Lora Markova and Roger Shannon, 'Leonora Carrington on and off Screen: Intertextual and Intermedial Connections between the Artist's Creative Practice and the Medium of Film,' *Arts*, 8:11 (January 2019): www.mdpi.com/2076–0752/8/1/11 (Accessed 22 February 2020).

66 Haraway, *When Species Meet*, 15.

67 Leonora Carrington cited in Joanna Moorhead, *Leonora Carrington—Britain's Lost Surrealist TateShots* (2015): www.youtube.com/watch?v=lqXePrSE1R0 (Accessed 1 April 2020).

68 Josh Appignanesi cited in Jennifer Higgie, 'How "Female Human Animal" Blends Documentary with Fiction,' *Frieze* (2018): https://frieze.com/article/how-female-human-animal-blends-documentary-fiction (Accessed 27 November 2018).

69 Appignanesi cited in Higgie (2018).

70 The mysterious male lead is played by Marc Hosemann, an actor from the Volksbühne, whom Aridjis knew from her years in Berlin. She first saw him in the role of Mephistopheles, and he reminds her of a character from Weimar Berlin. Correspondence with the author (August 2020).

71 Chloe Aridjis cited in interview with Natasha Stallard, 'In Conversation with Chloe Aridjis,' *Tank Magazine*, 77 (2018).

72 Chloe Aridjis cited in interview with Fernando Hernández Urías, '"Without disenchantment there is no change,"' *Chilango* (21 April 2020): www.chilango.com/cultura/chloe-aridjis-monstruos-marinos (Accessed 22 April 2020).

73 Sopinka cited in Toderash, 'An Intimate Discussion.'

74 Grateful thanks to Hannah Buckley.

75 Homero Aridjis, 'The Solitary Enchanter,' *The Child Poet*, trans. Chloe Aridjis (London: Archipelago Books, 2016), 105.

76 Julia Kristeva rewrites the Freudian perspective in her suggestion that the child has to abject themselves from the body of the mother in order to become an autonomous subject, *Powers of Horror: An Essay on Abjection*, trans. Leon S. Roudiez (New York: Columbia University Press, 1982), 12–13. Aridjis chooses to re-explore such subjective becoming in relation to the father's intellect.

77 Chloe Aridjis, 'Introduction,' *The Child Poet*, 8.

78 Aridjis, 'Introduction,' *The Child Poet*, 10.

79 Aridjis, *Sea Monsters*, 22.

80 Sopinka, *The Dictionary*, 18.

81 Leonora Carrington cited in Homero Aridjis, *News of the Earth*, 268–269.

5

Menagerie

I think a lot of my work sits on the borders of acceptability, so I expect
opinions to be mixed.

—Samantha Sweeting (2010)[1]

The mountains darkened into rude animal shapes …

—Leonora Carrington (c.1941)[2]

The medieval bestiary is one of the most characteristic features of Leonora
Carrington's art, and her meticulous attention to animals and animal iconography has been described by Gabriel Weisz Carrington as "a pictorial
menagerie."[3] Performance artists Lynn Lu (b. 1974) and Samantha Sweeting
(b. 1982), are among the many contemporary makers who have been drawn
to realising Carrington's animal picture and stories, producing practical
manifestations of such visual and literary human–animal relationships. In
the previous chapter, I argued that, in the spirit of Carrington, women have
to take back and prioritise their creative solitude before they can participate
in collective activism. This is true also for Lu and Sweeting, who both hold
dear the power of their subjective imaginations, while championing participatory engagement and audience interaction which completes their work.
Drawing on the legacies of a feminist-surrealism, with particular interests
in psychoanalysis and childhood memories, Lu and Sweeting are united in
their interdisciplinary and dialogic practices that spotlight empathy, wellbeing,
and grief, often prioritising non-traditional art audiences in the process.
They practice separately but, since 2011, have collaborated twice on a
multisensory performance installation based on Carrington's novel, *The
Hearing Trumpet* (1974), which this chapter will unpack as a form of what
Sweeting has termed "embodied storytelling."[4]

Lu and Sweeting hail from different cultural heritages, but were both born
in Singapore and have spent much of their careers in the art scene in London
as well as living rurally. Their respective approaches to art-making often
involve or evoke animal familiars. Their work thus continues Carrington's
thinking around a "female human animal," and they could be said to inhabit

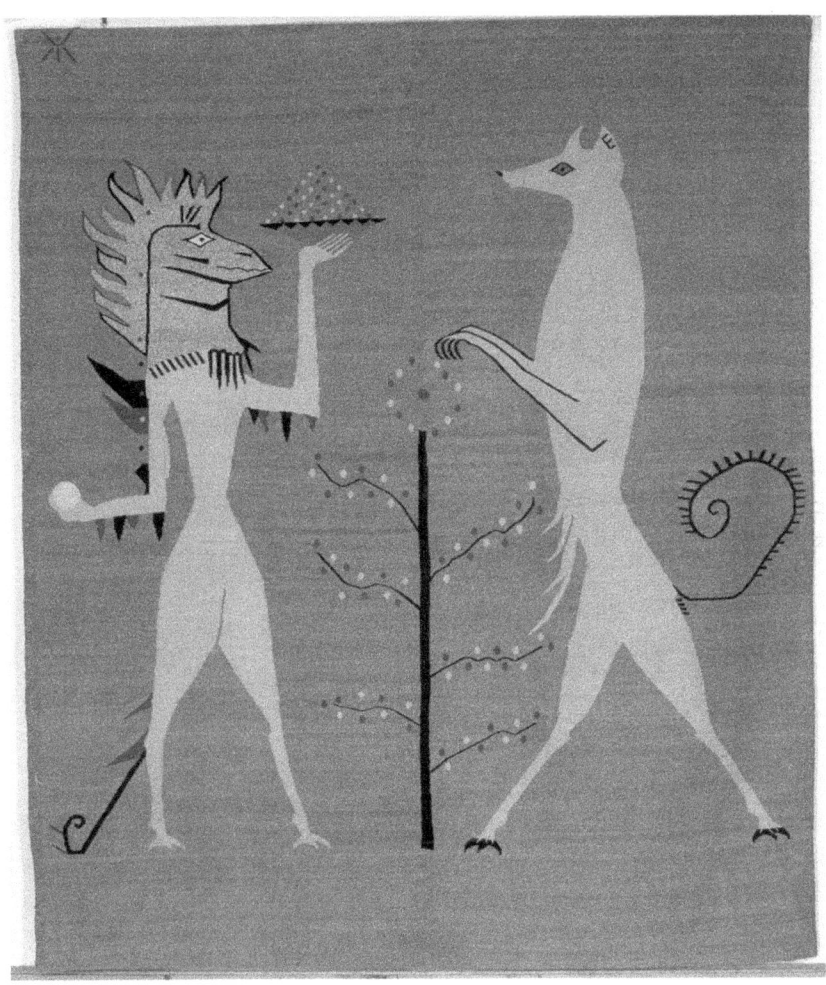

23 Leonora Carrington, *Iguana and Fox*, 1948–58

artistically many of her fantasy bestiaries. Both have produced significant bodies of work exploring the cultural history of lactation (for example Sweeting's performance photographs *In Came the Lamb*, 2009, and Lu's performance installation, *Adagio*, 2013). Both have involved their "companion species" in their artworks—Lu's dog, Ichiban, appears in her installation *Happily Ever After* (2007), while Sweeting's cat, Texas, was the subject of *Experiments in Cat Licking* (2016). Sweeting's adoptive lamb, Oscar, has also had cameos in several of Sweeting's video performances. For Sweeting, the zoo and the farm are some of the creative spaces and ecologies that form a baseline of her research. For Lu, absurdity and the participatory chance encounter are crucial to her practice. All such knowledges and experiences contributed to their *Hearing Trumpet* collaboration. First, let's explore how each arrived at Carrington.

Donkeyskin

Stepping outside art-world circulation towards the end of her art education in 2006–07 in rural Devon, Sweeting went into a period of creative hibernation or incubation, cohabiting with a variety of abandoned animals in a derelict farmhouse in the French Pyrenees. While the artist literally sought to rewild herself and more closely understand and embody animal behaviour, mythology, and inter-species dialogues, these experiences also seem to have raised her long-term interest in the aesthetics of care and de-hierarchy amid the animal kingdom. Much of this early work involved Sweeting broaching human–animal boundaries with close visceral contact—whether cradling dead lambs, feeding runts, rolling in the mud, or lying prone in fields of livestock.

In this respect, Sweeting could be said to embody expressively the uninhibited wildness of Carrington's literary icon, Virginia Fur, from the fairy tale 'As They Rode Along the Edge' (*c.*1937–41):

> Her name was Virginia Fur, she had a mane of hair yards long and enormous hands with dirty nails; yet the citizens of the mountain respected her and she too always showed a deference for their customs. True, the people up there were plants, animals, birds; otherwise things wouldn't have been the same … She, Virginia Fur, lived in a village long abandoned by human beings (26).

Virginia is a wild woman huntress who lives with a hundred cats and is seduced by a decorative boar called Igname. The image of the boar would later appear in Carrington's painting *Pig Rush* (1960) and among her late bronze sculptures. Sweeting's video performances, *Like a Pig in Shit* (2007) and *Experiments in Cat-Licking* (2016), seem to fold back onto Carrington's boar and cat imagery, in a sensorial gesture of getting to the heart of the source text as a mode of ecologically grounded, embodied storytelling. In the former, Sweeting writhes naked in the mud and attempts to eat a fallen apple using only her mouth. The snuffling, crunching sounds contribute a further layer of base instinct. In the latter, Sweeting inverts the feline gesture of washing by licking the fur of her tabby cat, Texas—an action the artist could only carry out for a few moments before gagging, as the fur clogged her tongue. *Experiments in Cat-Licking* is also an explicit homage to the multimedia performance artist and radical feminist Carolee Schneemann's *Infinity Kisses* (1981–89) and *Infinity Kisses II* (1991–98). In these photo-grids and later film (2008), Schneemann caresses and nuzzles her cats Cluny and

Vesper through a series of photographic close-up double portraits which are often intimately unfocused.[5] As Tess Thackara points out, cats are "something of a feminist symbol" in Schneemann's work, a fact that has become true for many feminist-surrealist exemplars such as Carrington's contemporaries, Leonor Fini and Remedios Varo, and more recently Chloe Aridjis (whom Sweeting has cat-sitted for in London).[6] *Experiments in Cat-Licking* therefore offers a clear indication of how Sweeting occasionally recycles and synthesises a range of feminist art histories.

Sweeting could be said to further inhabit the visual universe of Carrington. In a recent compartmentalisation of her art historical touchstones, Sweeting highlighted Carrington's painting *Pastoral* (1950) (Figure 20) as chief among her source texts and conceptual menageries.[7] *Pastoral* is one of several arcadian picnic paintings made by Carrington, following *Down Below* (1941) and *Pomps of the Subsoil* (1947). Here, the humanoid creatures are surrounded by both airborne and earthbound homunculi within a bucolic forest landscape. Ali Smith is also drawn to this artwork, reproducing it in her experimental text *Artful* (2012) as a typical example of Carrington's visual *œuvre* which, Smith claims, she is even more drawn to than Carrington's writing:

> That night in bed you showed me some of Carrington's pictures. They were dark and bright, playful, like pictures from stories, but wilder, more savage, full of sociable-looking animals and wild-looking animals, beings who were part animal and part human, looking like they were all having a very interesting conversation, masked beings, people who were turning into birds or maybe it was birds turning into people.[8]

The fact that both Sweeting and Smith should select *Pastoral* as an exemplar is telling in terms of their shared perspective on the eco-critical Carrington, as someone whose work promotes harmony with the natural world and animal kingdom. Sweeting says: "I approach animals as an artist informed by folk tales and mythology, and the resulting work is often allegorical."[9] The underpinning framework for both Sweeting and Carrington's artistic practices are akin in this respect.

A key achievement of Sweeting's has been to bring such two-dimensional, human–animal imagery into the experimental domain of the live arts. For example, Sweeting performed *La Nourrice (Come Drink From Me My Darling)* at the live arts festival *Visions of Excess* (2009), co-curated by performance artists Ron Athey and Lee Adams. For this intimate, one-to-one encounter, Sweeting sat on a milking stool mounted on top of a raw sheepskin in a dimly lit archway, creating a peaceful, nativity-like setting in which she invited audience members to suckle from a synthetic nursing system she wore. As with Carrington, Sweeting often toys with religious (specifically

Catholic) iconography, overlaying it with the sensorial realities of stable farming and extracting its bodily profanities: "I am exploiting the established tradition of religious devotional art and have added an incongruous element."[10] Between 2007 and 2011, Sweeting produced a controversial body of work, a series of lactation narratives in which she appeared to breastfeed kittens, lambs, and humans. One might be reminded of the lactating hyena from one of Carrington's earliest self-presentations, *The Inn of the Dawn Horse* (1937), Joseph Beuys's didactic performance, *How to Explain Pictures to a Dead Hare* (1965), or Tori Amos's *Boys for Pele* (1996) album cover art. Sweeting further explains the genesis of her own project, that she was struck by a William Lyman Underwood photograph (1921) of a woman nursing simultaneously a baby bear and human baby, which appeared in Marina Warner's famous study *From the Beast to the Blonde* (1994).[11] Warner, writes of our cultural discomfort with such imagery:

> The collapse of boundaries between the animal and the human is not altogether complete in this story, because the book itself—and the permission the foster mother was asked to give—attests to the shock which I, for one, certainly felt. Despite fairy tales' and folklore's intermingling of creatures, the talking and helpful animal familiars, despite continuing advances in ecology and changing attitudes to animal rights and human domination, it is startling and feels uncomfortable, even prurient, to look at a woman feeding a bear cub, as if she and he belonged to a common species.[12]

Such an unsettling interspecies dialogue is arguably consistent with Carrington's own disruptive mode of storytelling. Yet, Sweeting's work, like Carrington's, is ethically committed; Sweeting is a pescatarian and resists any urge to hold animals or human–animal audience members against their will. Sweeting highlights the complexities of interspecies power dynamics and often revises her earlier ideas through new lenses. What she finds in Carrington is a commonality of transgressive feral behaviour and maternal imagery. Their mutual intrigue in feminine bodily fluids also overlaps in their shared use of menstruation as an artistic medium. According to Alejandro Jodorowsky, Carrington infamously, possibly apocryphally, decorated Luis Buñuel's bedchamber with her menstrual blood as an act of defiance.[13] Sweeting, in turn, made around twenty diminutive pictures of her childhood home, playful "period drawings" entitled *La Casa del Bambino* (2013). This was a collaboration with her partner at the time, the artist and magician Luke Rodilosso, involving fingerpainting with Sweeting's menstrual blood, Rodilosso's penis serving as the paintbrush. While Carrington's reference to the maternal occurs through her use of egg tempera paint, Sweeting uses her monthly blood in a ritualistic gesture to present a longing for a maternal house or occupied womb.

During the 2020 lockdown, as animals reclaimed empty urban centres, Sweeting began engaging with local fox narratives.[14] Carrington herself frequently depicted foxes in her work, both as a key occupant of her beloved childhood bestiary and as a mythological, unifying force. Often it is an Arctic fox that Carrington depicts. Think, for instance, of Carrington's hieroglyphic-like tapestry, *Iguana and Fox* (1948–58) (Figure 23), a surrealist-like encounter of two different ecosystems, tropical and tundra. Or Carrington's *The Q Symphony* (2002), an Orphic remix of a painting in which musicians actively keep the company of wolves and other canine creatures that howl in response to a range of instruments being played. Carrington quips: "Once a dog barked at a mask I made; that was the most honourable comment I ever received."[15] Francis Alÿs's *The Nightwatch* (2004) has also become of enduring interest to Sweeting—an exploration of the wildness within the civilised—where a fox was released in the National Gallery in London and monitored through CCTV footage. The fox is a deeply talismanic animal for Sweeting through performances such as *Moon Dance* (2020), "the culmination of a series of dance scores I have been making with my midwife friend," where Sweeting communed with a local fox in a meadow in Dawson's Heights, East Dulwich, using her choreography training to mimic the fox's movements and thus attempting to forge an interspecies bond.[16] Donning her grandmother's red shawl, Sweeting performed the fairy-tale role of 'Little Red Riding Hood,' rewriting the well-known narrative and its chief iconography (the red cloak) for the contemporary moment and enchanting the antagonist from malevolent wolf to gentle fox. In this scenario, Sweeting displaced authorial intention and curiosity onto the fox itself, with the conversative moral of "straying from the path" predominantly directed or led by the non-human in this encounter. In doing so, Sweeting tried to dialogue with this fox in terms which we might understand through Donna J. Haraway's notion of companion species or animal encounters, or through Clarissa Pinkola Estés's idea of going feral to reclaim an intrinsic and genuine sense of the feminine self.[17] Like Carrington, both present eco-feminist perspectives on social reality. This chimes with the "lupine acoustic structures" which Heidi Sopinka uses in *The Dictionary of Animal Languages* (2018) to describe such animal research, a reading which reverberates throughout Sweeting's practice.[18]

Carrington's many images of her horse alter ego find their twenty-first-century artistic realisation in Sweeting's pony images, from talismanic readymades like Sweeting's miniature rocking horse to the involvement of donkeys within an animal-friendly performative domain. Collaborations with donkeys include *She Wants It, She Wants it Not* (2007), a filmed performance in the Pyrenees during which Sweeting dangles a carrot from a contraption on her head in order to commune with her "muse," a donkey called Gina:

"I called her name. She epitomised donkey strength and pathos. I was very fond of her and, in an expression of empathy, I made a mask for myself in her image."[19] The image of Gina in question was a donkey head fabricated by costume designer Nichola Kate Butland, and worn for Sweeting's epic, durational performance, *Bestilalia (I Never Imagined Life Without You)* (2008). As with her use of performance art to rewrite well-known fairy tales (another aspect she arguably shares with Carrington's short stories), here Sweeting adjusted Charles Perrault's 'Peau d'Âne' ('Donkeyskin,' 1697). While the well-known tale explores father/daughter incest and disguise, Sweeting adapted the story to speak to her own experiences of non-consensual sex with paternal figures in the artworld and experiences from her time working at a home for sexually abused girls in Singapore. *Bestilalia* might be seen to operate between Carrington's second-wave feminism and that of #MeToo. Weisz Carrington writes that "Leonora was often inspired by animal skins. This became a recurrent theme in her work and was often associated with transformation."[20] Indeed, Sweeting has frequently been cited for her shape-shifting abilities, and her instincts might be best understood through Warner's idea that "shape-shifting is one of fairy tale's dominant and characteristic wonders."[21] Sweeting has experimented with animal disguise and fairy-tale characters, not to mention earlier experiments with performance garb incognito in social fetish clubs such as the Torture Garden in London. In reprising the pantomime donkey head and in assuming the role of the beast for her installation, *Bestilalia*, she sat in a farm animal's trough, demythologising Cleopatra's legendary bath of ass's milk, and surrounded herself with feathers, home-made taxidermy, and bottled potions, as if performing a rite of passage or a witch's incantation. Two years later, she continued her experimentation with a similar range of shamanic paraphernalia in a tableau entitled *Still waiting for you to come back to me* (2009) (Figure 25). Sweeting describes this performance as follows:

> An invitation to dinner. On a dining table in a manor house on the edge of Dartmoor, I sat in a bath of milk plucking a pheasant. I was surrounded by glass bottles, bones, hair, feathers, wine, roses and fruit, as the bloody head of a freshly shot deer lay at the fore of the tableau. His carcass was served on a platter and guests were invited to feed themselves. I continued my action for the duration of the meal.[22]

The mixture of animal carcasses, candles, bottled potions, and female nudity is deliberately discomforting as a discourse on grief and the outpouring of sorrow, similar in its affect to the post-sanatorium imagery of narrative descent that Carrington produced during the Second World War. Performance installations like these might be read as a satisfying, if indirect, response to Carrington's picture-making, esotericism, and incantation. One might think

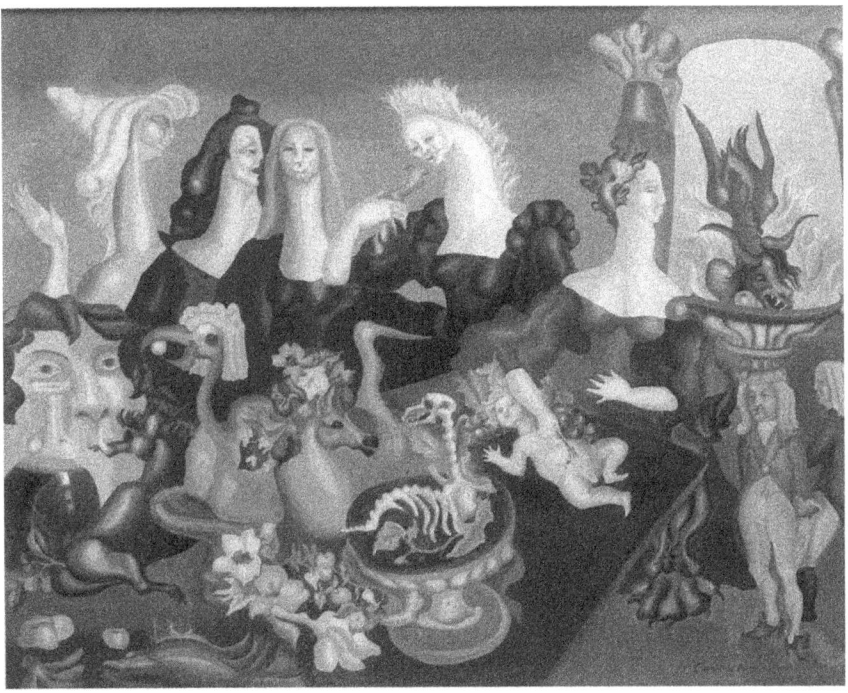

24 Leonora Carrington, *The Meal of Lord Candlestick*, 1938

of Carrington's extravagant pre-war painting, *The Meal of Lord Candlestick* (1938) (Figure 24), or other subversions of Crookhey Hall, the bourgeois mansion in which Carrington grew up.

Further "chance encounters" with animal behaviours and infiltration of dwelling spaces occur in Sweeting's filmed performance installation *The House Falls Down* (2009) (Figure 26), during which her adopted pet sheep, Oscar, wanders into the scene of Sweeting wearing a fairy tale-like red dress and performing the role of child-woman in an upward bow pose inside a circular metal frame reminiscent of a hula hoop. The shape of her body during this performance mimics the arch of hysteria found throughout surrealism (especially in work by Carrington's contemporaries such as Louise Bourgeois), while the presence of the sheep and ruined farmhouse suggest the feminist querying of domesticity that occurs in Carrington's dollhouse paintings such as *The House Opposite* (1945) (Figure 8). Carrington's picture features chambers where the dreaming activities open portals on to lush fantasy lands beyond the picture-plane and house walls. One thinks of the breaching of domestic boundaries as a mode of post-war escapist fantasy that occur in stories like C. S. Lewis's *The Lion, the Witch and the Wardrobe*

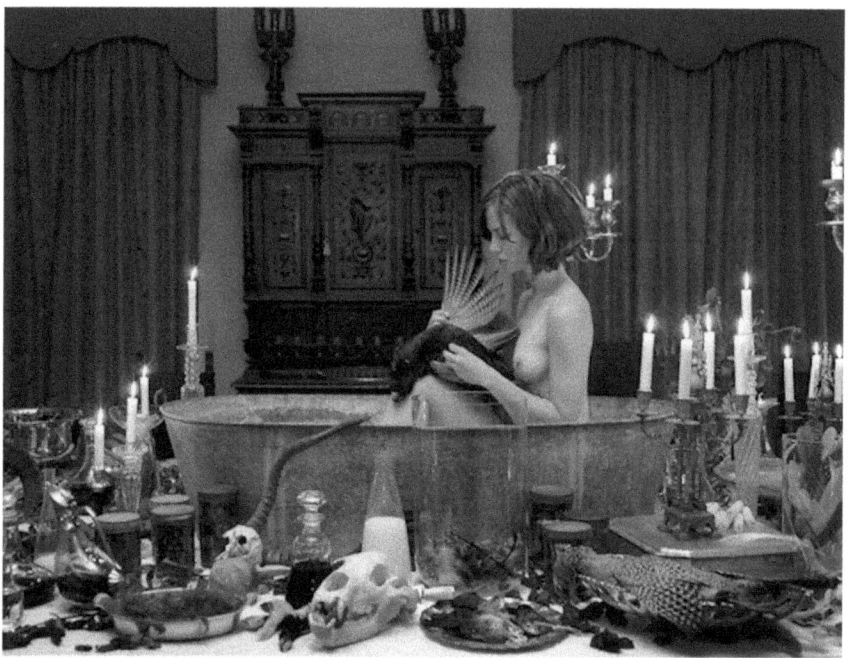

25 Samantha Sweeting, *Still waiting for you to come back to me*, 2009

(1950), although this would appear after Carrington's picture was painted. Sweeting is subtle in her more recent breaching of reality through her poetic presentations of marvellous in the everyday. For example, in Sweeting's dialogic video, *The Rhino and the Peacock* (2013), a white rhinoceros and a male peacock share an enclosure. This surprising yet harmonious juxtaposition of two rare and extraordinary creatures evokes the ubiquitous chance encounter as found in compositions by Carrington. Sweeting, the human-artist, is only present through her camera lens, and the image brings to mind Carrington's own peacock paintings such as *A Camelia for Anima* (1958). Sweeting's vignette suggests a common animal ground, that when it comes to shelter and cohabitation, we have more in common than what divides us. The chicken coop and snail shell are of further interest to Sweeting as structures for art-making, framing, and rethinking. For Sweeting's solo exhibition, *A History of the World* (2013), her archaeological investigation into farming and homesteads comprised a series of animal houses with snails occupying dollhouses and a reconstructed chicken roost tied with knotted ropes. The overall effect was a microcosm of the feminine as various modes of "house," but those which stand in diminutive rebellion against patriarchal suppression or anthropocentrism.

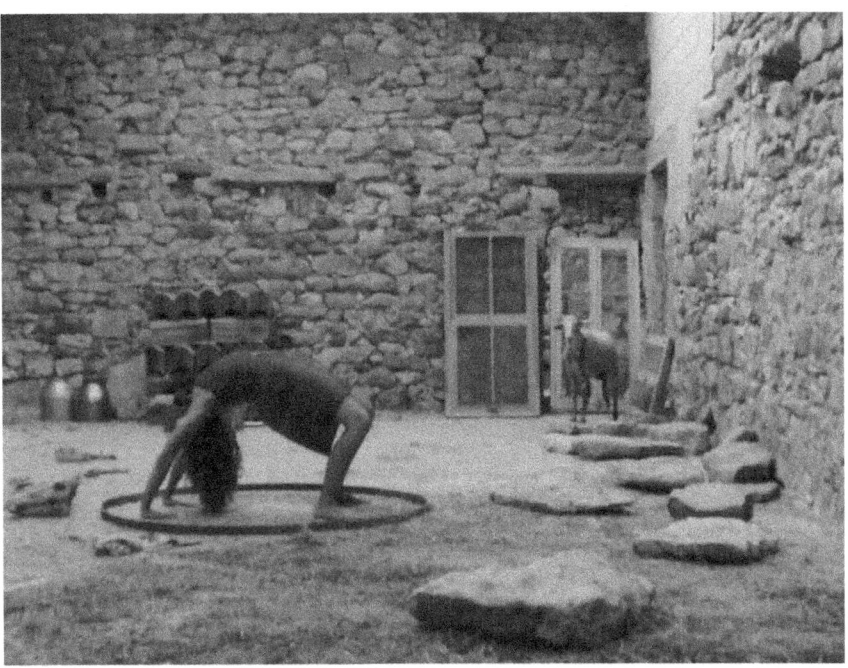

26 Samantha Sweeting, *The House Falls Down* (video still), 2009

Child-women

Who is the bride of the wind? Can she read? Can she write French without mistakes?

—Max Ernst (1938)[23]

Bullshit!

—Leonora Carrington (n.d.)[24]

Carrington's accepted narrative in the feminist scholarship has come to be understood as her rebellion against her child-woman status.[25] While I maintain that youth culture and *femme-enfant* status actually embody a significant degree of power and possibility through narratives of curiosity (epistemophilia being the active "desire to know"), it is interesting how this scholarly debate has been reinterpreted by artists.[26] To be sure, the unique iconography for which Carrington has become known can be traced back to an Edwardian girlhood—horse riding, zoo visiting, and longingly doodling in her exercise jotters. While many artists have flocked to this subversive picture-book aesthetic one hundred years later, others nuance the politics of girlhood and nostalgia through performative means.

In interview, Lynn Lu openly questions Carrington's youthful "apprentice-ship" to a much older surrealist in *Portrait of Max Ernst* (1939), commending Carrington's ability to question a potential power imbalance via Carrington's highly technical, early skill with paint. Here, Carrington self-represents as a miniature frozen horse inside a lantern, possibly lighting his way and guiding him through her aesthetic, rather than the other way around, as has too often been traditionally assumed. Such issue-raising through creative means breaks with accepted, anodyne, social, and art-historical narratives. This has been a constant throughout Lu's practice to date and seems to be a key area of commonality for Lu with Carrington.[27] Amelia Jones, has described Lu's *Haumapuhia Rising* (2018) as "gorgeous and disturbing" in its exploration of Maori mythology and in its challenging of misogynistic narratives through the visceral, "live" nature of performance.[28] Lu describes *Haumapuhia* as her "first consciously feminist work," and notes that her motivations behind it were in response to the #MeToo campaign, which was in the process of unfolding at that moment and still retains potential for giving formerly silenced women a framework, vocabulary, and medium through which to speak.[29] Kate Bernheimer recently pointed out that fairy tales were the first confessional narratives, and are thus to be read as pre-emptive of #MeToo.[30] As with Sweeting's use of the 'Donkeyskin' fairy tale, in *Haumapuhia*, Lu references another troubled father/daughter relationship. Carrington experienced difficulty with her own father, who wanted a more conventional path for his rebellious daughter, and Carrington explored this relationship in her stories 'Little Francis' (1937–38) and most potently in 'The Oval Lady' (1937), where the father burns his daughter's sentient rocking horse as an extreme punishment for the child-woman's resolute interest in make-believe. Carrington's railing against such patriarchy's refusal of magic is arguably one of the main contributing factors that led to her output as well as a leading reason for her contemporary appeal. Although neither Sweeting nor Lu makes direct reference to this Carrington's paternal complex, there is common ground to be found in the practices of all three regarding their nostalgic yet troubled ties to familial heritages.

Much of Lu's work engages with maternal practices, particularly the raw, bodily processes of lactation and menstruation, and the related substances of milk and blood. Again, Carrington's lactating hyena in *The Inn of the Dawn Horse* comes to mind. This blue-eyed creature has perhaps received more critical and creative fixation than any other iconographical detail throughout her wider *œuvre*, perhaps due to its defiant challenge to surrealist expectations around women's self-portraiture. Susan L. Aberth approaches the hyena in Carrington's work as a "witch's familiar," while Sopinka reminds us that "spotted hyenas live in large matriarchal clans and have a startling social intelligence ... Medieval bestiary says that hyenas are immortal. That they are highly sexualized and can change their gender."[31] Lu's interests in "folkloristic lactation" might be aligned with this leaky, chaotic animal body, while Natalya Lusty argues that Carrington's representation of older female bodies presents a direct challenge to the surrealist image of the *femme-enfant*.[32] In working through the legacies of Carrington, Lu uses her maternal status to do something similar, inviting her own maternal politics into her creative space, not only to reveal motherhood as a highly performative social activity, but as a way to reassert her own child-woman status, betwixt and between two registers of age brackets, appearances, and expectations. As a mother of a daughter, the need to reclaim and demonstrate her own artistic authority (and subjectivity) may be even more heightened—in *Adagio* (2013) (Figure 27), the five-month-old child and woman are reunited in the same womb-like space of the performance zone. Again, Carrington's dollhouse architecture might be evoked, especially works like *A Warning to a Mother* (1973). Lu explains she deployed her infant daughter, Kiki, as an "uncooperative prop," and explored the glacial slowness of "maternal time" through a melting block of ice and "the rhythmic drone" of her breast pump.[33] Both Sweeting and Lu are intrigued by French feminist, Julia Kristeva, and often burrow into the darker, more torturous implications of her writing. Current critical nostalgia for French feminism across artistic practice and academia often overlooks or sublimates the more challenging dimensions of such texts: the rejection of the maternal body, the notion of maternal failure, and the difficulty of reconciling the creation of life with the inevitability of death: "The abject confronts us ... within our personal archeology, with our earliest attempts to release the hold of maternal entity."[34] The scene for *Adagio* was composed almost classically, with Lu and Kiki appearing nude on dialogic, spotlit platforms, yet radically reworking the art-historical traditions of the Madonna and Child or even the Pietà. Not only does this performance installation demarcate mother and daughter as separate subjects, Lu depicts her own internal desire for and conflict with her child-woman status, corporeally conscious of her body's new meaning as a site of production and consumption. Far from whimsical idealisation, *Adagio* therefore emphasises the more torturous aspects of maternal separation as a kind of identity crisis of the *femme-enfant*, one of many critical conversations Carrington can be called upon to reopen intergenerationally.

Whispers

In the same year of Carrington's death, Lu and Sweeting collaborated on *The Hearing Trumpet* (2011), a dialogic, public engagement performance installation, based on Carrington's novel of the same title. The result was

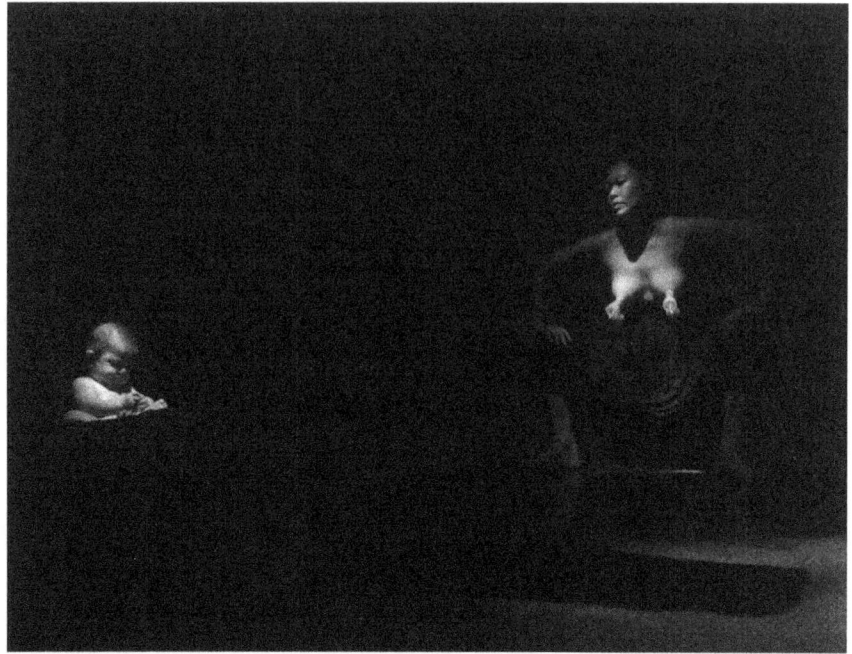

27 Lynn Lu, *Adagio*, 2013

a séance-like experience, with *The Hearing Trumpet* serving as the conceptual and thematic starting point for a two-part narrative performance exploring intimate personal memories. It was as if Lu and Sweeting were eavesdropping on Carrington's art-historical potency. Rather than a straightforward reprisal of the novel's narrative, their version highlighted its central motif, deploying Carrington's instrument as media. *The Hearing Trumpet* was first shown at *2Nights with 2Gyrlz* at Performance Space in Hackney, London (14–15 October 2011), and survives through documentary photographs taken by Marco Berardi on the first night and by Sweeting on the second night.[35] The diptych performance itself included an interactive game of Telephone (a playground or parlour game where secret messages are passed along a chain of participants, typically resulting in a very different end narrative from what was initiated). This game was recorded on the first night then played back through the static installation on the second night.

In the first act of the 2011 version, Sweeting collected previously untold childhood secrets from the audience before whispering these tales from memory through a brass hearing trumpet held up to Lu's ear. Lu then breathed onto a glass pane in front of her, which also served as a framing device, linking back to Carrington's visual output. With her index finger,

Lu then transcribed the stories into the condensation which visually hovered for a climactic moment before evaporating. In Sweeting's account, viewers were able to briefly decipher fragments of their own memories and those of other people before they vanished. The second act completed the dialogic circuit, replaying the tales exchanged on the first night back to the audience through the hearing trumpet, now installed as a spotlit, wall-mounted readymade with a concealed audio sound-piece. The combination of low-level lighting, murmuring sounds, and the raw immediacy of the artistic duet in this performance space appear to have served as the ideal environmental factors for a public confessional. The 18 anonymous, guilt-ridden micro-narratives related by members of the audience were revealing in their frank brevity, tragic tones and psychoanalytic content, for example:

> I used to read my sister's diary and cry over the bits about her sexual explorations with her boyfriend. She would find me curled up sobbing, and would try to comfort me. I never told her why I was crying. I was so afraid of losing her ...

> I stole from my grandmother's purse. Everyone thought she was going senile because she kept declaring that she was missing cash ...[36]

The combination of revulsion and desire was paramount. Many of the tales involve violence, humiliation, voyeurism, unrequited love, and fetishistic content. They echo the anecdotal asides and inner monologue of Marian in *The Hearing Trumpet*, for instance: "I had a faint idea of stealing one or two chocolates from Muriel which she hides behind the bookcase. Muriel is very mean about sweets and she wouldn't be so fat if she were more generous" (7). The suggestion that Marian has dementia is further taken into account through the partial loss of message between audience and performers and its creative reconfiguration. As Carrington's novel is told from Marian's point of view, even as an unreliable narrator, there is logic to her situation and experiences rendering the rest of the world and its characters as the true arbitrators of the nonsensical. Susan Rubin Suleiman, among others, has elucidated on the dynamics of empowerment, rewriting and shifting perspectives within the novel: "Only by having the old 'senile' crone tell her own story is the contradictory effect achieved. Marian's sharp wit counteracts her 'decomposing flesh' and her dependent status is belied by her narrative mastery."[37] Moreover, the polarity between youth and old age is dramatised, reminding us of the fact that Carrington was only in her thirties when she was writing about the "surrealism" within this particular nursing home. For the 2011 performance, audience members were invited to assist Sweeting and Lu in "writing" and shaping the event by means of transference and intersubjectivity. Lu describes the public engagement event through the micro-narrative economy of the curatorial text panel:

The audience is invited to think of a childhood experience they have never told anyone. They are then asked to tell it to their neighbour, who passes along what they hear—in a game of Chinese Whispers—until the story reaches Samantha.

Samantha murmurs what she hears into a hearing trumpet held against my ear. I breathe on the glass and transcribe what I hear in the condensation.

The audience catches glimpses of their secrets spelled out by my fingers. A few moments later, the words evaporate.[38]

Sweeting, meanwhile, describes her version of events as follows:

Night 1: Performance. The audience is invited to think of a childhood experience they have never told anyone. They then tell it to their neighbour, who passes along what they hear, in a game of Chinese Whispers, until the story reaches me. I murmur what I hear into a hearing trumpet held against Lynn's ear. Lynn breathes on a pane of glass and transcribes my words into the condensation. The audience catches glimpses of their secrets spelled out by Lynn's fingers and cast in shadow on the adjacent wall. A few moments later, the words evaporate.

Night 2: Sound installation. The hearing trumpet is attached to a wall. The audience places their ear to the mouthpiece to hear the stories I had whispered to Lynn the previous night.[39]

As with the chance encounter, and well-known surrealist parlour game of consequences or the exquisite corpse, here the initial game of Telephone created an oral/aural communicative chain in which, inevitably, some of the narrative content and detail got lost, transformed, or misheard in the process. This led to a reconfiguration and variation of the source tales. Thus, the performance quoted Carrington in a lively and resourceful manner, actively embodying and reimagining the novel rather than merely imitating it. The generational split of emerging artists and grand matriarch is bridged through the processes of embodied acting and adaptation. One could easily interpret Lu and Sweeting as performing the roles of the well-documented historical friendship of Carrington and her surrealist contemporary Remedios Varo, who appear in Carrington's novel as the fictional characters Marian and Carmella. Lu and Sweeting's minimal twinned costumes of uniform grey dresses, evening gloves, and red shoes further characterised them as participants in the iconographic universe of Carrington and Varo and provided a uniformity and contemporary edge to their visual tale-telling remote from the original script.

Turning to analysis of the performance object itself, the very process of oral storytelling is transferred from the speaker (she who quotes) to active listener; Carrington prefiguring the dynamics of sound art. As the title of her novel suggests, Marian is gifted an antique hearing trumpet, an *objet trouvé* or found object, from a surrealist flea market, by Carmella. This gift is an antique-like heirloom or art object and is described as follows:

> The trumpet was certainly a fine specimen of its kind, without being really modern. It was, however, exceptionally pretty, being encrusted with silver and mother o'pearl motifs and grandly curved like a buffalo's horn. The aesthetic presence of this object was not its only quality, the hearing trumpet magnified sound to such a degree that ordinary conversation became quite audible even to my ears (1).

The reader then learns that Carmella is clairvoyant and foresees that the device will enable her friend Marian to eavesdrop on some significant conversations such as her younger family's intentions to move her to a nursing home. Later, it enables Marian to overhear a murderer's plans and intervene. For the purpose of the contemporary performance, Lu acquired the brass prop from a specialist instrumental shop called Phil Parker Ltd in Marylebone, London. The owner sawed the horn off an old, battered trumpet and fitted a mouthpiece into the end. As an ad-hoc, assisted ready-made, the item used in the performance was a second-hand reinterpretation, a musical trumpet instead of the more prosthetic hearing aid used in the novel. Again, this detail is consistent with the story; when Marian is given the item, she is at first somewhat confused about its true purpose before Carmella demonstrates its application. As Lusty expands, metonymically the ear, or hearing more generally, is fetishised within the novel via the trumpet apparatus.[40] Meanwhile, Ali Smith suggests that "Fundamentally, *The Hearing Trumpet* is a book about profound disconnection; at its centre are people unable to hear each other, or unwilling to."[41] The novel is concerned with the prejudices and short-sightedness related to cultural views on ageing and dementia, and, less pejoratively, the empowerment and therapy associated with trust and friendship. Weisz Carrington has noted the parallel ability of his mother's paintings to speak to those that have "been denied the right to exist outside their clinical diagnoses."[42] Lu and Sweeting's performance and sound installation thus detail the themes of secretive communication, audibility, and lucidity, or lack of, that are so vividly highlighted in Carrington's novel. Moreover, for Lu and Sweeting, the presence of the reinvented hearing trumpet is vital to their performative interaction as a dialogic bridge, connecting both halves of the performance and installation as an audio-visual experience as well as a historical bridge linking past with present, namely the avant-garde practices of Carrington with this contemporary happening. By this logic, the trumpet also turns into an art historical heirloom, conceptually "passed down" the creative generations as new way of conveying Carrington's narrative.

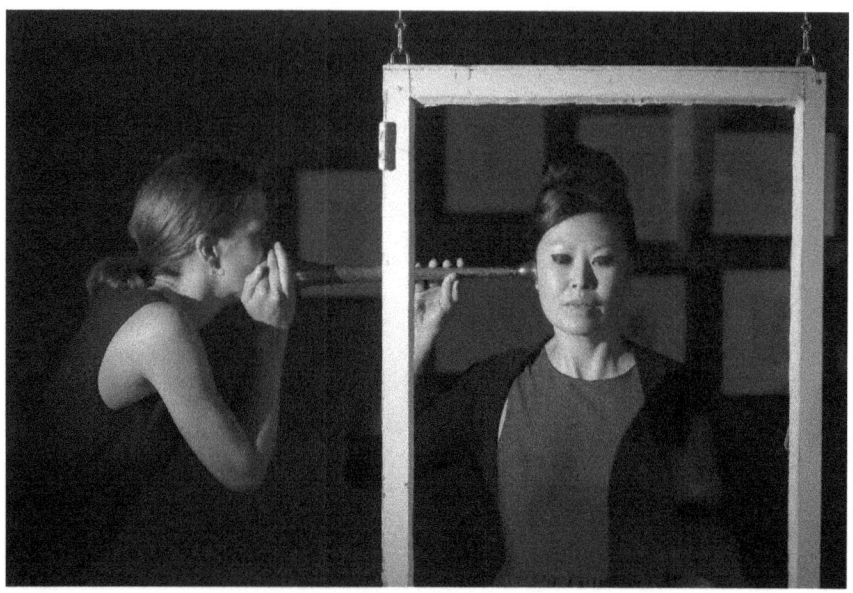

28 Lynn Lu and Samantha Sweeting, *The Hearing Trumpet*, (2011) 2016

In 2016, Lu and Sweeting reprised *The Hearing Trumpet* for an exhibition I curated in Leeds (Figure 28). The antique trumpet performance object was exhibited for the duration as a relief sculpture attached to the wall with a hidden sound component—if audience members bent down or leaned into the instrument, they heard Sweeting whispering secret stories from anonymous audience members. Reviewing this repurposing, Derek Horton described the installation as a "quiet intervention. The aural equivalent of looking through the wrong end of a telescope, you put your ear to the trumpet's mouthpiece to hear whispered confessional accounts of intimate misdemeanours."[43] The performative element occurred during the closing event. On this occasion, Lu and Sweeting invited me as curator to perform the role of ringmaster and dispense Victorian-inspired animal-snap cards with an instruction sheet advising audience members to: "Think of a childhood experience you have never told anyone; Find other animals the same as you to whisper to; When you receive a story, pass it on." The vintage cards used for the performance were *Animal Grab* by Thomas De La Rue (*c.*1900), and the deck's cast call is reminiscent of a Carrington picture or fairy tale, including pigs, sheep, turkeys, cockerels, cats, crows, cows, ducks, donkeys, dogs, frogs, and owls. These alternative "wild cards" were distributed at random, and individual audience members were encouraged to find their "familiar" (often a stranger) by making the animal call indicated on their card, and then tell them their most intimate childhood secret. Once again, secrets were collected, then whispered by Sweeting through the antique hearing-trumpet prop, and into the ear of Lu, who then breathed onto a glass window and wrote with her finger, so that secret words would be legible for a moment before disappearing. Due to the relatively large audience of over 52 people, two packs of animal-snap cards were required for circulation, and so little groups of animal familiars started congregating. The three toads formed a monthly lunch club, which was an unanticipated but empowering outcome of this performance intended to break the ice and forge connections between potentially like-minded audience members.[44]

In conclusion, Lynn Lu and Samantha Sweeting's spontaneous, participatory practices could be said to evoke Carrington's visual and textual animal narrativity and maternal politics. The titular hearing trumpet becomes a new kind of storytelling medium, articulating Carrington's continued relevance. In doing so, they produce an intergenerational dialogue, immersing Carrington's framework into a millennial vernacular language. Through bringing her ethos into the domain of the live arts, Lu and Sweeting experiment with and extend her eco-feminism, rewriting her legacy through their preferred medium of a queer, feminine body art. Through spare, conceptual, DIY means, both Lu and Sweeting are capable of conjuring high aesthetic drama. What does it mean when Carrington's artworks become the starting point for larger scale theatrical productions? The final chapter explores Double Edge Theatre's Carrington cycle.

Notes

1 Samantha Sweeting cited in *The Rebel Magazine* (2010): http://therebelmagazine. blogspot.com/2010/10/interview-with-samantha-sweeting.html?m=1 (Accessed 19 June 2020).

2 Leonora Carrington, 'As They Rode Along the Edge,' *The Debutante and Other Stories* (London: Silver Press, [1941] 2017), 34.

3 Gabriel Weisz Carrington, *The Invisible Painting: My Memoir of Leonora Carrington* (Manchester: Manchester University Press, 2021), 29.

4 Samantha Sweeting, 'Artist's Statement'(2014): www.samanthasweeting.com (Accessed 19 June 2020).

5 Lynn Turner, 'When Species Kiss: Some Recent Correspondence Among Animots,' *Humanimalia: A Journal of Human/Animal Interface Studies*, 2:1 (Fall 2010), 63–64.

6 Tess Thackara, 'Carolee Schneemann's Lifelong Love Affair with Her Cats,' *Artsy* (14 February 2018): www.artsy.net/article/artsy-editorial-carolee-schneemanns-lifelong-love-affair-cats (Accessed 15 April 2021).

7 Samantha Sweeting, 'Familiars and Shape Shifters: On Fur and Foxes' (2020). Unpublished.

8 Ali Smith, *Artful* (London: Penguin, 2012), 110; Interview with Ali Smith.

9 Samantha Sweeting interviewed by Jareh Das, *Bomb Magazine* (29 January 2014): https://bombmagazine.org/articles/samantha-sweeting (Accessed 22 April 2021).

10 http://fillermagazine.com/culture/gallery/though-the-looking-glass-samantha-sweeting (Accessed 22 April 2021).

11 Personal correspondence with the author (19 August 2013).

12 Marina Warner, *From the Beast to the Blonde: On Fairy Tales and Their Tellers* (London: Chatto & Windus, 1994), 305.

13 Alejandro Jodorowsky and Marianne Costa, *The Spiritual Journey of Alejandro Jodorowsky* (Rochester, NY: Park Street Press, 2005), 25–26; see also Porochista Khakpour, 'Surreal Talk: The Otherworldly, Magical Writing of Leonora Carrington,' *Book Forum* (2017): www.bookforum.com/print/2403/the-otherworldly-magical-writing-of-leonora-carrington-18463 (Accessed 23 April 2021).

14 As early as March 2020, Chloe Aridjis and I were discussing the positive environmental effects of human quarantine, that pollution was decreasing, and that dolphins had returned to the Venetian canals (personal correspondence with the author, 20 March 2020). Aridjis also encouraged me to sign an online petition through Humane Society International to ban the very wildlife markets believed to have caused the virus.

15 Leonora Carrington, 'Commentary,' *Leonora Carrington: A Retrospective Exhibition* (New York: Center for Inter-American Relations, 1976), 23.

16 Personal correspondence with the author (9 June 2020).

17 Clarissa Pinkola Estés, *Women Who Run with the Wolves: Contacting the Power of the Wild Woman* (London: Random House, 1992), 214.

18 Heidi Sopinka, *The Dictionary of Animal Languages* (London: Scribe, 2018), 6.

19 Samantha Sweeting, 'Clicker Training,' *Encounters with Animals* (29 April 2013): https://encounterswithanimals.wordpress.com/page/3 (Accessed 15 April 2021).

20 Weisz Carrington, *The Invisible Painting*, 105.

21 Warner, *From the Beast to the Blonde*, xv.

22 Samantha Sweeting, 'Still waiting for you to come back to me' (2010): www.samanthasweeting.com/performanceinstallation/stillwaitingforyou.html (Accessed 19 June 2020).

23 Max Ernst, 'Preface, or Loplop Presents the Bride of the Wind,' *The House of Fear: Notes From Down Below* (London: Virago, 1989), 26.

24 Leonora Carrington cited in Whitney Chadwick, *Women Artists and the Surrealist Movement* (London: Thames & Hudson, 1985), 66. Thanks to Rachael Grew.

25 According to Chadwick, the woman-child's presence "inevitably, and perhaps more than any other single factor," worked "to exclude woman artists from the possibility of a profound personal identification with the theoretical side of Surrealism," *Women Artists*, 33.

26 Laura Mulvey, 'Pandora's Box: Topographies of Curiosity,' *Fetishism and Curiosity* (Bloomington and Indianapolis: Indiana University Press, 1996), 59.

27 Interview with Lynn Lu.

28 Amelia Jones, 'Writing as Doing: Performance Arcade…Counternarratives,' *The Live Press: Performance Arcade* (2018), 2.

29 Interview with Lu; Lynn Lu, 'Haumapuhia Rising,' *Lynn Lu* (2018): https://lynnlu.info/haumapuhia-rising (Accessed 24 April 2021).

30 Kate Bernheimer, 'Power Imagined: Fairy Tales as Survival Strategies,' *Woman Power: The 2020 SBS Downtown Lecture Series* (2 October 2020): www.youtube.com/watch?v=C28-paZlJtA (Accessed 12 May 2021).

31 Susan L. Aberth, 'Animal Kingdom,' *Leonora Carrington: Magical Tales*, eds Tere Arcq and Stefan van Raay (Mexico City: Instituto Nacional de Bellas Artes, 2018), 249; Sopinka, *Dictionary of Animal Languages*, 85.

32 Lynn Lu, 'Creative, Academic, and Personal Responses to Breastfeeding Research' (6 May 2021): www.youtube.com/watch?v=mAIr1nlJXUU (Accessed 15 May 2021); Natalya Lusty, *Surrealism, Feminism, Psychoanalysis* (Aldershot: Ashgate, 2007), 62.

33 Lu, 'Creative, Academic, and Personal.'

34 Julia Kristeva, *Powers of Horror: An Essay on Abjection*, trans. Leon S. Roudiez (New York: Columbia University Press, 1982), 12–13.

35 2 Gyrlz Performative Arts is the collaborative brainchild of Lisa Newman and Llewyn Máire; Samantha Sweeting, 'The Hearing Trumpet' (2011): www.samanthasweeting.com/performanceinstallation/hearingtrumpet.html (Accessed 23 May 2015); Lynn Lu, 'The Hearing Trumpet' (2011): www.lynnlu.info/projectItem.php?Pid=125&PP=8&NP=10 (Accessed 23 May 2015).

36 Anonymous members of the audience cited in Lu, 'The Hearing Trumpet' (2011): www.lynnlu.info/projectItem.php?Pid=125&PP=8&NP=10 (Accessed 23 May 2015).

37 Susan Rubin Suleiman, *Subversive Intent: Gender, Politics, and the Avant-Garde* (Cambridge, MA and London: Harvard University Press, 1990), 170. See also Whitney Chadwick, 'Muse Begets Crone: On Leonora Carrington,' *M/E/A/N/I/N/G: An Anthology of Artists' Writings, Theory and Criticism*, eds Susan Bee and Mira Schor (Durham, NC: Duke University Press, 2000), 419.

38 Lynn Lu, *The Hearing Trumpet* (2011; 2016): https://lynnlu.info/hearing-trumpet/497orls7yfoze76g460m6309ivix79 (Accessed 18 June 2020).

39 Samantha Sweeting, *The Hearing Trumpet* (2011): www.samanthasweeting.com/performanceinstallation/hearingtrumpet.html (Accessed 19 June 2020).

40 Lusty, *Surrealism, Feminism, Psychoanalysis*, 64.

41 Ali Smith, 'Introduction,' *The Hearing Trumpet* (London: Penguin, 2005), xii.

42 Weisz Carrington, *The Invisible Painting*, 104.

43 Derek Horton, 'Review: Leonora Carrington/Lucy Skaer,' *Corridor 8* (2016): https://corridor8.co.uk/article/review-leonora-carrington-lucy-skaer-leeds-college-of-art (Accessed 19 June 2020).

44 Grateful thanks to Charlotte Cullen and Gail Earnshaw for sharing this outcome.

6

Edgework

Inhabiting these pages are odd boundary creatures ... These boundary creatures are, literally, monsters, a word that shares more than its root with the word, to demonstrate.

—Donna J. Haraway (1991)[1]

On a former dairy farm in Ashfield, rural Massachusetts, a radical metamorphosis, amounting to a paradigm shift, is occurring, involving the practical application of our elusive subject's eco-feminism and the re-embodiment of her characters and artistic principles. Through long-term study of her multifaceted iconography, Double Edge Theatre present a microcosm of Leonora Carrington's thinking as a lifestyle choice. Devised, directed, and created by international artistic director, Stacy Klein, *Leonora's World* (2018) offers an immersive autumn spectacle where select artworks by Carrington are transformed into a series of theatrical tableaux. The weather and elemental factors have led the company out of doors: in the trees, through the carefully tended gardens, down the stream, around the labyrinth, and through the pond. The whole complex has been meticulously landscaped and tenderly cultivated in order to bring Carrington's visual narratives and eccentric archetypes to the forefront of the critical imagination.

Since 1982, Klein has become known for her feminist theatre company—her directorial debut presented an all-woman cast and crew for *Rites*, a contemporary reinterpretation of the *Bacchae*, set in an English lavatory. "Double Edge" itself is named after the double-edged axe wielded by the priestesses (or Bacchae) who served Dionysus, the god of theatre. Klein's approach also has origins stemming from the Eastern European tradition of theatre. Polish theatre-maker and actor, Rena Mirecka, has been one of Klein's mentors since 1976, and a sun shrine has been installed in the heart of Double Edge Theatre's grounds in her honour. Mirecka herself was a founding actor of Jerzy Grotowski's experimental school of theatre, Teatr Laboratorium. Grotowski's poor theatre would seem the very opposite of the rich esotericism represented by Carrington, two tendencies that are difficult to reconcile, but again one might think back to those spare, inverted conceptual strategies

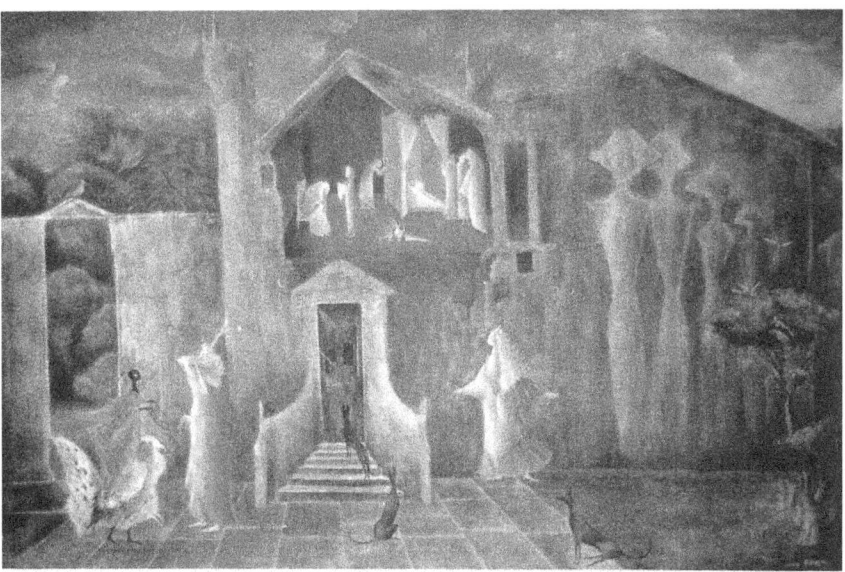

29 Leonora Carrington, *The Dog Child of Monkton Priori*, 1950

deployed by Lucy Skaer and Tilda Swinton to work through their known interests in Carrington as an artistic medium. Klein explains how her own approach to theatre direction has developed:

> The way we use the whole farm in the spectacles—the pastures, the barn, the pond, the trees—is a big change from my early work which used to be much more "poor theatre," the images drawn by the actors alone. Now I design and paint in full color. The land has given me a sense of place—a humble understanding that we humans are a small part of life, full of wildness and hope. Still, while I love creating the spectacles, I also need to return to the inner work of the imagination.[2]

As with Carrington's long-term dissociation from surrealism, over time Klein has detached herself from her foundational poor theatre training in order to immerse herself more fully in her imagination and a more layered, colourful approach to the *mise-en-scène*. Like Carrington, Double Edge welcome high theatre and deep narrative. For Double Edge, further techniques for their adaptations include iconographic extraction and relocation for their distinctive mode of promenade theatre. The archive room in their bespoke pavilion includes over 39 years of material relating to the history of the company, and demonstrates a spatial commitment to research, and how a scholarly community underpins the overarching thinking and programming of the company. A major part of the display in this archival resource

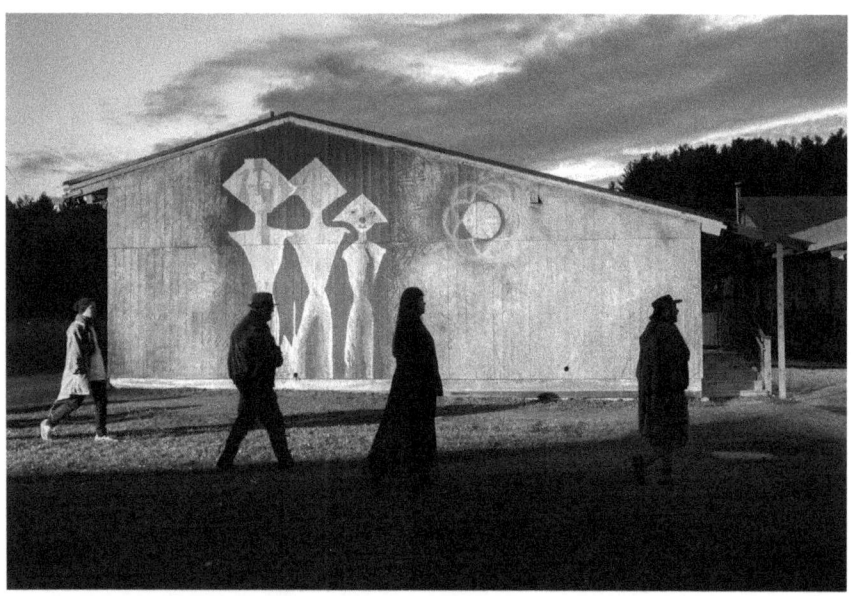

30 Michelangelo Noel Aurello, mural for Double Edge Theatre, 2018

is a giant mood board, a collage that transforms Carrington's artworks into a series of *tableaux vivants*. Such "living pictures" are consistent with the company's political emphasis of "living culture." This is followed through in the topographical approach to the programme, a map indicating where the selected scenes will be performed, leaving audience members enough choice and agency with which to shape their journey. Indeed, Carrington's detailed scenes lend themselves readily to theatrical adaptation.

That the majority of actors are women or those who identify as gender non-binary further speaks of the role model the artist has become in the age of #MeToo.[3] Carrington's aesthetic recipe offers both matriarchy and de-hierarchy, both being useful strands of revisionary thinking for the promotion of minority views. In the aftermath of Hillary Clinton's concession speech (2016), Klein henceforth resolved to have a woman and/or gender non-binary person cast in the lead role in all Double Edge productions as an act of resistance. Double Edge were looking for a Latin American woman to follow, and Leonora Carrington became apparent as their posthumous figurehead, described by one reviewer as a "free-spirited Anglo-Mexican painter-sculptor-feminist-mystic."[4] "I am in a Carrington-cycle," Klein tells me.[5] Having previously worked through a *Marc Chagall* cycle (2010–15), Klein was already invested in a visual realm and close study of the art history. While Klein's feminist attitude had long been present in the company's underlying philosophy and in her own practice since at least the 1980s, her *Leonora* cycle represents the stepping up of commitment to a radical politics that seeks to bring about structural change, both within, as well as beyond, the liminal nature of performance. Again, the mission statement of "living culture" commits Double Edge to embedding the ethics of artmaking at every level, including farming the very land on which they live and work; harvesting fruit from the orchard and growing vegetables in the produce garden, as well as keeping chickens for eggs and providing a sanctuary for rare goats—all spaces that double as theatrical platforms. There is thus also a de-anthropocentricism at play, one that seeks to work in harmony with the non-human.[6] Klein and the ensemble champion local, sustainable politics and a model of direct democracy. In a recent 'in conversation', Klein made their world mission clear:

> I think local is the only way we are going to transform our society, and that doesn't mean we can't have huge exchanges in other places, it just means that our focus needs to be on the local and whatever that means to people because we really need to grow our communities and strengthen our communities, and for me it has totally been proven, and over and over again, everyday there is another effort.[7]

The ensemble, thus, shares Carrington's practice of esotericism and eco-political concerns, embedding her ideas into their own thinking. Over the last three to four years especially, their work has attempted to get inside her imagination and live her politics.

The sheer abundance of research for the project further demonstrates this level of commitment. Carrington expert Susan L. Aberth was brought on as a consultant and notes that Klein "had already purchased not only the primary texts on this artist but many of the more obscure as well. These items were worn with use, tagged with notes, and clearly had been carefully read and memorized."[8] In Klein's office, books about tarot, folklore, puppets, and the historical significance of masks mingle with rare exhibition catalogues and compendiums of essays on Carrington. Again, such literature is followed through in a dedicated study centre, which is by and large a homage to Klein's mentors, Mirecka and Carrington, among others. Indeed, Carrington becomes a connecting principle for Klein, a force that binds all these props and theatrical devices and brings people together.

The fact that Carrington herself designed and wrote for theatre is noteworthy and positions her as an even more apt choice. One thinks of her numerous plays: 'The Invention of Molé' (*c.*1960), 'The Holy Oily Body' (co-written with Remedios Varo, 1956), 'Penélope' (co-written with Alejandro Jodorowsky, *c.*1957), and 'Opus Siniestrus: The Story of the Last Egg' (1970).[9] Scriptwriting and set design were necessary expressive vehicles in Carrington's sense of world-building and present a case for her entire *œuvre* as a form of *Gesamtkunstwerk*. Moreover, Carrington's interest in and fabrication of masks is also of crucial interest to Double Edge Theatre, who place a powerful emphasis on this theatrical device in order to summon a sense of character. For example, one of the tomes on display in the archive room is Andreas Lommel's multicultural study, *Masks: Their Meaning and Function* (1981): "Originally, every mask was imbued with significance, and the mask itself or the person wearing it mysteriously represented some power or spirit."[10] The mask is a performance object, a conduit that imbues the wearer with the power to channel magical transformations, which is why they are so often used in rituals and rites, practices to which Carrington and Double Edge Theatre both subscribe. One might also recall the symbolism in Carrington's short story 'The Debutante' (1937), where the hyena tears off the face of the maid to wear as a disguise to the social obligation of the coming-out ball.[11] In any context, the mask is an uncanny object—when one dons a mask, and peeps through its eyeholes, one becomes me/not-me. Poet and cultural theorist Susan Stewart tells us: "the mask, the costume, and the disguise find their proper context in carnival and festivity ... where hierarchy is overturned."[12] Again, such overturning of hierarchies is of keen interest to both parties and one might think through the alternative logic of the hybrid, carnivalesque, and grotesque. Stewart further notes the connecting forces of quotation and carnival as mutual "process[es] of restoration and disillusionment, for the boundary of the text is both fixed and made suspect," surely a definition for the kind of theatre presented here.[13] Bill Marx writes that *Leonora's World* is "[a]s close to Mikhail Bakhtin's anarchistic vision of carnival as New England is ever going to get."[14] By prising open these marvellous coordinates, Double Edge Theatre guide audiences to a site where Carrington's feminist intertextual grotesque is released.

Harvest surrealism

The effects are riveting: this is not carnival; it is magic.
—Jonathan P. Eburne (2019)[15]

Let's bring this performance back to the present tense. The scene is twilight on the evening of 11 October 2019. Upon arrival, the Carrington theme is immediately apparent in the shape of a large mural by Michelangelo Noel Aurello (Figure 30) that has combined iconographic details from her paintings, *The Dog Child of Monkton Priori* (1950) (Figure 29) and *Hod's Polyèdre* (1965) (Figure 5). Carrington's portrait has been inscribed onto the tallest apparition of elongated figures alongside the geometric motif from the latter painting. The sensibly dressed audience have been equipped with their programme, a map of the farm based on Carrington's schematic drawing from *Down Below* (1944). The curation of this outdoor museum is partly audience-led. Carrington is played by co-artistic director Jennifer Johnson, who appears nonchalantly in androgynous riding garb as in the famous self-portrait, *Inn of the Dawn Horse* (1937). She serves as a guide throughout *Leonora's World*, beckoning the audience through scene after scene. Appropriately, Johnson begins the journey by leading us through the yellow-curtained proscenium, a portal to the outdoor realm. The audience are offered a choice of two directions left and right. We are immersed instantaneously in this otherworldly space and are witnessing what feels like a harvest ritual. In front of me, a tall, feline creature straight out of *Are You Really Syrious?* (1953) roams around a small field. Its stilted limbs elegantly patrol and traverse this magical terrain. Alongside this Syrious cat character, I recognise the elaborate moon-face of *The Giantess* (1947), another companion on stilts. Monumentally doll-like, she is a paradox like the painting, gliding her way around, commanding the space. Suddenly, I find myself in a fairy-tale forest, an ornamental garden in which a flurry of medieval sprites are dashing around. One is in a tree house playing a glockenspiel, while another is upside down within a spiral trapeze, flying! The frantic spirits of the painting *Nine Nine Nine* (1948) (Figure 31) are conjured as if by an act of sorcery, and dash about the ornamental garden. Further theatrical realisations of Carrington's well-known paintings and sculptures await us in the scenes that follow.

The protagonist reappears, this time in a black cloak with a ram-horn headdress denoting an older, visionary Carrington. She quotes from her subject in a deep, English accent: "Time was, time is, time has passed," a potent anachronism from the drawing, *Brothers and sisters have I none* (1942). The next time I see her, she is carrying the ubiquitous glowing egg that appears in numerous paintings from Carrington's mid-career, including *Ab Eo Quod* (1956) and *Who Art Thou White Face?* (1959), as well as her aforementioned play, 'Opus Siniestrus.' Meanwhile, an alchemist, immersed in consulting his books and potions, weighs two glass spheres on a pair of brass scales hanging from a tree. A typewriter is positioned by a small bonfire. Across the river, I spy *The Temptation of St Anthony* (1945); the tall white figure of the hermit saint dwarfs the water carrier standing nearby. The congregation next to the saint in the painting process towards me with tambourines and flowing garments.[16] They are chanting and humming soothingly. This gathering will recur later. Chance encounters are frequent in this semi-structured yet improvisational approach to theatre. I find myself at the heart of a wordless, yet profound, dialogue between a cloaked figure from Carrington's *Tower of Nagas* (1991) (Figure 33) based on the Hermit card in tarot, played by Argentinian co-artistic director, Carlos Uriona, and

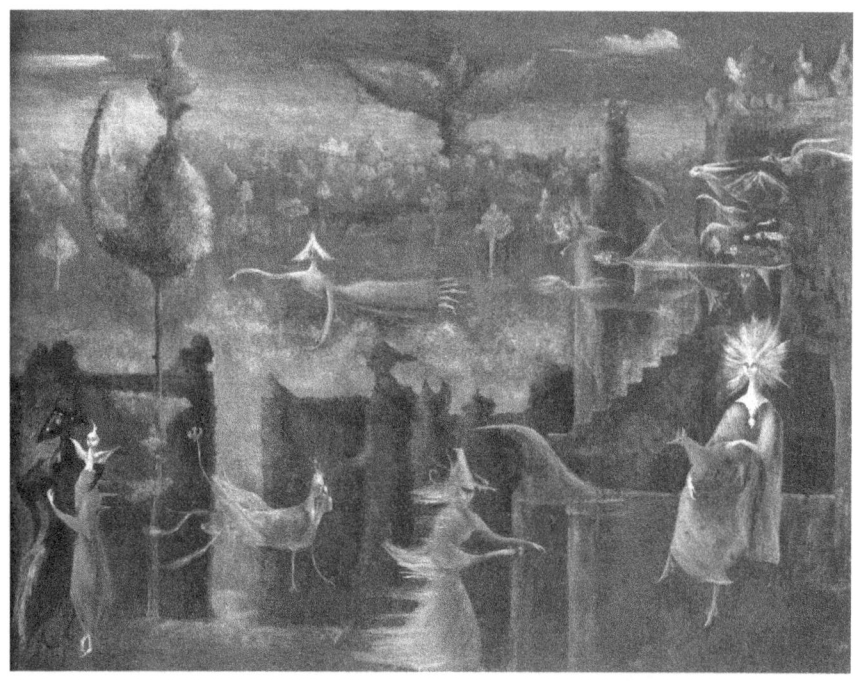

31 Leonora Carrington, *Nine Nine Nine*, 1948

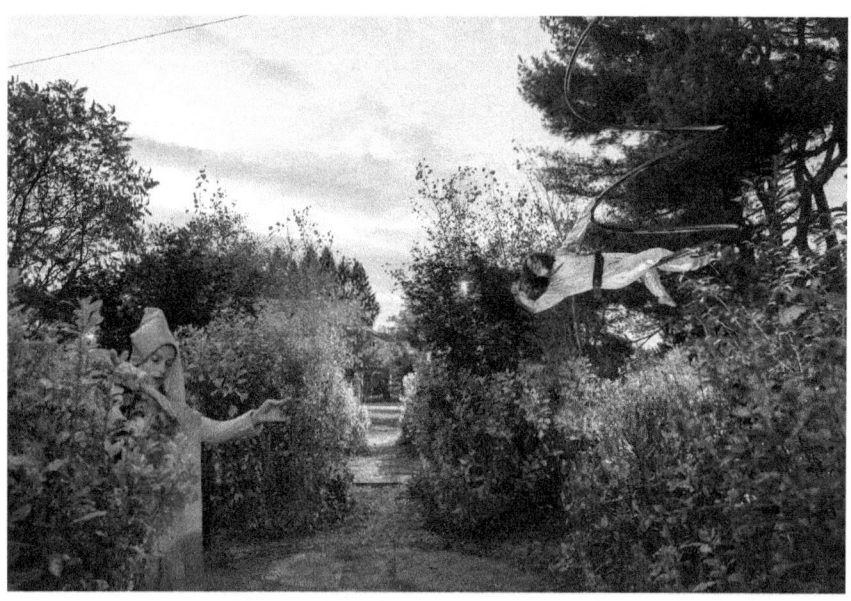

32 Double Edge Theatre, *Leonora's World*, 2019

a sorceress performed by Nipmuc actor, Jasmine Goodspeed—a convergence of cultural backgrounds brought about through this fantasy encounter.[17] This is what Carrington's work is capable of enabling—think of her multicultural, archaeological comingling in *El Mundo Mágico de los Mayas* (*The Magical World of the Mayas*, 1963). As Carrington herself wrote in *The Stone Door* (1976), which underpins much of Klein's thinking: "The frontiers onto the unknown are constructed in layers. One layer opens into a fan of other layers which open new worlds in turn."[18] Double Edge adapt this conceptual challenge to offer an enticing sense of what might happen if two or more of Carrington's detailed in-scapes were to collide or overlap. Moreover, the longevity of Carrington's art history and eight-decade career is at times collapsed anachronistically into a matter of minutes.

I wander past a malevolent picnic in progress, conjoined thinking from Carrington's paintings *Pastoral* (1950) (Figure 20) and *Edwardian Hunt Breakfast* (1956), and possibly also *Pomps of the Subsoil* (1947) and the painting version of *Down Below* (1941), depending on one's mood and how one chooses to interact with this. I cross over to an epic earthwork re-creation of the *Labyrinth* (1991). Appropriately, the sun is still setting as I enter, and when I finally exit, the seasonal lights have gone out. I loop around two concentric spirals—creatures, masks, and golden orbs emerge through the undergrowth. There is an exhibit to see around every corner, something to surprise, delight, and tempt. This gigantic temporary structure makes reference to an archaeological sense of ancient theatre. I reach the centre and find a soldier-like figure frozen mid-pose. He then comes to life and guides us out of this Fibonacci-like maze. A horn, presumably borrowed from the imagery of *The Hearing Trumpet,* sounds a short, tribalistic blast summoning us on to the next chapter. We emerge from this domain and are beckoned into the baby barn where dioramas from *Grandmother Moorhead's Kitchen* (1975), and lullaby paintings, *Night Nursery Everything* (Figure 3) and *Neighbourly Advice* (both 1947), can be glimpsed in each of the stables, comprising decorative horse murals in Carrington's signature carousel style by Jeremy Louise Eaton. I notice a sculptural re-creation of *How Doth the Little Crocodile* (2000) on the arbour above and wonder how I missed this before. There is so much to see: a new Carrington vista there; a quotation brough to life there; a unique happening in every direction. My eyes are hungry, yet I find I am starved of time. And then I am confronted by a lone figure, a jester from *El Juglar* (1954). We lock eye contact. They are exquisitely beautiful, glittering and haunting in their pierrot collar, twinkling in the sudden darkness which has enveloped us. They make strange, unhuman noises and gestures in semaphore. Reluctant to leave them, I realise I am at the tail end of the audience queue and hurry to the large barn, where a cacophony of voices can be heard, and soup is being served.

I am now inside *The House Opposite* (1945). Bird-actors with Venetian beak masks are in the rafters squawking and tittering, and our protagonist communes with them, crooning back and conducting this feminist-surrealist orchestra. The space is activated and the energy in the room is palpable in every nook and cranny, mimicking the compartmentalised scenes of the dollhouse architecture in the painting. The overarching soundscape is hewn from the alchemical and gnostic language found within *The Stone Door*. By my count, in the painting there are approximately 15 matriarchs and young girls, as well as their familiars, which are predominantly domesticated animals such as birds and cats. This is carried over into those performing within this particular domestic set as a feminist command of space.[19] We might recall that Tere Arcq points out that the original painting depicts "a house inhabited only by women," and, in the case of Klein's vision, this category of "woman" is expanded to include members of the queer and trans community.[20] As for Heidi Sopinka and Chloe Aridjis, Double Edge use this scene as a space with which to present a feminist ecosystem.

Throughout the spectacle, I am particularly struck by the multisensory, elemental nature of the performance. The shamanic soundscape is augmented by the smells and tastes of woodsmoke and spicy soup. *Leonora's World* could be said to present a kind of harvest surrealism; the performance is carefully timed in relation to the seasonal, lunar cycle, and occurs deliberately at twilight. There are phantasmagorical dimensions to the penultimate scenes, conjuring a sense of ancientness and inheritance of magical practices and bonfire-lit storytelling traditions. We are led outside through a back door in the large barn towards the pond for the finale. The gallows of *The Gibbet Birds* (1971) add an ominous atmosphere to the penultimate procession. In the distance, one can perceive the precarious rocking and frantic activities found aboard the chequered ship in the *Nunscape in Manzanillo* (1956). The mood of trepidation is quickly dispelled by another enchanting spectacle. The scene is a fairy-tale woodland pond illuminated by a soft green light. The colours seem to shore up Carrington eco-feminism as presented in her predominately green poster, *Mujeres conciencia* (*Women's Awareness*) (1972). The poster includes a soaring, winged creature, and pre-empts Double Edge Theatre's philosophy by representing a double-Eve, one black woman, one white woman, sharing the apple of knowledge.[21] In the closing scene of *Leonora's World*, characters swoop across the scene like comets and a boat full of cardinals sets sail. Carrington becomes a vehicle for imaginative crossings into different dream states. Johnson's Carrington boards the monochromatic crocodile gondola straight out of the iridescent painting *Tower of Nagas* and sails across the pond, proclaiming from *The Stone Door* that "it is a great thing to be errant in time and space."[22]

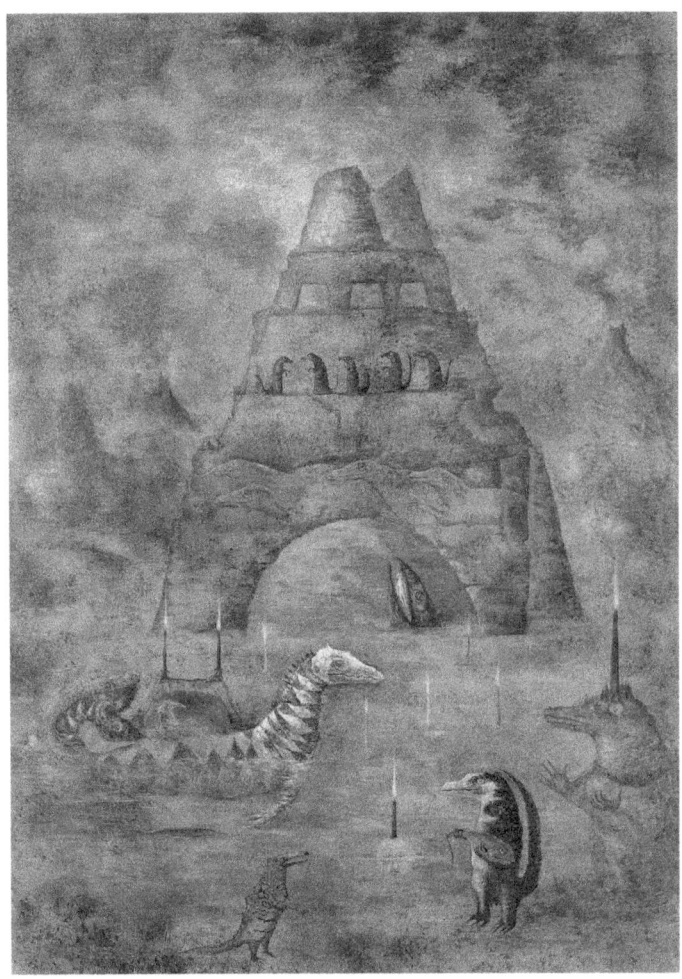

33 Leonora Carrington, *Tower of Nagas*, 1991

The magician and the teacher

Silence, let us not disturb the mystery.

—Leonora Carrington (*c*.1957)[23]

In the genesis of the Leonora cycle, Double Edge Theatre's indoor production, *Leonora: La Maga y el Maestro*, presents an even earlier stage of creative evolution. Klein reveals that *La Maga y el Maestro* began its journey with Carrington's imagery at its foundations. Through close investigation of Carrington's imagery, the company collaborated to create a "visual script."[24]

The lead actors, Jennifer Johnson and Carlos Uriona, then mined the key texts of their characters, Leonora and Adan (meaning "everyman" as a loose reference to Jodorowsky), including 'The Oval Lady' (1938), *Down Below* (1944), and *The Stone Door* (1976) in Carrington's case, and *The Spiritual Journey of Alejandro Jodorowsky* (2005) and *The Way of Tarot* (2009), among others, for Jodorowsky—sampling key ideas, quotations, and narrative possibilities but ultimately rewriting the raw script as their own. Carrington's texts are duly dominant while Jodorowsky's riddles and tarot were, Klein explains, "layered in as responses."[25] Klein would then edit the developing script along with her fellow dramaturgs in the company.

La Maga y el Maestro translates as "the magician and the teacher," suggesting that this is the story of a sorcerer and her apprentice. Jodorowsky was quick to recognise Carrington as someone whom he might follow as a fantasy guru. Jodorowsky claims that on his quest for eternal life, he encountered Carrington in Mexico: "When I realised that Leonora used the symbols of the Tarot in her work, I begged her to initiate me."[26] In the 'Surrealist Master' chapter of his *Spiritual Journey*, Jodorowsky further explains that his spiritual teacher, Ejo, had encouraged him to seek out a feminine archetype and align himself with Carrington in order to cure himself of his angry childishness.[27] One might see such a pattern repeated in the relationship between Uriona and Klein, whom Uriona chose to follow in terms of showing him the feminist way.[28] Klein and Uriona have long been interested in Latin American artistic precedents, so Jodorowsky's following of Carrington must have appealed to them both as source material. That said, it is important to note that Jodorowsky's devotional model of homage does not necessarily hold true for the range of creative responses to Carrington discussed throughout this book, many of which prefer to dialogue or query. While Double Edge Theatre claim Carrington as a figurehead, they respectfully champion her as a lifestyle choice and research her work in depth in order to produce new and authentic work. It is this level of critical engagement and a sense of working through which saves them from idolisation. This dynamic is borne out in *La Maga y el Maestro* in its careful exploration of re-gendered hierarchies.

Associate artistic director, Travis Coe, plays the Flying Hyena, an evolution of the creature from Carrington's short story, while Amanda Miller plays the ubiquitous Pajaro, a nod to Max Ernst's bird alter ego Loplop from Carrington's early career but a creature Carrington increasingly adopted within her own imagery. The bird and the hyena prowl the stage throughout the show as crucial aspects of Carrington's imaginary bestiary. The cast also includes the Cook, a Trio of Shadows and the Giantess. The set includes multiple movable stairways, designed to mimic the dollhouse architecture in *The House Opposite*, with each compartment functioning as a potential scene change. As we know, Carrington's painting appears to open a dollhouse façade so that the viewer can witness the multiple storeys, layers, and going-on inside.[29] The eventfulness and myriad scenes coexisting in one image continue to prompt the shape, tempo, and rhythms of *La Maga y el Maestro*. In the set design, iconic details from *The Inn of the Dawn Horse* (1937), such as the rocking horse and yellow-curtained proscenium arch, have been realised in three dimensions. One can also discern key props such as the glowing egg from *Ab Eo Qoud* (1956). Glockenspiels and other analogue percussion contribute to the childlike atmosphere of wonder and the nursery scene presented, though interestingly the majority of the script and events take place when Carrington was an adult woman—Jodorowsky sought Carrington out for counsel in the 1950s when she was in her late thirties/early forties.

In *La Maga y el Maestro*, Carrington's character is quick to demythologise any idea of her perceived surrealist persona as a mad witch. She reads from Lewis Carroll's narrative poem, 'The Walrus and the Carpenter' (1865), before lecturing the Jodorowsky character on the core ideas of ancient knowledge. She describes her childhood self as a ram. There are flashbacks to her time in the sanatorium. When tarot is read, she is surrounded by the chanting shadows from the painting *The Bird Men of Burnley* (1970), who later return as the masked figures in *Lepidopteros* (1969) to help her cast a spell. The play then segues into moments from *The Stone Door* and *The Hearing Trumpet*, including reading a letter from Carmella. At one point both Carrington and Jodorowsky mirror each other in red and blue velvet cloaks. A ram's skull is passed ceremoniously between them before Carrington covers the bird's feet in mustard. Whilst warning of the dangers of over-interpretation and psychoanalysis, she covers the doors with red handprints to represent her menstrual blood that Jodorowsky reports she once used to decorate Luis Buñuel's walls.[30] Then, in her horned headdress, she chants manically over a cauldron, in what is possibly the most malevolent episode in this production, before dancing under the billowing skirts of *The Giantess*. The force field then transforms into the ghostly figures that haunt her many depictions of *Crookhey Hall* (1987). In one of the penultimate scenes, Carrington and Jodorowsky perform a circular dance, the former in white, the latter in black, as if to demonstrate two parts of the whole or sides of the Taoist yin-yang (a symbol which Carrington includes in her tapestries, such as the undated *Beast with a Feline Head*). This offers a prophecy of the final moments in *La Maga y el Maestro* where the stone door is opened, and the Carrington character reveals her true self to be the moon.

Both the indoor and outdoor productions serve as inversions of one another, each a part of the whole. Given that they both form part of Klein's overarching Carrington cycle, it is interesting to compare *La Maga y el*

Maestro and *Leonora's World* in terms of what essential elements and key aspects have been retained and carried over, many as signatures of Double Edge Theatre: the yellow proscenium curtains, the Giantess figure on stilts, the spiral corkscrew that enables flight, the glowing egg, some of the recipes and some of the lines. Johnson's Carrington appears in both, yet she improvises more in *Leonora's World*, given its looser structure that enables spontaneity. The selection of adapted Carrington artworks are slightly different in each production, although there are inevitable crossovers.

Boundary creatures

the acrobat, the astronaut, and even the porn star ... had been able to escape their own bodies and, for a few moments, flee their condition and enter something more hypnotic.

—Chloe Aridjis (2013)[31]

The logo for Double Edge Theatre has an archaeological backstory—the bacchanalian figure with the double-bladed axe, their original logo from the 1980s, has subsequently been streamlined, and, in recent years, has come to represent a winged woman.[32] This is apposite given that one of the company's signature performative practices is "flying," including trapeze acts, aerial choreography, and intricate stilt-work, much of which is derived from ensemble members' backgrounds in circus and puppet theatre.[33] Klein explains that she had "always wanted training to not only deal with the ground," and, like the logo, such gravity-defiance has evolved over time through a commitment by particular members of the company to aerial training.[34] Klein's directorial style has even been likened by one reviewer to that of a "ringmaster extraordinaire."[35] Such Icarian ambitions make Carrington's imaginary sites all the more appropriate given the number of airborne vehicles and winged creatures that inhabit her imaginative universe. Double Edge found this was particularly the case in their performance of the soaring figures that occur in her paintings *La chasse* (1942) and *Nine Nine Nine* (1948). Co-producer Cariel Klein astonished audiences in their rendition of the latter picture, their body twirling and undulating upside down, their spiral flight a conduit for the alternative realities on offer (Figure 32). Later, Travis Coe soared across the pond at night in a *deus ex machina* as if inhabiting the floating islands of Carrington's wartime painting, *La chasse*. Again, it is interesting that flying should be the preserve of the women and non-gender binary members of the ensemble. Serenity Young, who has written a cultural history of flying women, explains how acts of flying rail against "patriarchal definitions of womanhood" as a metaphor for actively breaking restraints and taking control of one's destiny.[36] Writing further on the paradoxical figure of the aerialist, Helen Stoddart points out the simultaneity of the illusion and the reality of their body politics, highlighting this figure as a synecdoche for the whole cultural phenomena of circus:

> There is ... congruence between the presentation of the female aerialist's body and the image that the circus as a whole has presented itself ... the circus self-image is at heart a paradoxical one since it promotes an idea of itself in the popular imagination as embodying a lifestyle unfettered by conventionality or by social and legal restraint: a freedom which was echoed in performances which foregrounded the illusion of ease. Behind this image lie levels of physical discipline, bodily regulation and hardship which are unrivalled by any other western performance art.[37]

For the Double Edge ensemble, such commitment to physical discipline and dedication to circus techniques and training all contribute to making the theatrical spectacle appear seamless and effortless. On one level, it is illusion, on another, it is a lived reality that suspends disbelief. This is what makes productions like *La Maga y el Maestro* and *Leonora's World* such successful practical inquiries into surrealist techniques in the early twenty-first century. The figure of the aerialist also has much to tell us about Carrington the artist, and her ability to enable us to imagine the impossible.

Donna J. Haraway's notion of the "boundary creature" offers a useful way of defining how the winged beings and raw material of Carrington's imagination have been adapted so authentically into Double Edge Theatre's sense of flight.[38] The creatures that Haraway has in mind are anomalous cyborgs, mermaids, and women, "wild cards" that inhabit "possible [feminist] worlds," marginal beings that Haraway repositions at the heart of her "blasphemy."[39] While Haraway's biotechnologies might seem out of sync with Carrington's organic universe and Double Edge's farmland, Haraway maintains that "the boundary between science fiction and social reality is an optical illusion."[40] Her emphasis on the repositioning of myth, hybridity, and "possible bodies" are therefore allied: "The boundary is permeable between tool and myth, instrument and concept, historical systems of social relations and historical anatomies of possible bodies, including objects of knowledge. Indeed, myth and [biotechnological] tool mutually constitute each other."[41] Such a statement may be closely aligned with Double Edge Theatre's Carrington cycle and might be pushed even further when it comes to Carrington's philosophical aftermath.

Elaborating on Haraway, Mary Russo and Frances S. Connelly further probe the compelling idea of the boundary creature as the very manifestation of the grotesque: "something that creates meaning by prying open a gap, pulling us into unfamiliar, contested terrain."[42] Connelly does this by re-reading the grotesque through the architectural grotto, arabesque, carnivalesque, and caricature: "[the grotesque] is earthy and material, a cave, an open mouth that invites our descent into other worlds. It is a space where the monsters and marvels of our imagination are conceived … fusing humor with horror, wit with transgression, repulsion with desire."[43] This is true also for Russo who describes study of the grotesque as "claustrophobic," and "position[s] … the grotesque—as superficial and to the margins."[44] Although Carrington's work is not mentioned specifically in either study, both conclude that the grotesque is typically associated with "the attributes of the feminine."[45] Such languages of the feminine grotesque are germane when it comes to appreciating Carrington's underlying haunting of maximal theatrical spectacles and liminal trapeze work. Double Edge Theatre's flying figures present the physical manifestation of such edgework, not only parading Carrington's own boundary creatures but demonstrating Carrington *as* a boundary creature herself. Some of the most successful adaptations of Carrington are cognisant of this aspect of her legacy, the significance and political potency of prowling the fringes, as well as being acknowledged in the limelight.

In closing this chapter on flying beings, eco-farming, and theatrical adaptation, I would like to suggest that the grotesque boundary creature has become the very manifestation of Leonora Carrington for Double Edge Theatre and beyond, an embodiment of feminist intertextuality and mythological rewriting. Along this edge or line of inquiry, I find another Venn diagram linking many of the examples already touched on in this study, from the performative bodies of Tilda Swinton's *The Maybe* (1995) and Samantha Sweeting and Lynn Lu's *The Hearing Trumpet* (2011), to the trickster-like entity of Lucy Skaer's *Harlequin is as Harlequin Does* (2012), and to the ecological introverts in novels by Chloe Aridjis and Heidi Sopinka. In evoking Carrington as an epistemological framework, Double Edge's multifaceted production makes its audience reflect and seriously consider the possibilities of communal creative living, the benefits of existing in closer proximity to agriculture, and a proactive awareness of the native Nipmuc culture that have left their mark on this land. In total, Double Edge Theatre can be seen to interweave all aspects of adaptative gestures inherited from Carrington, from narrative costumes to esoteric conceptualism, from animal rights and intertextual dialogue to the importance of an eco-feminist creative solitude.

Notes

Double Edge Theatre's response to the global pandemic is noteworthy, having to cancel their spring 2020 tour half-way through. Double Edge Theatre opened for socially distanced tours, hosted Tai Chi classes, and presented their Summer Spectacle under the heading '6 Feet Apart, All Together' (2020) for limited audience numbers around 12 key locations across their 105-acre farmland. This spectacle continued their reference to Carrington with a scene entitled, 'Leonora's Labyrinth of Tarot.'

1 Donna J. Haraway, *Simians, Cyborgs, and Women: The Reinvention of Nature* (New York: Routledge, 1991), 2. Grateful thanks to Kim L. Pace for introducing me to this idea.

2 Stacy Klein cited in Richard Schechner, 'Double Edge Theatre in its Ashfield Community: An Interview with Stacy Klein,' *TDR/The Drama Review*, 64:4 (December 2020): 69. For more on Klein's history with Rena Mirecka, see 50.

3 Josh Appignanesi cited in Jennifer Higgie, 'How "Female Human Animal" Blends Documentary with Fiction,' Frieze (2018): https://frieze.com/article/how-female-human-animal-blends-documentary-fiction (Accessed 24 October 2019).

4 Chris Rohmann, 'Love Letter to a Nightmare,' *Valley Advocate* (4 February 2020): https://valleyadvocate.com/2020/02/04/love-letter-to-a-nightmare (Accessed 14 April 2020).

5 Interview with Stacy Klein.

6 Janet Lyon, 'Carrington's Sensorium,' *Leonora Carrington and the International Avant-Garde*, eds J. P. Eburne and C. McAra (Manchester: Manchester University Press, 2017), 164.

7 Frank Hentschker, 'In Conversation with Stacy Klein and and Stephanie Monseu,' *Segal Talks* (8 May 2020): https://youtube/SOzefa8J_Bc (Accessed 12 May 2020).

8 Susan L. Aberth, 'Programme Notes,' *Leonora: La Maga y el Maestro* (2018), 6. More recently, Klein has continued to remind audiences that Aberth was there from the beginning of their research into Carrington, 'Leonora Carrington and the Theatre: Susan L. Aberth and Stacy Klein In Conversation' (7 March 2021): www.youtube.com/watch?v=gJUTP82shOY (Accessed 28 March 2021).

9 For more on Carrington's theatrical interests, see Tara Plunkett, 'Dissecting *The Holy Oily Body*: Remedios Varo, Leonora Carrington and *El Santo Cuerpo Grasoso*,' *Leonora Carrington and the International Avant-Garde*, 74.

10 Andreas Lommels, *Masks: Their Meaning and Function* (London: Ferndale Editions, 1981), 7.

11 Natalya Lusty reads this mask in terms of class and "*faceless* wage labour," *Surrealism, Feminism, Psychoanalysis* (Aldershot: Ashgate, 2007), 34.

12 Susan Stewart, *On Longing: Narratives of the Miniature, the Gigantic, the Souvenir, the Collection* (Durham, NC: Duke University Press, 1993), 107.

13 Stewart, *On Longing*, 20.

14 Bill Marx, 'Best Stage Productions of 2019,' *The Arts Fuse* (28 December 2019): https://artsfuse.org/192651/theater-feature-best-stage-productions-of-2019 (Accessed 24 April 2020).

15 Jonathan P. Eburne, '"All Artwork Is a Magical Act,"' *ASAP/J* (10 October 2019): http://asapjournal.com/all-artwork-is-a-magical-act-an-interview-with-susan-aberth-and-stacy-klein-jennifer-johnson (Accessed 16 April 2020).

16 Tilda Swinton performs the same detail in her fashion story with Tim Walker for *i-D Magazine* (2017).

17 Carlos Uriona was interested in his native gauchos (horse-people or cowhands) when defining this role, personal correspondence with the author.

18 Leonora Carrington, *The Stone Door* (New York: St Martin's Press, [1976] 1977), 21.

19 Thanks to Hannah Buckley for this notion.

20 Tere Arcq, 'In the Land of Convulsive Beauty: Mexico,' *In Wonderland: The Surrealist Adventures of Women Artists in Mexico and the United States*, eds Ilene Susan Fort et al. (Los Angeles, CA and Mexico City: LACMA and Prestel, 2012), 81.

21 For more on this poster, which was originally a gouache painting, see Jonathan P. Eburne and Catriona McAra, '*Mujeres conciencia* (*Women's Awareness*): Leonora Carrington's Agit-prop,' Manchester University Press Blog (July 2019): https://manchesteruniversitypress.co.uk/articles/mujeres-conciencia-womens-awareness-leonora-carringtons-agit-prop-by-catriona-mcara-and-jonathan-p-eburne (Accessed 12 July 2020).

22 Carrington, *The Stone Door*, 21.

23 Leonora Carrington cited in Alejandro Jodorowsky, *The Spiritual Journey of Alejandro Jodorowsky* (Rochester, NY: Park Street Press, 2005), 29.

24 Personal correspondence with the author.

25 Personal correspondence.

26 Alejandro Jodorowsky and Marianne Costa, *The Way of Tarot: The Spiritual Teacher in the Cards* (Rochester, NY: Destiny Books, 2009), 5–6.

27 Jodorowsky, *The Spiritual Journey*, 25.

28 Thanks to Carlos Uriona for confirming this.

29 Dawn Adès, 'Carrington's Mysteries,' *Leonora Carrington* (Dublin: Irish Museum of Modern Art, 2013), 100.

30 Jodorowsky, *The Spiritual Journey*, 25–26.

31 Chloe Aridjis, *Asunder* (London: Chatto & Windus, 2013), 120.

32 Double Edge Theatre, 'From Allston to Ashfield: Historical Highlights from 1982-Present,' *Medium* (24 April 2019): https://medium.com/@DoubleEdgeTheatre/from-allston-to-ashfield-historical-highlights-from-1982-present-931c35c0714d (Accessed 23 April 2020).

33 Co-producer, Carlos Uriona, founded the Argentinian puppet theatre Diablomundo, and Cariel Klein trained at the New England Center for Circus Arts, among other places.

34 Klein cited in Schechner, 'Double Edge Theatre,' 45.

35 Marx, 'Best Stage Productions of 2019.'

36 Serenity Young, *Women Who Fly: Goddesses, Witches, Mystics and Other Airborne Females* (Oxford: Oxford University Press, 2018), 5. Grateful thanks to Cariel Klein for suggesting this reference, which could be said to function as a sourcebook for their aerial practice.

37 Helen Stoddart, *Rings of Desire: Circus History and Representation* (Manchester: Manchester University Press, 2000), 175.

38 Haraway, *Simians, Cyborgs, and Women*, 2.

39 Haraway, *Simians, Cyborgs, and Women*, 4.

40 Donna J. Haraway, *A Cyborg Manifesto: Science, Technology and Socialist-Feminism in the Late Twentieth Century* (Minneapolis: University of Minnesota Press, 2016), 6.

41 Haraway, *A Cyborg Manifesto*, 33.

42 Frances S. Connelly, *The Grotesque in Western Art and Culture: The Image at Play* (Cambridge: Cambridge University Press, 2012), 8; 2; Mary Russo, *The Female Grotesque: Risk, Excess and Modernity* (New York: Routledge, 1994), 15. The notion of the "boundary creature" is adapted from Haraway, *A Cyborg Manifesto*, and further mentioned in Haraway, *Simians, Cyborgs, and Women*, 2.

43 Connelly, *The Grotesque*, 1.

44 Russo, *The Female Grotesque,* 1; 5.

45 Connelly, *The Grotesque*, 2; 116–117; Russo, *The Female Grotesque,* 1. Such arguments chime closely with Susan Rubin Suleiman's "feminist intertextuality," *Subversive Intent: Gender, Politics, and the Avant-Garde* (Cambridge, MA: Harvard University Press, 1990), 173; 142.

Afterword

I call it a tendency to look around the corner.

—Mieke Bal (2017)[1]

perhaps this "finished feminism" is somewhere so simple, but nowhere I have been.

—Mary Russo (1994)[2]

This study of Leonora Carrington's currency within the contemporary arts has begun to track a resurgence of creative interest and fandom, especially in the decade since her death. In her critical afterlife, she has become a tangle of behaviours, a medium or mode of practising in the contemporary cultural landscapes of the early twenty-first century. Her lifespan undoubtedly helped shape how her subsequent legacies would unfold—many of the key figures discussed in this book had the chance to meet her as a primary source of surrealist activity. Yet despite the sheer number of biographies, memoirs, and homages, there is a noticeable tendency, in the practices of those discussed, to distance or detach themselves from her biography. Throughout this book, I have referred to Carrington as a philosophy or site of knowledge, a lifestyle choice with much still to do. I have found the appeal of her work is related to a range of factors, not least her own ability to combine a unique, and potentially infinite, range of animals, symbols, and source materials that crucially speak an ecologically invested view on gender politics. Her reach has forged a bond between the archetypal-primeval and the modern-contemporary, demonstrating how these distinctive episte-mologies might inform, recapitulate, and fold back onto one another rather than stand as opposing historical forces. She enables us to channel a con-temporary grotesque for feminist purposes. Her growing appeal gives many, especially women, creative licence to explore or dedicate themselves to imagery that was once dismissed as marginal, childlike, or insincere. Many of her contemporary legacies utilise associated surrealist techniques of juxtaposition and marvellous interactions, while harnessing the possibilities of more recent technologies and medial approaches. For some, Carrington continually prompts an entire practice; for others she underpins the realisation of a single work. I will close with a selection of examples by men and what they reveal about Carrington's hold over contemporary arts and politics.[3]

Reflecting on the surrealist era and reimagining a post-apocalyptic scenario in which the Nazis had triumphed, China Miéville galvanises Carrington's drawing *I am an Amateur of Velocipedes* (1941) (Figure 35) as a "manif" of the French Resistance in the opening of his novella, *The Last Days of New Paris* (2016): "The Amateur of Velocipedes. Lurching through Paris on her thick-spoked wheels singing a song without words ... She landed hard on the Surrealist side of the street."[4] Here, a motif from Carrington's wartime *œuvre* is collaged intertextually, demonstrating the extent to which Carrington's work can be co-opted for a hard left ideology. The photographer, Sam, a thinly veiled disguise for war journalist Lee Miller, adds further feminist dimension to this predominantly masculine environment. Sam is not only documenting New Paris but is also a collector of manif imagery. With a background in witchcraft, Sam "spit[s] magic" as an undercover agent from Hell.[5] She is later symbolically eviscerated by Hitler's unfinished self-portrait:

> She is in the air and the self-portrait looks at her and she
> is just gone.
> Gone. Sam is unpersoned.[6]

With this literary image, Miéville critiques a misogynistic fascism. Sam's deletion also constitutes a self-reflexive metafictional transfer of the responsibility of writing up *The Last Days of New Paris* from Sam to the protagonist Thibaut, an elderly version of whom later relays this whole tale to the author in a hotel room in London. Such intergenerational inheritance is common ground across Carrington's legacies.

A lively painting-assemblage that draws from Carrington's compelling use of the feminist grotesque is Simphiwe Ndzube's *As They Rode Along the Edge* (2020) (Figure 34). Ndzube evokes Carrington to raise awareness around the mistreatment of elderly African women associated with witchcraft.[7] Three hybrid figures can be discerned within the painting. Each wears a theatrical mask or alternative mode of disguise such as a hat and feather boa. A couple of two-dimensional figures in piggy-back formation are flanked by a third three-dimensional, condensed figure comprising a mouth with an exaggerated tongue, white wig, trousers, and boots. The use of readymade found objects for this third, herald figure enables them to step outside the picture plane, grounding this sur-real work and connecting it with the viewer's own space—riding along the edge of reality and illusion. As well as the titular story of Virginia Fur, Ndzube's characters might also be compared to the heavily costumed figure in Carrington's *The Artist Travelling Incognito* (1949) (Figure 10) as a form of eccentric masquerade or alter ego. Indeed,

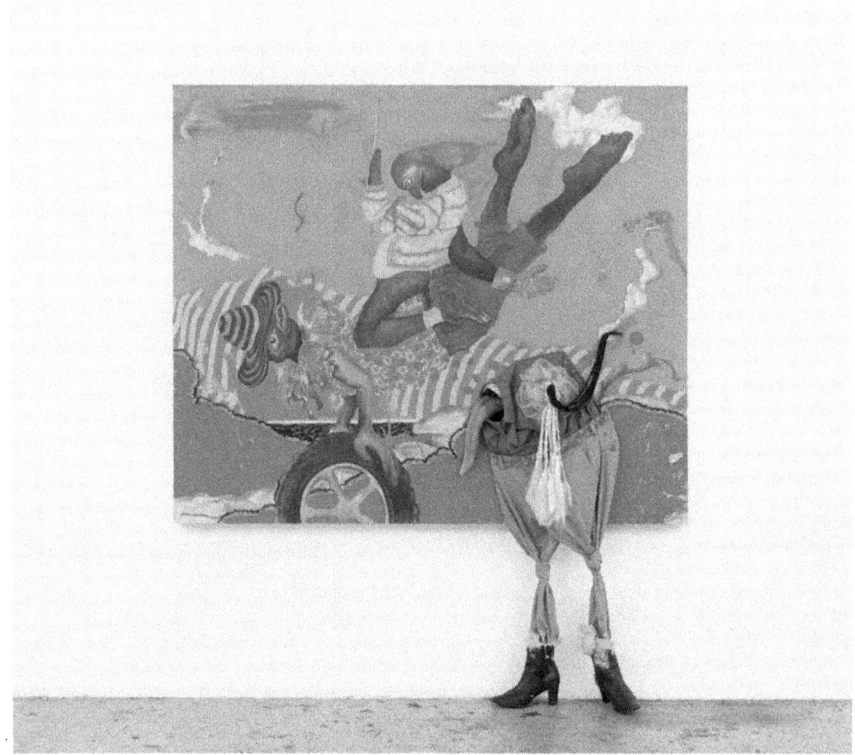

34 Simphiwe Ndzube, *As They Rode Along the Edge*, 2020

Ndzube appears to have brewed several iconographic ingredients from Carrington's *œuvre* to realise this vivid composition, again, for example, the tenacious unicyclist, *Velocipedes*, which seems to be a direct visual quotation. The blue glove of Ndzube's riding figure further references the broader surrealism of André Breton's novella, *Nadja* (1928). The overall effect can be compared to the surrealist game of the exquisite corpse as a (dis)organising method infinitely available for pictorial construction.

A short story by Fernando A. Flores, 'The Performances of Liliana Krauze' (2018), offers a micro-allegory for Carrington's twenty-first-century inter-generational meaning. The story begins with a Belgian dream that leads a fictional Leonora Carrington to a hospital in Mexico City. The protagonist, Liliana, is born under the watchful eye of Carrington who, mistaken by hospital staff for a doula or grandmother, symbolically cuts the baby's umbilical cord. Liliana, the daughter of an art historian, grows up to be a performance artist working between San Francisco, Montréal, New York, and Mexico City. The botched outcome of her third performance, involving

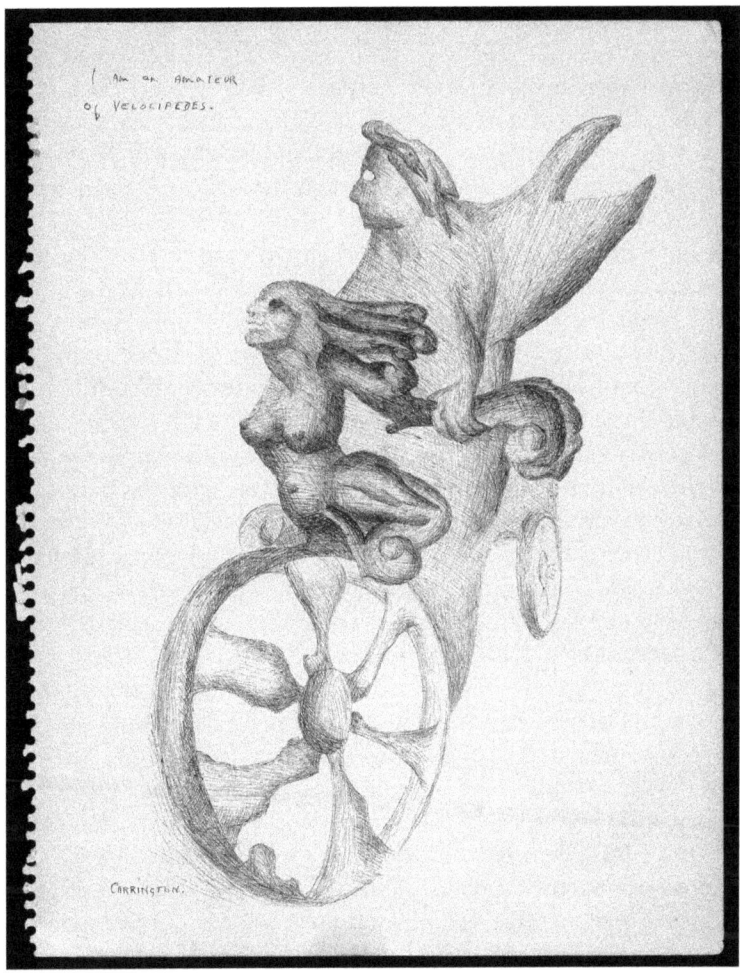

35 Leonora Carrington, *I am an Amateur of Velocipedes*, 1941

taped conversations, a red dress, yellow petals, and a caesarean-like stabbing action to her abdomen, takes her back to the same hospital, the site of her birth. Flores's tale feels recursive, a statement on Carrington's legacies in alternative media, and a snapshot of how she has come to operate inter-generationally as a marvellous entity in the contemporary arts, ever elusive yet always pulling the strings.

While we may or may not consider ourselves superstitious, study of Carrington inevitably makes one question their belief systems. Although I maintain that demythologisation is crucial to what Carrington-as-medium gives us, through this research, I have come to both understand and deeply respect how Carrington makes believers of her audiences.[8] As her activist legacies in the recent arts demonstrate, we are in deep need of this kind of contemporary shamanism. Carrington triggers and bewitches the imagination whilst reminding us of a mode of social critique. "Leonora's work brings some sort of re-enchantment to a world that seems a little too sure of itself," proclaims Chloe Aridjis, "Her inspiration came from something much more interior."[9]

Through Carrington, I have also sought to inquire after the scholarly meaning of feminist intertextuality and its practical manifestation in the early twenty-first century. What has changed since Susan Rubin Suleiman first used this term to describe Carrington's writing in the early 1990s?[10] Moreover, what has occurred since Gloria Orenstein's 1975 call for greater attention to be paid to the women of surrealism?[11] While we can confidently state that Carrington's profile has been raised exponentially since this time, we should continue to probe whether or not the irrepressible practice of quoting from Carrington's statements, artworks, and writings has enabled feminist intertextuality to achieve its aims of dismantling patriarchal norms and unsettling the canon. What techniques and strategies of the surrealist marvellous have prevailed? Do such makers offer a more poetically accurate way of understanding the history of Leonora Carrington? Close study of a range of examples, from performance to the literary field, arguably helps us understand Carrington better, but what does the curation of such findings tell us?[12] Throughout this study, I have been specifically interested in why Carrington is providing such a productive site for feminist investigations into ecocritical concerns such as animal rights and climate change. I think of this study as a form of appropriation itself, intersecting with different generations of feminist-surrealist politics. Placing Carrington into dialogue with contemporary creative responses from the 1980s, 1990s, and especially those from the early decades of the twenty-first century promotes this vibrancy of intergenerational awareness. Through channelling Carrington, we can prophesise the future, mapping out what must be done, what actions must be taken to ensure life survives on this planet, and that it may even retain some cultural meaning if it does.

The fandom around Carrington increasingly intersects with an ethics of consciousness around diversity and environmentalism. Such issue-raising abilities within the contemporary arts demonstrate that creatives have important political work to do, redressing the past for more equitable and sustainable futures. *The medium of Leonora Carrington* has presented one framework for forward-looking revisionary pursuits, rethinking an artist/writer/figurehead who offers an unprecedented democracy and infinite possibilities to those who choose to quote from her legacies. Yet we should remain wary of those who would seek to institutionalise her feminism.[13] In

2018, former UK Prime Minister, David Cameron, made a surprising appearance at Carrington's *Magical Tales* exhibition in Mexico City—a gesture of international relations, perhaps, but a simplistic and awkwardly staged photo opportunity given the complexity and political histories of the left-leaning avant-garde which Carrington and her work can be said to directly represent.[14] Let us not forget Cameron's role, however supposedly reluctant, in bringing about Brexit, nor the many environmental failures and empty promises of Westminster and beyond.[15] One could argue that all appropriation is a misappropriation, sometimes a violent decontextualisation and wresting of meaning, but I cannot help but feel troubled by this particular breed of establishment hypocrisy. We should resist and critique those who would attempt to align Carrington's power and profile with the very conservative, right-wing politics she (and much of her legacies) have demonstrated time and time again not to stand for. We must remain vigilant of commercial capitalisations and institutionalisations which would try to deny, neutralise or contain such transgressive clout. Rather we must look towards supporting artist-histories which do not pin down but ever expand Carrington's reach.

Notes

1 Mieke Bal cited Anna Kérchy and Catriona McAra, 'Interview with Mieke Bal,' *European Journal of English Studies*, 21:3 (2017): 231 https://doi.org/10.108 0/13825577.2017.136926916 (Accessed 16 July 2020).

2 Mary Russo, *The Female Grotesque: Risk, Excess and Modernity* (New York: Routledge, 1994), 40.

3 Carrington herself represented men, often in a humorous and/or ominous way. Think of *The Daring Young Men on the Purple Balloon* (1970), or her portraits of Max Ernst and Chiki Weisz.

4 China Miéville, *The Last Days of New Paris* (London: Picador, 2016), 4–5.

5 Miéville, *The Last Days*, 152.

6 Miéville, *The Last Days*, 163.

7 Simphiwe Ndzube @simphiwe_ndzube (20 November 2020).

8 Angela Carter, 'Notes From the Front Line,' *Shaking a Leg: Collected Journalism and Writings*, ed. Jenny Uglow (London: Penguin, 1997), 38.

9 Chloe Aridjis cited in Josh Appignanesi, *Female Human Animal* (London: Minotaur Film, 2018). This statement echoes Hal Foster's reading of the surrealist marvellous: "the reenchantment of a disenchanted world, of a capitalist society made ruthlessly rational," *Compulsive Beauty* (Cambridge, MA: MIT Press, 1995), 19.

10 Susan Rubin Suleiman, *Subversive Intent: Gender, Politics, and the Avant-Garde* (Cambridge, MA: Harvard University Press, 1990), 173.

11 Gloria Orenstein, 'Art History and the Case for the Women of Surrealism,' *Journal of General Education* 27:1 (Spring 1975): 31–54.

12 Mieke Bal, *Quoting Caravaggio: Contemporary Art, Preposterous History* (Chicago: University of Chicago Press, 1999), 7.
13 Thank you to Natalya Lusty for this idea.
14 'David Cameron visits Mexico,' *Office of David Cameron* (10 May 2018): www.davidcameronoffice.org/david-cameron-visits-mexico (Accessed 24 June 2021).
15 Selena Chambers, 'The Hyena's Escape Plan: Leonora Carrington's Advice on Surviving Brexit,' *The Debutante*, 1 (2020), 4.

Appendix: interviews

The archetype of the Wild Woman and all that stands behind her is patroness to all painters, writers, sculptors, dancers, thinkers … for they are all busy with the work of invention, and that is the Wild Woman's main occupation.
—Clarissa Pinkola Estés (1992)[1]

The following interview material appears in two parts. In-depth interviews with novelists Chloe Aridjis (CA) and Heidi Sopinka (HS) were carried out in person in 2014 and 2018, respectively, and, in Aridjis's case, updated via email in 2020. Further bespoke interviews with artists Samantha Sweeting (SS) and Lucy Skaer (LS), and novelists Ali Smith (AS) and China Miéville (CM2), were conducted via email in 2020–22.

The second set of interviews are arranged by medium, and were conducted remotely via email in 2018–22, in a format that became increasingly necessary given the global Covid-19 pandemic. They conform to a standard set of inquiries that became useful to the research but might be best read through the unfolding surrealist game of consequences or exquisite corpse.

Interestingly, Carrington's literary works *Down Below* (1944) and *The Hearing Trumpet* (1974) are most frequently cited here as touchstones, with her most popular visual artwork being *The House Opposite* (1945) (Figure 8). Out of 33 responses, 24 identify as feminist, with the remaining nine eager to nuance the term for contemporary arts and politics.

Part 1: bespoke interviews

Interview with Chloe Aridjis

31 July 2014, London (updated 15 May 2020, via email)

Catriona McAra (CM): Leonora Carrington makes a brief cameo in your first novel, *Book of Clouds*, in a rare exchange between your protagonist and the historian Doctor Weiss. Here it seems that you're conflating the real-life with the fictional domain. Often there is this overlap; you and

Tatiana have both spent time in Berlin, for instance. I was wondering if you could talk about how you relate or diverge from your central characters?

Chloe Aridjis (CA): That's something I am always happy to discuss since there's such a tendency to conflate author and first-person narrator, especially with women writers, and it can be frustrating. *Asunder* is more autobiographical than *Book of Clouds*, for instance, though most readers assume that the young Mexican woman in Berlin is my alter ego. I tried to create someone quite detached from the outside world, whereas my years there were much more social. I did go through solitude as well but it was a different sort of solitude, less acute. I wanted to create someone who had a real aversion to intimacy yet was still experiencing the city in a similar way to me. I would go out with my notebook and wander the streets and take notes. Years of notes and observation. At first I went out a great deal at night, to parties and art openings, like a bee collecting pollen, and then I started to write. I had in mind a collection of short stories but one of the short stories grew into what became *Book of Clouds*.

Another autobiographical difference is that I am not Jewish-Mexican. My mother is Jewish and my father is Mexican but we grew up in a very secular household, completely separate from the Jewish community, whereas Tatiana is escaping from it. People have sometimes asked me whether my family own a deli in Mexico!

CM: On the one hand, I am so cautious of "the author" after Roland Barthes but then, of course, the work comes from you and your experiences.[2] I am interested in the notion of embodiment.

CA: Exactly. You do inhabit those people. It is an act of ventriloquism; you are giving them a voice, one you have shaped. No matter how much you try to distance yourself, it is you who creates it. It is a very complicated question to answer. Truthfully or thoroughly.

CM: Even in art history there is still this primacy of the author. For example, for Carrington the work will be invested in emotionally and financially, but it is still the name that carries those works together under one banner. My second question was actually about Carrington. What was your relationship with her? Do you think she has had any impact on your writing?

CA: My father had met her in the 1970s but the friendship with our family was launched in the early 90s through our doctor Teodoro Césarman, who was doctor to most of the artists and writers in Mexico City. We met Leonora at his house at lunch one Saturday and immediately sensed a kinship. She invited us for tea the following day. From then on, nearly every Sunday we would go and have tea at her house. It became a ritual, and part of an ongoing dialogue. She was such an inspiring force, so uncompromising! Perhaps not directly or on a conscious level, but I think her spirit is always present. With her it is very tricky to use the word "imagination." She always insisted that things just happened.

CM: Were you aware of her back catalogue?

CA: Slowly, not all at once.

CM: So she was a friend first?

CA: She was a friend first. I had seen some of her paintings and loved them, but the immensity of her world and her output was extraordinary and there was a great deal yet to discover. Then I started reading the books. There wasn't any line between her person and her work. She could have been a character in one of her own paintings or short stories! She seemed to embody so many of her own creatures. Leonora was extremely modest, she never boasted or name-dropped; on the contrary, she mumbled. She was beyond that and had no interest in any of the superficial aspects of the art world. There were a few times when during her own exhibitions in Mexico City, her sons would plead with her to put in an appearance at the opening, but often she would be hiding in a room upstairs. Unlike many famous artists with suffocating egos she never lost her authenticity. She was always that way, it wasn't age. I still often think about her.

CM: It is interesting that you mention going for tea at her house because I feel like I know it from Lucy Skaer's work (2006) which was recently acquired by the Hunterian in Glasgow. There are also photographs by Skaer of Carrington's kitchen in *Tate Etc.* magazine featuring a bricolage of postcards on Carrington's kitchen cupboard (Figure 15).[3] Scholars are starting to read quite a lot into this.[4]

CA: The kitchen in her house was the centre of the universe. That's where we would nearly always sit during our visits. (I don't know if you noticed but the table is covered with a Liberty's oilcloth I once bought her.)

CM: I am interested in all these bits and pieces of ephemera and found objects.

CA: It was part of the mosaic of her daily life.

CM: I am intrigued by the fact that she was both an artist and a writer. Your novel *Asunder* is also so visual, an amazing conflation of images. There is such an economy of imagery.

CA: My greatest frustration in life is that I am not a painter! This is the closest I could come.

CM: I have a question about intermediality and topography. I was wondering about the transition from the narrative content to the surface of the painting?

CA: I have had a relationship to paintings since going to museums as a child. For a long time, I interacted with the narrative of paintings and responded in perhaps a more predictable way, but once I began reading about craquelure and thinking more about the history of paintings I began seeing them on a more microscopic level too, as vulnerable physical objects prone to cracking. The craquelure provided an additional topography. A landscape within a landscape. For a while it made it difficult for me to see the paintings I loved. I didn't set out in the same spirit but as I did research I began thinking about what the themes would be. I realised it was very similar to the method I had in terms of cracks and fissures and where meaning lies within a text. It's that rupture, where there's a release of tension. It became more apparent to me over time that something could happen in the narrative—I was guided by the themes that began emerging in the book and what the character was drawn to. For example, the Velázquez painting of the *Rokeby Venus*, which I've always been aware of as a remarkable painting, but I have to admit it was not the first painting I would visit myself or even think about when I thought about at the National Gallery. But then it acquired a whole new significance in the book.

CM: And the William Dyce?

CA: *Pegwell Bay* was a painting I only got to know a few years ago, although I'd been going to Tate Britain since my adolescence. For some reason I only discovered it the year before I started working on *Asunder*. And I loved it from the moment I saw it—I felt a strange attraction, as though it were calling out to me, asking to be deciphered.

CM: Thinking about notions of intertextuality and ekphrasis, you collage real-life works of art into the fictional domain and there are lots of references in *Asunder* to other paintings in other galleries that you've visited. We could think about this as a kind of mapping both geographically in terms of Berlin, London, Mexico City, but also in terms of the patterning of how you go about structuring your novel. Are these chains of thought linked?

CA: With both novels there is a lot of echoing and doubling, where certain characters prefigure others, and wandering is an important element. I don't map out my books much before I write them so I too am wandering and waiting for patterns to emerge. With *Asunder* I did have to give a great deal of thought to structure since it involves rather disparate themes—the suffragettes, the craquelure, the museum, the goth, and the chatelain. That was my biggest challenge writing it because these things were pulling me in different directions. I had to come up with some sort of metaphorical framework in which to accommodate them all.

CM: I noticed that both novels have quite a sharp climatic moment. In *Book of Clouds* it is the mugging scene or moment of the attack, and in *Asunder* it is the encounter in the chateau when the character scratches her face. Both are such sharp moments of rupture compared to the pacing of the rest of the novels.

CA: Yes, I was leading up to those moments. For me that is the most important scene in *Asunder*, and the chatelain is one of the most important characters even though he may come across as more of a cameo. Marie has her goth in Camden but then she meets an even more authentic goth living in his chateau. Suddenly something is awakened, and there is something thrilling and dangerous about him. Unlike the National Gallery, the goth and his home are unprotected heritage. In both novels these climactic moments spell a great release of tension. In *Asunder* it is prompted by Marie changing location, from London to France, which somehow allows her to break out of a passive state.

CM: I think boredom can provide a useful process too. Boredom can conjure such brilliant images.

CA: It is underrated! And a necessary state for interesting thought to emerge.

CM: A penultimate question I have is about feminism, mainly because you have conducted so much research on the suffragettes. I'm interested that that history features so much in your novel. Was the grandfather character in your novel (who tries to stop the suffragette) entirely fictional?

CA: Yes. I had been interested in the suffragettes but I hadn't known much about them previously. Very early on, while researching the history of the National Gallery, I came across accounts of Mary Richardson, and found her story spectacular. I knew I wasn't going to write a historical novel but I thought, this story will be haunting my character and loom in her psyche. I began reading more and more and was obviously quite shaken and appalled. We've had some formidable women in Mexico but we haven't been as organised, and I was struck by the incredible social movements across Europe. They had more agency. I was extremely moved and became quite fixated. When writing a novel you have to absorb the research and then gradually make it your own. Many thoughts and ideas didn't make it in.

It wasn't until I went to university in the States (after growing up in Mexico) that I saw how young women could be self-assertive and self-possessed. Culturally one isn't imbued with that strong sense of self early on. Yet my main activism has been environmental: I am above all interested in animal rights. If I were going to picket outside somewhere or go chanting down the street, it would be for the animals, who are completely voiceless. They matter more to me than anything.

Leonora herself was fiercely independent and autonomous and simply having access to someone like that as a friend for nearly two decades really left its mark. As much as I love her work, her very being was a tremendous inspiration. Of course, only later do you realise how someone has affected you. I really thought she was one of those people who was going to live forever!

CM: Why is Carrington's legacy proving so productive a site for creative work today? She suddenly feels very relevant again in 2020. Why do you think this might be?

CA: It has indeed been wonderful to see the growing interest in Leonora over the past years. What to attribute it to? She's a splendid hybrid, an Old World being who spent most of her life in the New World, her work a magical blend of different mythologies and cosmologies and strange worlds all her own. She was a muse yet refused to be one. She is considered a surrealist but never called herself one. She refused all categorisation. She was simply and categorically herself and believed in a fluidity of identity. One could be, and have, many selves at once.

Interview with Heidi Sopinka

22 May 2018, London

Catriona McAra (CM): It feels appropriate to be recording your voice. I wanted to start by asking about the cast list in your book. I really like how you represent friendship figures like Remedios Varo as Tacita, Lev as Max Ernst, and maybe even yourself as the Mexican journalist? Marcel Duchamp and Leonor Fini also make cameo appearances. To what extent is your protagonist Ivory Frame a portrait of Leonora Carrington?

Heidi Sopinka (HS): I actually wrote a draft of the book before I'd ever met or heard of Leonora. I'd written a draft about a woman in two time periods at 19 and at 92, and at 19 had fallen in with the surrealists. So it had those basic events. I happened upon *The Hearing Trumpet* of Leonora's when I was at the library looking for a different book. And I read it, and was, of course, intrigued because the character Marian Leatherby is 92, which is the same age as my character, and it is very rare to find book with a nonagenarian heroine. So that immediately intrigued me to her. And then I started looking up elements of her life and reading a lot about her and eventually I did meet her.

   The ghost of her was already in the draft before I'd even known of her, which is very odd. Her time period was exactly the same time period of my heroine. I'd already written this unrequited love story because I was interested in the notion of how people are haunted by the incomplete rather than something which has been taken to its final extent. It is a real blurred line between what existed before and what existed after meeting her. But certainly the events of her life and herself were a huge inspiration.

CM: I want to ask a question around the importance of creative ageing. The age 92 is recurrent—the age Carrington was when you interviewed her, the age of Marian in *The Hearing Trumpet*, and the age of Ivory Frame. What is your interest in nonagenarians or the nonagenarian moment?

HS: It actually came from the flipside of that. The whole book came from after I gave birth to my first child. I instantly started to look at death and the end of life. In the extreme of giving birth, it led me to that spot. Just as a baby seems to come into the world from nowhere, I wondered, where do we go? I wanted to look at people who live on the edge of that every day, so it had to be someone who was older, quite old, not just in their 70s. Someone who is contending with death.

The book started with a series of images, and one of them was of an old woman that was working. Older women particularly are one of the most underwritten aspects of the female experience. Ironically it is at a time when we are at the height of our power! Certainly in terms of artists, especially women artists that don't get recognised until their very late years until they have a big body of work and *finally* they are noticed. In Leonora's case that was certainly true. So, I wanted to explore someone living in a liminal state and being at the height of their powers yet not quite seen that way by others.

CM: That really chimes with me. During my doctoral studies I was interested in the figure of the *femme-enfant* or child-woman, so I was looking at that early period of work. Then for my post-doctoral studies, I became interested in nonagenarian and centenarian artists; the idea of a late practice. Then I had my son and I started looking at Carrington's maternity paintings, the *Night Nursery* pictures (*c.*1947) (Figure 3). Her life spectrum is absolutely fascinating but one of the problems in the scholarship is that it tends to focus on her 1930s and 40s period. So, I find it interesting to look at her as an older woman and to think about our historical overlap with her.

HS: Her own childhood loomed so large for her. You can see from her paintings and from studying her work, but also from speaking with her. I think that is another interesting aspect about ageing, that at the very end spectrum of your life, everything is amplified in different periods, and her childhood seemed to be very large for her. And obviously the time in Paris as well. Those were the big ones. And then a period as a young mother, she talked about as well.

CM: Can you tell me what it was like to interview Carrington for *The Believer* magazine (2012)? She seems intent throughout that interview on her refusal to be pinned down and again that really comes across to me in your novel. Can you talk a little about that experience?

HS: I found it quite unsettling to be in the room with her at first because she lived this grand life. It seemed like such a long shot! It was such a weird, serendipitous way of getting to her. I imagine in her prime she would have been very unnerving. She was so direct: "what do you want to know?" Not like anyone else I'd ever spoken with. It was really fascinating that she would come up with anecdotes about Picasso!

It gave me licence in my own work to understand that, at that age, you experience your life and memory in a different way. Nothing was linear. She did talk about making those posters for the Women's Liberation movement in the 1970s in Mexico, and at the same time she talked about her contribution to the *Temptation of St Anthony* competition (1945). It was all melded into one. An amazing moment where you realise that a life is glimpsed like driving quickly in a car.

CM: I sadly never got to meet Leonora Carrington. When she died, I realised I would have to conduct my future research in a completely different way. So, for me, it is now all about meeting people, especially creative practitioners like yourself, who did meet her and did know her. To explore her through other people's encounters.

HS: My friend is a photo-editor and my other friend is an artist who did a series of bookbinding of Leonora's work. With really beautiful leathers and fish scales. She made one that opened like a cabbage. We went down there but we didn't have an address so we didn't know if we would ever find her. We did these performance pieces to try and conjure her. We used a lot of her iconography to make these picnics across Mexico City. It was amazing, we'd dress up in these costumes and conceive of what it would look like. Leonora loved it when we told her! We showed her some of the imagery. I think she felt it was about time! She was finally starting to get a bit of a taste of people seeing her and her work in a larger context.

CM: Why is Carrington's legacy proving so productive a site for creative work? She suddenly feels very relevant again.

HS: I think surrealism really went out of fashion, even for the male practitioners. They were such radical thinkers yet so conservative when it came to their views and representations of women. Someone like Frida Kahlo became huge because of her subversion of that, and I think Leonora was the same; she had no time for the Freudian theoretical elements. She followed her own path towards magical realism and the alchemical. She thought that the kitchen, where she and Varo did all of those experiments, was a site of power rather than one of degradation. She was clearly a staunch feminist her entire life. I think only now we have been able to embrace feminism as part of the mainstream.

CM: Yes, I think there is a lot of work for us to do as the next generation in terms of rescuing those voices. One of the aspects of your book which I find very productive for rethinking Carrington, is the idea of her extending her practice into birdsong, biology, and eco-feminism. I feel that Carrington was a trailblazer for that cause, particularly in the realm of eco-feminism as we understand it today. I, therefore, read your book this way and you do include a lot of reflection on the female condition. Where is your feminism located?

HS: I remember when I was at university I saw Margaret Atwood speak, and someone put up their hand and asked if she would consider herself a feminist (this is when "feminism" was a dirty word in the early 1990s), and she replied, "what, do you mean do I think that women are human beings?" I think that was a perfect answer! It is an issue and I am really happy to see it in the mainstream.

I see the struggle looking at Leonora's life. She was such a radical thinker but she had to be satisfied with practising her art in a way that she felt was symbolic of what she wanted to do. It obviously wasn't without struggle; she obviously wanted to have some recognition. I feel lucky to be born in a time which is not 1917 but it is obviously not still without struggle! My own personal issues were around how to balance motherhood with a creative practice. I wish I had talked to her more about this. To go deeply into work, you have to really disappear. And that doesn't exactly bode well for motherhood. Women tend to be seen in a more nurturing role, and I think it is harder for us to fully commit ourselves. I loved the notion of getting at the heart of dedication with a woman. With a man they can get into their work and no one will say they are a bad father. How does a woman navigate love and nurture? I wanted to look at all those issues and turn them over and examine them and persevere in them. Someone asked me if Ivory really had to end the relationship, and I replied that, yes, to be fully herself, she does. I had that in the book before I had even met her, and I found that such an interesting aspect of Leonora, that she had to leave Max.

CM: I think we definitely need more conversations around creative practice and motherhood. I tried to emulate Carrington after I gave birth to my son (holding the paintbrush, or pen in my case, in one hand and the infant in the other) because I needed to maintain a sense of self-identity. I was also so amazed by having a little creature in my arms and could empathise with the human animal in Carrington's work, especially that lactating hyena! All those characters are at the forefront of rethinking the maternal body.

HS: I asked her about children and work, and she said, "well, I had help." In Mexico she must have had an affordable nanny. She said she could never have done this had she lived in London. She would never have had the life that she had, the freedom. A really basic thing but essential. When I asked what her biggest accomplishment was, she said it was her children, which surprised me! I think those categorical questions are difficult anyway, but she was clearly a dedicated mother as well as a dedicated artist.

CM: I often hear Carrington's voice in your writing, such as "procuring an omelette with hair" (2018, 48), "speaking French without mistakes" (56), and the idea of being "more animal than human" (116). These details are jewels for the Carrington scholar! How did you conduct your Carrington research for this book?

HS: I read all of her writings, and then I read the Susan Aberth book, and other people's accounts. There wasn't a lot around at the time in the early 2000s, so minimally. It was not an afterthought, but it was just so interesting that her world existed without me even knowing about her. Then I met her.

I did really struggle with the notion of switching from art to science. But after a traumatic experience, especially with women I find, one has to discard their self. I wanted it to be believable enough. It goes back to eco-feminism and the surrealist interest in animals as the ultimate non sequitur! I love the notion that we exist in a language-less place with them, and yet we see our own humanity reflected back at us when we look at them, and she really explored that.

CM: How did you (or Ivory Frame) structure *The Dictionary of Animal Languages*? How did you/she select the animals?

HS: That was another struggle, because I know in academia you end up focusing on a very specific creature! But I felt like she had to look at all the animals. It was a bit ad hoc, there wasn't necessarily a design around it.

CM: Birds do seem to populate her *oeuvre* (alongside the horses). There are perhaps more birds in your book than any other animal.

HS: I think birds are obvious because we coexist with them most commonly. I came across a book called *Wild Birds and Their Music* (1904) – it was how I imagined initially how *The Dictionary of Animal Languages* would work, with technical and biological illustrations and bars of music to explain what their song sounded like.

CM: Have you seen *Female Human Animal* (2018)? It stars the novelist Chloe Aridjis. The film is "haunted by Leonora."

HS: It sounds fascinating! It's the name of the film?

CM: Yes, Carrington wrote about the idea of being a 'female human animal' in an essay entitled 'What is a Woman?' (1970). It seems so parallel to your thinking!

HS: I'm so curious to know what the scholarship is on surrealism and feminism now …

Interview with Samantha Sweeting

3 September 2020 (via email)

Catriona McAra (CM): I wonder if we might begin by thinking back to your initial encounter with the work of Leonora Carrington. You have said it was through our mutual friend, the artist and collector, Viktor Wynd. Can you tell me a little more about how that came about? Can you remember what it was by Carrington that he shared with you? What was it about Carrington that initially piqued your interest?

Samantha Sweeting (SS): I was definitely taken with her animal imagery, and her striking ability to re-imagine her life as something other than the one she was born into.

I had just returned from living in an isolated stone farmhouse in a forest in the French Pyrenees. It had been a wild fairy tale existence, with feral animals, mountain lakes, and log fires to stay warm through the never-ending winters. I packed what I could carry and travelled back to London by train, landing in a tiny attic room above the kitchen at Wynd's warehouse flat in Hackney. I'd been reading Unica Zürn's *The Man of Jasmine: Impressions From a Mental Illness*—a gift from Wynd that excited the unanchored state of mind I was in at the time.

I began working at bookartbookshop, where I was introduced to other surrealist and pataphysical texts published by Atlas Press, as well as the works of outsider writers and artists like Madge Gill, Ruth Lakofski, and Niki de Saint Phalle. Wynd was in the middle of setting up his museum and avidly collecting Carrington's art, alongside shrunken heads, mortuary tables, and an articulated skeleton of a lion named Mortimer, so her fantastical animals and otherworldly scenes fed into this general atmosphere. There was also the personal connection, through Chloe Aridjis's family, which made the anecdotes of Carrington's sharp wit and eccentricity feel especially vivid. I became intrigued by the playful and at times harrowing nature of Carrington's biography and writing, in particular her experience of mental breakdown she recalls in *Down Below*. I have since trained in psychotherapy and worked closely with people experiencing psychoses and other severe mental health issues.

CM: I am interested in coincidences which enable us to glimpse into the inner workings of the surrealist marvellous. You and I met shortly after this moment at the *Alice in Wonderland* exhibition at Tate Liverpool. Can you tell me about the specific artwork you showed? Do you see any parallels between Lewis Carroll and Leonora Carrington?

SS: I showed my video, *Run Rabbit, Run Rabbit, Run, Run, Run* (2007), which depicts my hands gently manipulating a dead rabbit as though it were a marionette. I made it in Wistman's Wood, an ancient and mythical oak woodland in Dartmoor, Devon. I had found the rabbit killed on the road the night before and wanted to give it a burial. By the time I arrived in the woods, its rigor mortis had eased and its limbs were malleable. I played with it like a child trying to understand death. I moved its legs making the rabbit slowly leap back into life. When exhibited, the two-minute video is played on continuous loop. Like Carroll's White Rabbit, my rabbit continues to run in defiance of its mortality.

Carrington and Carroll both create marvellous imaginary worlds, with their own rules and anthropomorphic creatures. There's a performative and bodily nature to their illustrated texts, which came out of oral storytelling. While Carroll is writing in the literary nonsense tradition, Carrington's work, for me, veers more towards mysticism and magic. She had a psychotic breakdown, survived it and wrote her own narrative. There's a sense of reverie and fearlessness, in which she is her own muse, seamlessly walking in and out of the dreamworlds she paints.

Carroll had more of a divided life, as the children's book writer under his pseudonym Lewis Carroll, and as Charles Lutwidge Dodgson, the Oxford mathematician and photographer. Dodgson was friends with children, notably Alice Liddell and her sisters Lorina and Edith, and entered their world in a way that was troubling and voyeuristic, dressing them up, photographing them, and entertaining them with his fantastic stories.

CM: In previous interviews, you have explored why Carroll's text remains so intrinsic to contemporary art making and thinking ("generation after generation").[5] Why do you think Carrington's legacy is proving so productive a site for creative work today?

SS: There's more of an appetite for work made by women and gender queer artists, and a desire to reappraise the very white phallocentric art world and history. In London, there have been notable retrospectives of Dorothea Tanning at Tate Modern, Claude Cahun at the National Portrait Gallery, Frida Kahlo at the V&A, as well as programmes like *100% Women* at Richard Saltoun Gallery.

The world at large feels quite mad at the moment and there's a great need for role models. Carrington had a prolific output and longevity. She rebelled against the expectations imposed upon her, endured a psychotic breakdown, rejected the fetishisation of madness that her male surrealist contemporaries had, and avoided being trapped in the role of muse. She seemed able to step between internal and external realities, disrupting conventional notions of body and mind. Her writings and images have a timeless quality, combining humour, violence, play, and wonder. Engaging with her work is like entering a deep well of knowledge about life and death.

CM: In 2011 you collaborated with Lynn Lu on the performance-installation adaptation of Carrington's novel, *The Hearing Trumpet*. I was subsequently fortunate enough to work with you and Lu on curating a public engagement variation of this at Leeds Arts University in 2016 for my *Carrington/Skaer* show. Can you tell me more about the origins of this performance and its subsequent development encompassing the animal snap cards? Did you conceive of it immediately after Carrington's death in May 2011, or were the bones of it already there? It felt very responsive and powerful for two contemporary artists to do this, very sisterly. Is a sense of dialogism (or co-authoring) important to your practice?

SS: Lynn and I have overlaps in our performance interests and the way we engage with audiences, setting up intimate situations to collect participant stories. Although we met in London, we are also both from Singapore. I left when I was 12 and often return to my childhood home in my dreams. Our connections, and the feeling of time travel between past and present were important to me.

Lynn had been working with a tin can telephone and I had recently read *The Hearing Trumpet*, where Carrington's 92-year-old protagonist uses a hearing trumpet to overhear her family's furtive plans to commit her into care. Lynn and I wanted to unearth hidden childhood memories and look at how they get told and distorted.

We introduced the cards to turn the performance into a playful parlour game. The vintage animal illustrations of cats, owls, crows, and toads felt aligned with Carrington's work. The participants needed to find their animal kin and pass their secrets on to one another, before I gathered them and whispered them down the trumpet to Lynn. She breathed on the pane of glass and transcribed what she heard in the condensation. For a fleeting moment, the words are cast in shadow on the adjacent wall.

The framed glass window was like a mirror and Lynn and I echoed each other in our clothing and red shoes. This twinness and obscuring of individual identities is terrifying and yet compelling, like falling through the looking glass. It came up again very strongly in a wild ritual performance work I made with Canadian-Czech artist Misha Horacek in Wales last year. We wore a costume with red fabric and human hair, left breasts exposed, and built a nest, and danced, slept, stitched, howled, and cleansed ourselves together over 48 hours.

CM: What are you currently working on?

SS: Over the past year and a half, I've jumped into contemporary dance, attending classes at Siobhan Davies Studios. This physical research has helped me process my work in mental health and opened up a creative space to bring together ideas around trauma, materiality, and the body.

In a course on improvisation led by Seke Chimutengwende, I directed a score for a group of performers based on dog movements, drawing on a childhood photograph of myself as a 4-year-old wearing a lion mask, and lying on my foxy-looking pet dog (named Badger—a touch of Carrington). My research references the dog women paintings and imagery of Paula Rego, Dorothea Tanning, Kiki Smith, and Ana Mendieta.

I was planning to move into a series of improvised duets with dogs, but this changed course over the recent lockdown. Instead, I started spending time at a local medicinal garden and keeping a diary of fox sightings, meanwhile reading fairy tales and recording my dreams every morning. A midwife friend, Jess McArdle, and I co-devised a series of domestic choreographies, culminating in a cycle of solitary moon dances at civil twilight. My final dance took place during a Full Strawberry Moon in the grounds of Dawson's Heights in East Dulwich. There was a restlessness in the air. As I began moving, a juvenile ashen-coloured fox emerged from the undergrowth and watched me. We spent an hour dancing and playing together until he disappeared back into the foliage, like a magical shape-shifting messenger.

Interview with Lucy Skaer

3 February 2021 (via email)

Catriona McAra (CM): You first met Carrington in 2006 and then returned to Mexico City after her death to make more work about her in 2012. What do those bodies of work mean to you now almost ten years since her death? Will you continue to use Carrington as a "disassembling logic" for your practice?

Lucy Skaer (LS): I was suspicious of myself when I made the work. It felt like a very uncertain move to associate myself with a senior and much more well-known artist and, although I absolutely knew I had to go and meet her, I didn't understand why. Looking back at the body of work I realise it crossed a threshold of sorts for me, and I stepped into the world in a different way after. I think it was because my esoteric thought, once it was made actual, also had meaning for others. This expanded what I understood as conceptual, it being utterly indistinct from whim and desire. And so, I became more interested in taking an unjustified position as an artist. I think this is in part why I returned to Leonora's house after her death, to not meet her. This set in motion a whole backwards motion in my practice, where I revisited, reworked, melted down previous works or compiled new works by adding ears and eyes to older ones. The last work of this retrograde phase landed me at my father's house making works from the floorboards and stone steps, dwelling in scenes from my own childhood and verging on biographical. The experience of meeting Carrington and of making my work have gained importance to me, and while I no longer need to disassemble in the same way, maybe the experience somehow helps me reassemble differently and with more breadth.

CM: Which of Carrington's artworks or writings are you most drawn to and why?

LS: Right now I am drawn to *The Giantess* (*Guardian of the Egg*). Specifically, the wheat around the Giantess's shoulders and neck. I'm interested in it appearing as a zone of matter, like an attribute that the Giantess possesses, rather than as a physical object. To me it seems like a combination of a symbol and a sensation. I'm fascinated with "stuff" being used in that way. I've just been making pelts of imaginary animals, each pelt corresponds to a word, such as Forest, or Fire. The word (and imagined animal) is depicted by the texture of the fur. I see a parallel in the way the Giantess wears her crop.

CM: Why is Carrington's legacy proving so productive a site for creative work today? She suddenly feels very relevant again. Why do you think this might be?

LS: I think ambiguous and various practices like Carrington's sustain ideas. Maybe the "return" of her work is due to its initial difficulty, or to it being thought of as biographical rather than looking outward. It feels non-binary in some way that is not specifically to do with gender.

CM: Would you describe your practice as feminist in any way? What does this word mean to you in 2021?

LS: Yes, I think my way of thinking is feminist. Thanks to organisations, such as If I Can't Dance, I think there is more acknowledgment of how crucial feminist thought is to contemporary art. Feminism in 2021 still means to me to struggle for equality for women, but it seems more united in 2021 with other causes to stop oppression and injustice.

Interview with Ali Smith

15 October 2020 (via email)

Catriona McAra (CM): You wrote a very insightful introduction for the 2005 Penguin reissue of Leonora Carrington's *The Hearing Trumpet*, and your seasonal cycle (2016–20) has been described as experimentally rethinking the novelistic format. Has the surrealist novel informed your practice in any way?

Ali Smith (AS): It will have. Though I think surrealist visual art is more likely to have influenced me. There's a hinge moment in Lee Miller's photographic *oeuvre*, for instance, as she moves with the troops at the end of WWII through the places the allies are liberating, where the surrealism she employed in the late 20s and 30s as a means of seeing the world as it really is becomes a vision of reality so stark and obvious, and also somehow so calm, that the relationship between the imagined and the unimaginable (and not so unimaginable after all) reveals itself to us—so that we can't and mustn't look away, and so that we start to understand dimensionally.

CM: Carrington is mentioned in *Artful* (2012) as an "expert in liminal space." When did you first become interested in Carrington? What specifically about Carrington and/or her work interests you? Which of her artworks and/or writings are you particularly drawn to?

AS: I read a collection of her short stories about twenty years ago, and then her memoir of her incarceration and escape, and I *loved* this writer who sees through the conventional forced and false structures of things to the real thing. Then I found some of her artworks and it was wounding that she'd been so underrated, especially in her early years. I love all of it. I think I especially like her sculpture. Because she's all about dimensionality, when she makes consciously three-dimensional works something enchanted happens bodily, in the world.

CM: Why is Carrington's legacy proving so productive a site for creative work today? She suddenly feels very relevant again in 2020. Why do you think this might be?

AS: See my answer to question 1 re: Miller. It's another hinge time, politically, repressively, divisively, technologically, and in terms of the shift of power in the real world, a time of blatancy and subterfuge both at once. The times when then the realities both cloak *and* reveal themselves—this is when we need the visionary more than ever.

CM: Are there any other surrealism-associated women that you have read, seen and/or referenced within your writing?

AS: Probably. But as I said, that's because to me realism isn't really real / ism unless it admits its own surreality.

CM: Would you describe your practice as feminist in any way? What does this word mean to you in 2020?

AS: Of course. It's natural. The word means the same as it's always meant to me: a natural and positive thought practice/activism working to re-address an endemic and false gender inequality that's ancient, historical, contemporary, cyclic, mythical, societal, political and personal, at every level.

Interview with China Miéville

14 July 2021 (via email, updated 31 January 2022)

Catriona McAra (CM): What is your creative practice, and can you explain how Leonora Carrington has become manifest within it?

China Miéville (CM2): Forgive me, I don't think I understand the first part of this question. Unless you mean "writing"? The bulk of my creative practice (a term that, unfamiliar to my usage, feels ungainly as a gobstopper in my mouth) is the writing of fiction: in addition, and increasingly, I write non-fiction; and, distantly third and mostly for my own interest, I draw. The presence of some of Carrington's graphic images appeared in my novella via the third: I love cross-hatching in monochrome art, and her cross-hatched shading in *I Am an Amateur of Velocipedes* (Figure 35) and *Do You Know My Aunt Eliza?* spellbound me. To the best of my memory, the first of these was the first surrealist image that I wanted to literalise in *New Paris*.

CM: What specifically about Carrington and/or her work interests you? Which of her artworks and/or writings are you particularly drawn to? When did you first become interested in her?

CM2: I've been interested in Carrington as long as I've been interested in surrealism, which would be since I was a young teenager—so more than 30 years. I think it may have been *Green Tea* (Figure 6) that was the first I saw. I came later to her writing and graphic works, and I must say that for me her drawing and graphic work draws me more even than her colour work.

CM: You interestingly describe *The Last Days of New Paris* as an idea you had for a video game but had to realise in your medium of writing.[6] In addition to *I am an Amateur of Velocipedes* which provides a herald image to your novella, are there any other Carrington artworks or writings that you could imagine or would like to see existing as video games?

CM2: I'm aware of the vulgarity and ridiculousness of the idea of adapting the works of Carrington and others into video games, and I can only hope that the surrealist love of pulp would mean that they, and she, would respond with amusement to the idea. As to others of her images that might work—I can think of many. A figure like *The Surgeon*, from the 1970 pencil drawing of the same name, could be a scary antagonist, the rather celestial-looking minotaur from *And Then We Saw the Daughter of the Minotaur* (Figure 12) could be an ally, and the terrifying dark figure who *doubles* as a doorway in the back of *Friday the Thirteenth* (1965) could be the entrance to the lair of the "boss baddy," the end-of-level antagonist in a game. And such an antagonist couldn't come much more intimidating than some of Carrington's bronzes, for example, blown up giant and animated: the terrifying body-horror bruja-esque figure, *La Madre de los Lobos* (2007), say, or the ghastly and astounding hollow-eyed *El Sueño del Fuego*, from the same year.

CM: Why is Carrington's legacy proving so productive a site for creative work today? She suddenly feels very relevant again. Why do you think this might be?

CM2: Truly I have no idea. It's been startling to see her ascent to cultural prominence over the last five or so years. Perhaps to some extent this is part of the tendency to a long-overdue (if still very inadequate) recovery of hitherto underrecognised or ignored women artists and artists of colour, including in the surrealist tradition. I think perhaps, more ambivalently, one of the reasons that she is particularly a go-to is that her work, unlike (say) that of Unica Zürn's or the Yoyottes or Suzanne Césaire or Toyen's or even Dorothea Tanning's, can from a certain perspective be viewed as more whimsical than frightening. I'd want to stress that I'd resist that reading, but her aesthetics have a touch of the Moomins to them, if you want to see them that way.

Part 2: Shorter interviews

Art history

1. **What is your creative practice, and can you explain how Leonora Carrington has become manifest within it?**

   Susan L. Aberth: I am an art historian—teacher, researcher, writer—and I first discovered Carrington in 1987 in New York City. I was in graduate school and came upon her work in a gallery and was from that moment on obsessed with it. I had always been interested in the occult and in her work I saw, or rather felt, the presence of some very important magical lessons. I am still learning magical lessons after almost 30 years from her work; I am very grateful for that. She also taught me patience and that most people will not understand, but the right people will. That was an important lesson.

2.   **What specifically about Carrington and/or her work interests you? Which of her artworks and/or writings are you particularly drawn to? When did you first become interested in her?**

Susan L. Aberth: I love all of her paintings and visual work, and they never cease to teach me something new about myself and the world. This is so surprising to me and after 20 years it is still the same, whenever I begin to work on one of her paintings, I find so much new material, things I never saw before. Each time I look, I see something different. The writing I admire the most, and that I think is the most neglected is her novella *The Stone Door*. This is endlessly fascinating to me.

3.   **Why is Carrington's legacy proving so productive a site for creative work today? She suddenly feels very relevant again. Why do you think this might be?**

Susan L. Aberth: I strongly feel that Carrington was never not relevant as she was light years ahead of anyone in her vision of a new world. There are so many ways to connect with her work—ecology, spiritually, magically, feminist, mythology, humour, etc. – it always amazes me how so many doors open into her work … artists, writers, actors, dramatists, all manner of creative people find something to connect with and explore.

4.   **Would you describe your practice as feminist in any way? What does this word mean to you?**

Susan L. Aberth: My practice is very much informed by feminism and in 2021 it means more to me than ever. My teaching, research, and writing are all seen through a feminist lens and my students are more engaged with it than ever before—in terms of methodology, theory, and most of all activism. It makes me very happy that after a decade or more of neglect, young men and women are once again motivated by issues of gender equity, even if that interest often means dismantling all gender categories.

Filmmaking

1.   **What is your creative practice, and can you explain how Leonora Carrington has become manifest within it?**

Joanna Lipper: I am a filmmaker, photographer, and writer in the early stages of developing a narrative feature film interweaving Leonora

Carrington's memories of her life with images from another dimension—the realm of her imagination. Made with the collaboration of the Leonora Carrington Estate and biographer Joanna Moorhead (*The Surreal Life of Leonora Carrington*), this film has access to invaluable source materials including Leonora Carrington's paintings, short stories, and her memoir, *Down Below*. Innovative visual effects will be used to bring to life Carrington's self-portraits and shape-shifting avatars in human, animal, bird, insect, goddess, and hybrid creature forms.

2. **What specifically about Carrington and/or her work interests you? Which of her artworks and/or writings are you particularly drawn to? When did you first become interested in her?**

Joanna Lipper: I first encountered Carrington's work when I was an undergraduate at Harvard, enrolled in a course on Surrealism and the Avant-Garde. I am drawn into Carrington's paintings by sensations of vertical and horizontal movement evoked through images of ladders, trapdoors, staircases, boats, bicycles, carriages, horses, and chariots. Images etched in my mind include: *The House Opposite* (1945) (Figure 8), *Inn of The Dawn Horse* (1937), *Chiki Ton Pays* (1944), and *Amor Che Move il Sole et l'altre Stelle* (1946). For me, these paintings are celebrations of freedom and forward movement in the life cycle.

In contrast to this kinetic momentum, *Green Tea* (1942) (Figure 6) evokes the sensation of entrapment that Leonora carried with her from her experience being drugged and incarcerated against her will at an asylum in Spain, during World War II. Life and death, motion and stasis, violence and peacefulness, truth and deception, beauty and ugliness, sanity and psychosis, entrapment and liberation, defeat and resilience, petrification and transcendence, seduction and repellence, and the conscious and unconscious—all these dualities coexist within the paintings *Green Tea* and *Down Below* (1941). Similarly, they inform my quest to evoke and distil Carrington's essence cinematically on screen. The stories behind *Green Tea* and *Down Below* are just a few of the many examples of the layers of meaning within Leonora Carrington's paintings and their compelling connections to the fascinating story of her life, defined by her relentless quest for integrity and self-preservation.

Carrington lost the original manuscript of her memoir, *Down Below*. In Mexico City, in 1943, she was persuaded to dictate what she remembered of this lost memoir, with Dr. Pierre Mabille listening and his wife transcribing Carrington's words on an old typewriter. As a filmmaker I am separated from this moment in time by continents, an ocean, and nearly eight decades of history, yet while reading *Down Below*, I always have the sense that I am adjacent to Leonora Carrington—situated in the position of a companion trusted to listen, decipher, and assist in the reconstruction of her thoughts and memories in real time. This is the intimate perspective I intend to carry with me when I commence the process of directing the film.

3. Why is Carrington's legacy proving so productive a site for creative work today? She suddenly feels very relevant again. Why do you think this might be?

Joanna Lipper: In today's new world shaped by the pandemic, Black Lives Matter, and the #MeToo movement, Carrington's capacity to visualise change and represent transformation, adaptation, and progression towards new and alternative realities has proven to be vital and necessary. I believe that Carrington's legacy is a productive site for creative work because she always embraced uncertainty, daring to imagine both the unknown—and the unknowable. As scientists raced to discover and manufacture an effective vaccine to battle the Coronavirus, they became acutely aware of its shape-shifting capacity to mutate. Carrington's work is full of symbols of alchemy, eggs, cauldrons, and healing rituals that are relevant today as inspiration for reflection on the quest for a cure and the endless need for the hatching of new ideas, new solutions, and new perspectives in response to constant mutability.

4. Would you describe your practice as feminist in any way? What does this word mean to you?

Joanna Lipper: Leonora Carrington's painting *Kron Flower* (1987) features three elderly women in the foreground transfixed by an irrepressible bright red flower poking robustly through cracks in the pavement. This painting sums up how I feel as a feminist filmmaker in 2022. For me, the word "feminist" carries the weight of authenticity and integrity. My having a feminist vision entails producing and directing films that go deeper, wider, and further, taking risks and breaking through boundaries to expand the ways in which women's lives and legacies are portrayed on screen.

Choreography

1. What is your creative practice, and can you explain how Leonora Carrington has become manifest within it?

Michelle Man: As a choreographing dancer, facilitator, and pedagogue, Carrington's work has become increasingly more present in my practice, especially in terms of embracing playfulness as a creative tool and understanding how artistic energy can speak through different mediums. Coming closer to Carrington's work has allowed me to consolidate with greater conviction my fascination for dancing with cabbages and how that combines vegetable ecologies with feminist thought, and mysticism.

2. What specifically about Carrington and/or her work interests you? Which of her artworks and/or writings are you particularly drawn to? When did you first become interested in her?

Michelle Man: I first learnt of Leonora Carrington through the Mexican aerial circus artist Julia Sanchez, when we were working together in Madrid where I had been living since 1989. We were mutually shocked that I had not come across Carrington, who was a household name in Mexico, and this triggered my curiosity to find out more about "my lost" British surrealist.

With Carrington's work I experience an immediate visceral magnetism which allows me to believe that I recognise something familiar in the exquisitely strange fantastical worlds she paints and writes. The tender elegance she draws, combined with unapologetic and mischievousness gestures, become choreographic provocations that urge me to venture under the skin of her paint, and between the words on the page, to embody and give flight to the energies she conjures.

Of Carrington's work I have met in the flesh I am utterly mesmerised by *The Magical World of the Mayas* (1964); it combines secretive underground existences with cosmological wonder in a soul-seducing palette. My experience of this mural at the Tate, Liverpool was immersive; it was as if I was journeying this world from within the canvas.

And of her short stories the transgressive nature of 'As They Rode Along the Edge' is astonishing; each time I re-read the tale of Virginia Fur I am profoundly excited and disturbed into new ways of thinking the female-human-animal.

3. **Why is Carrington's legacy proving so productive a site for creative work today? She suddenly feels very relevant again. Why do you think this might be?**

Michelle Man: Carrington's work dialogues with living forms—animal, vegetable, bacterial, and other—all of which have received across her art a space of equal respect and consideration. She does so, combining ancient wisdom with sharp contemporaneity. In our age of climate emergency where crucial questions of how we co-habit the planet with these different life forms, Carrington's voice offers a catalyst for re-thinking and manifesting through art ways of caring and connecting to the living. In her adopted country of Mexico, Carrington would have been very aware of what has become identified as Southern Epistemologies—different ways of knowing the world that have traditionally suffered under Western political dominance. The embracing of diversity we can experience in Carrington's work creates a gateway for accessing wisdoms of marginalised, oppressed peoples, and their practices, thus opening a space to be more radical in our ecological thinking and actioning.

4. **Would you describe your practice as feminist in any way? What does this word mean to you?**

Michelle Man: In my choreographic and performance making processes, I bring to the creative working space what I would define as feminist sensibilities and qualities: use of language, questions around female positionality, and knowing through the female body. Feminist as a word for me is: defiance; questioning; a reminder that our worlds and the majority of our languages are constructed through patriarchal dominance; it is also a call for action and hope.

Literature

1. **What is your creative practice, and can you explain how Leonora Carrington has become manifest within it?**

Alyssa Harad: I'm a writer, currently at work on a novel inspired by Carrington's life, art, and times. However, this is not the first time I've written about Carrington. In a former life as a would-be academic, I wrote my MA thesis on her memoir, *Down Below*. (Specifically, I was interested in the ways it broke with expected trauma narratives.) The word "manifest" is interesting here—I do feel that Carrington manifests in my life periodically, almost always at moments of rebellion or resistance to a prescribed path.

Fernando A. Flores: I am a Mexican-American short-story writer and novelist who discovered Leonora's work around 2007, when her books were very hard to come by in central Texas, where I live. Leonora's work struck me even then as highly unconventional, challenging the dominating realist aesthetic of popular literary fiction, which encouraged me to be as weird as I felt like being in my own work.

Claire Dean: I'm a writer, primarily of short stories. I'm also a full-time academic, lecturing in creative writing and undertaking practice-as-research to explore the entanglement between writing practices, technologies, and the environment. My fiction is often inspired by fairy tales, folklore, non-human nature, and the post-industrial Lancashire landscape in which I live. In my stories, extraordinary things tend to happen in very mundane northern English settings. I'm always playing with wonder and trying to see how far I can push the fantastic in a story without the need to explain it. Explaining kills the magic but carrying readers with you when the setting is a contemporary one can be tricky. Leonora Carrington is an expert guide in how to do this. There are no explanations for the bizarre and wondrous in her artworks or her fiction. There's a boldness to Carrington's prose style—things are what they are. A reader must accept that or else accept that they are not the right reader for the story.

Carrington's work has directly inspired some of my own short fiction, in particular the short story 'Leonora, Fly!' in which I drew on Carrington's writing, artwork, and biographical details from her childhood to create a new fairy tale. I wanted to apply the methods of fairy-tale retelling to Carrington's *oeuvre* (Max Lüthi writes about there being an old Greek saying—the fairy tale has no landlord). Instead of drawing on traditional tales, I was borrowing from, and imagining with, materials found primarily in Carrington's work. Subsequently, I was inspired to explore her work through my practice-as-research to develop *A House Book*. This hybrid story object is simultaneously a book, map, and miniature house. The reader opens it up to find narrative elements that respond to their movements, the direction they're facing, and the level of light around them. Rather than a linear story, the book is an invitation to wonder and consider the narrative possibilities of domestic space.

Michaela Carter: I am a poet and a novelist. My novel is called *Leonora in the Morning Light*, and it is about Leonora Carrington, Max Ernst, and Peggy Guggenheim before and during World War Two, when their lives intertwined as they escaped Europe ahead of the Nazis.

2.   **What specifically about Carrington and/or her work interests you? Which of her artworks and/or writings are you particularly drawn to? When did you first become interested in her?**

Alyssa Harad: I discovered Carrington's work in 1993 when I picked up a copy of Whitney Chadwick's *Women Artists and the Surrealist Movement*. When I told a friend about the exciting new painter I had found she laughed and handed me her favorite novel, *The Hearing Trumpet*. I went on to read everything I could find by or about Carrington and wrote about *Down Below* for my MA thesis in 1997, in spite of the fact that no one in my department knew who she was.

Or maybe because of that fact. Carrington and her work always appear in my life at times of great change and resistance to the status quo, moments when I'm in transit from one identity to another. Call it synchronicity or haunting, whatever it is I've come to expect it, even to rely on it.

For years my access to Carrington's images was very limited. In 1996 I sent ten dollars in an envelope to the administrator of a Carrington fan email list and got a huge poster of *The Giantess*. It's hung opposite my bed ever since. I stared for years at reproductions of her self-portrait before seeing it in person. Now I can look at all of them online and have too many favorites, but a few that live permanently in my head include *Crookhey Hall*, *Bird Pong*, *The House Opposite*, and *I Took My Way Down …*, the little bronze *Barco con* Chango and *La Cuña*, the wooden boat/cradle Jose Horna and Carrington—both exiles who had crossed an ocean—made in anticipation of Norah Horna's birth.

Fernando A. Flores: I first heard of Leonora in an interview with the Chilean filmmaker Jodorowsky. I've come to admire the entire body of Leonora's work, and it's hard for me to separate her writing from her visual art. The sheer anarchy of *The Hearing Trumpet*, her novel, still resonates strongly with me, and this theme/style in her work still attracts me to her.

Claire Dean: I first came across Leonora's work in the incredible *Angels of Anarchy* exhibition curated by Patricia Allmer at Manchester City Art Gallery in 2009. It was astounding to discover there was this incredible artist born and brought up in Lancashire (where I am from), who I had never heard of before that exhibition. It feels a bit silly to say it as our lives are so incredibly different, but I also felt points of resonance in our Lancashire upbringings and the fact we both have two sons. Some time after that first encounter, a friend sent me a copy of the out-of-print Virago edition of her stories *The Seventh Horse and Other Tales* as a present and I was thrilled. There's no way I'd ever be able to buy any of her paintings to hang her worlds on my walls, but books can carry them into the house.

In terms of works I'm particularly drawn to, I think it's the works that emphasise the extraordinary in domestic settings that call to me most, from the forest in the attic in *The House Opposite* (Figure 8) to the New York houses that look as if they've issued from the Fire of London in the story 'White Rabbits.' I'm also really drawn to her works that centre older women. I love the way she made the imaginative leap to much older age in *The Hearing Trumpet* (and I'm also thinking of the painting *Kron Flower*). It feels like her work can be approached as a map to every stage of a woman's life. Nothing is linear in terms of its creation or our understanding of it but rather it's life as a space to be ranged around at will.

Michaela Carter: In 2013, when I was researching the surrealist artists for what I thought would be an entirely fictional novel set among them, with a young, fictional, female artist as its protagonist, I discovered Carrington. My husband and I were at the Tate Modern, and when we saw her piece in the surrealist section, we both fell in love. In the gift shop he bought Susan L. Aberth's book on Carrington, and I promptly stole it from him.

Reading Aberth's book, I knew right away that Carrington's was the story I needed to write. I was drawn especially to her individuation—how she became the artistic force she became—which I saw as beginning at the start of the Second World War, when she was 22 years old and her lover Max Ernst was imprisoned by the French government for being German.

The more I delved into Carrington's art and came to realise the magnitude of her genius, the more intimidated I became by the prospect of telling her story. But it wouldn't let me go. And, finally, my desire to know her—to understand her trials and the inner power that saw her through them—overpowered my fear of not doing her justice.

3. **Why is Carrington's legacy proving so productive a site for creative work today? She suddenly feels very relevant again. Why do you think this might be?**

Alyssa Harad: I have two answers to this. The slightly silly one is: Instagram Witches. I think we're living in a moment when glamour with a witchy edge is a desirable look for young feminists and no one does that better than the elegant young women and fierce old crones—note the striking lack of photos of these women in middle age—associated with surrealism. Carrington and her milieu have always mixed with the world of fashion, dance, and music (I think of Eileen Agar writing in her memoir about the women of surrealism in their Schiaparelli dresses, but also about Madonna stealing from Varo and Carrington's paintings) and their image worlds do well on the internet. I don't mean to dismiss this popularity as superficial. I see in it a hunger for the possibility of magical high femme rebellion and I too have that hunger.

My more serious answer is that Carrington knew what it was like to live through the end of the world—more than once. She helps us think about what it's like to be swallowed by history and spat back out again. She shows us how to resist the relentless presentism of catastrophe by pinning the deep structures of myth to the everyday. She teaches us that magic is a necessary grammar of trauma, and that allegory, oblique angles, and displacement can allow us to tell otherwise unbearable stories. She offers strategies for survival: jokes, persistence, a taste for blasphemy, a refusal to be defined by anyone, and plain stubbornness. Most of all, Carrington is a trickster, and I think we will all need to learn the trickster's ways if we are going to survive this particular bend of history.

Fernando A. Flores: People seem to be more open to new genres and literary styles, at least in the English-speaking world, which tends to stick to the conventions of the market. In the past, and even today, the artistic work of women was not taken as seriously as the work of men, so this recent shift in wanting to excavate the previous work of women artists that weren't given their due in their lifetimes perhaps has something to do with it.

Claire Dean: When I first read Carrington's essay 'What is a Woman?' I was full of despair at the fact she had written such an urgent and lucid call to action against the enslavement of the imagination and the destruction of the planet and organic life in 1970 and yet so little has changed since. In the essay she writes, "*I am* may have been a dishonest invention meaning multitude." This chimes with so much of the posthumanist writing of luminaries whose work I love such as Donna J. Haraway and Jane Bennett. Carrington's work is full of chimerical and boundary-blurring tendencies that can offer new ways of understanding the world. We so desperately need thinking like this when climate breakdown and ecocide are no longer a nightmarish "what if" narrative, but an inescapable part of everyday life. This makes Carrington's works rich sites for exploration and inspiration. They echo forwards in time and resonate strongly here and now.

Michaela Carter: In addition to being a brilliant artist, Carrington was her own woman. As she continued to make art into her nineties, she seemed undeterred by age. In a society that is ageist, especially when it comes to women, we need her now. 2020 has seen the anthropocentric world in a dizzying tailspin. I see Carrington and her work as an antidote. Multidimensional, alchemical, and powerful, her art celebrates the magical, divine feminine, as well as the Earth and the numerous creatures on it. I think we need to find new ways of seeing the role of humans in respect to nature, and her life and art can offer us inspiration.

4.   **Would you describe your practice as feminist in any way? What does this word mean to you?**

Alyssa Harad: Oh gosh, yes. I am an old-fashioned feminist who learned how to be one from writers like Adrienne Rich, Audre Lorde, and Cherríe Moraga, which is to say, for me feminism is less an identity and more a method of analysis and a politics, one that seeks the equality of women, the destruction of white supremacy and heteropatriarchy, and works simultaneously at a cultural, social, and economic level. I often feel very confused about how the word "feminist" is used in mainstream discourse but I've been encouraged lately by a rejection of the watered-down neoliberal, individualist go-girl version and a return to some of the writers I mentioned above along with a whole new slate of poets and critics.

Fernando A. Flores: I was raised along the South Texas/Mexico border, which is a highly conservative, patriarchal region, and, though my Mexican mother didn't have words like "feminism," this is the way she raised me. To be intersectional feminist in this world, whether you're an artist or not, is the only way forward. Though I would not necessarily describe my work as "feminist," there are definitely feminist themes throughout my body of work, and I am always trying to learn more and be better.

Claire Dean: Yes, absolutely. I was born in 1981 and thought I was growing up into a world where everyone was equal. I was in my late teens when my experiences began to teach me this was still very far from the case. The disillusionment was/is like an ongoing body blow, and I'm a cis white woman, so I have a ton of privilege compared to many people. I tend to write stories with women as protagonists and I am unapologetic about this focus. The cultural spotlight has been on men's stories and men's writing for far too long. I often write from aspects of my own situated experience, but I also try to research and imagine other women's experiences. Feminism is an ongoing practice for me, it means engaging in and educating myself every day. Striving to practice intersectional feminism feels vital, and I'm constantly engaging critically with what I read and see around me and with my own thoughts and assumptions.

I'd describe my practice and my work as feminist, but perhaps what I'd consider to be the most feminist act for me, and the one I have yet to be successful in, is to put my own practice first. I have the Mary Oliver poem 'The Journey' pinned above my desk, in which she notes it's only as you move away from the clamouring voices that you begin to hear your own, striding "deeper and deeper / into the world, / determined to do / the only thing you could do—determined to save / the only life you could save." It is too easy to let the needs of my children, students, and workplace come before my own desire and drive to make and create new work. As a lecturer, I think a lot about how we each develop our own creative practice and advise students to discover their own creative guides. I'm so grateful to have Leonora Carrington as one of mine. She inspires me to aim to be bolder than the constructs around me expect me to be.

Michaela Carter: I am a feminist through and through. I love what Carrington said in the commentary to her 1976 retrospective in New York City:"A woman should not have to demand Rights. The Rights were there from the beginning; they must be taken back again." She was an eco-feminist (which I also consider myself to be) and, as such, she believed in the rights of the Earth. She ends her commentary with the assertion that "[f]ootprints are face to face with the firmament." This is exactly how I feel, and she said it better than anyone.

Visual art

1. What is your creative practice, and can you explain how Leonora Carrington has become manifest within it?

   Lynn Hershman Leeson: I have a multi-dimensional practice consisting of visual art, photography, drawing, site-specific work, computer-based and net art including AI, writing, and film. I have always been fascinated with the multi dimensions that Carrington used in her work, both in writing, mask making, writing plays, and painting. This multi-disciplinarity was frowned on and "authorities" said it meant that the artist was not serious.

   Kim L. Pace: Ideas about transformation, and a playful undermining of rational methods of knowledge have driven my cosmology of human-animal/plant hybrids in sculpture, animation, and drawing for over 15 years. Carrington's singularity of vision and the work's richness in its own lore bewitches me.

Aleksandra Niemczyk: I am a painter and a filmmaker working with abstract forms and subjects reaching into a fantasy world rather than documenting reality. My films tend to turn into dreamlike stories, often with personalised symbols, metaphors, and inner logic left for interpretation. Since my roots are in Fine Art, visual narration dominates over a conventionally understood linear plot. Theme-wise, I am interested in paranormal events, and characters connected deeply with their inner world. Often my work researches and illustrates visions, dreams, and a lucid state of mind. I am interested in the ways the human mind deals with traumas, hardships, mental conditions, transforming them into hallucinations that become true for the "beholder." My latest project, *The Siren's Scream*, reaches into the dreamy images of Carrington to explore a world built from memories and traumas. It's a continuation of my interests from previous projects, where paranormal events are a part of reality. My previous project, *Baba Vanga*, is a portrait of a Balkan visionary, who predicts the future and preaches it with conviction. Her words can be interpreted as facts or treated as interesting poetry. They are surreal but rooted in the reality she was living in. This experience advanced my interest in surrealism and the way it uses dreams. For *The Siren's Scream*, I decided to develop this further. Instead of portraying the visionary, I made an attempt to create a world of visions inspired by my research. I didn't want to be literal and adapt the images as they are, but rather research Carrington's work as a whole and let it become an inspiration for the film I was creating.

Elizabeth Cheche: My creative process begins with long morning walks through the forest with my dogs. In this quietness I come up with new ideas, solve creative problems, and visualise imagery from some of my favourite surrealists. Carrington's painting *Syssigy* (1957) always stirs my creative juices.

Anita Elias: I work with mixed media, including acrylics, ink, and resin, among others. Carrington was a strong presence since my childhood and growing up with her paintings made her subjects familiar and comforting to me. Her characters come to life through my work in subtle ways, emerging at will. A face emerges and suddenly the fantastic body follows. It's almost an automatic painting of abstract forms into humanoid figures.

2. **What specifically about Carrington and/or her work interests you? Which of her artworks and/or writings are you particularly drawn to? When did you first become interested in her?**

Lynn Hershman Leeson: I was quite moved by the book *Down Below* and wanted to make the film on it as early as 1994. I became aware of her in the early 1980s. I bought one of her drawings. It took two years to pay it off in small monthly payments, but having a drawing was important as an inspiration for creative sustainability and inspiration.[7]

Kim L. Pace: When studying Fine Art in the early 90s, there were two publications about women and surrealism (by Mary Ann Caws and Whitney Chadwick) that became important discoveries for me. These books introduced me to the context of Carrington's work—events in her life, her ideas and references—that brought her work alive. I'm particularly struck by her drawings through which we glimpse *Down Below*.

Aleksandra Niemczyk: I am very interested in her attitude towards illustrating, through symbols, different aspects of being a woman. From dreamy to harsh, based on her own experience, she reflected on the limitations of society, the role of the woman, the sexuality, the fertility, the motherhood, the ageing, many issues that are still relevant to a contemporary world and myself. I don't have a specific artwork that I could point out. I am drawn to them as a body of work manifesting a bigger picture, a complex meaning. When I study Carrington's paintings, I see not only what's "given" but also a movement, the sound, the dialogue between the creatures. So, each painting becomes a scene in my imagination, and another painting can become a continuity of previous one. Looking at them as a whole made me see the thick line connecting them into a slight narrative story. It's strictly personal and based only on my own perception, but it was strong enough to fertilise my mind. I knew Carrington's paintings for a long time but didn't turn to them as a subject of research before my art practice of analysing dreams and visions led my interest that way.

Elizabeth Cheche: a) I love Leonora's paintings and fiction in equal measures, she really walked her own path! b) I feel Leonora's painting *The Meal of Lord Candlestick* (1938) (Figure 24) exemplifies her unorthodox style, and true spirit. c) I first discovered Leonora when my boyfriend bought me the book *Leonora Carrington: Surrealism, Alchemy and Art* by Susan L. Aberth, as a gift. Her work opened me up to new possibilities, and I treasure it!

Anita Elias: I saw her work for the first time when I was six years old in a museum in Mexico City. Growing up in the 60s in Mexico meant being immersed in surrealist art and magic realism. Her scenes spoke of magical stories, dreamlike scenes, and gentle, mysterious beasts. I absolutely love paintings such as *And Then We Saw the Daughter of the Minotaur* (Figure 12). As with Remedios Varo, I find the narrative fascinating full of questions and surprises. The ethereal nature speaks of something not of this world, which I adore. Actually, I yearn to be able to live in a world like hers.

3. Why is Carrington's legacy proving so productive a site for creative work today? She suddenly feels very relevant again. Why do you think this might be?

Lynn Hershman Leeson: She was a strong person and continued to work despite oppression and repression. She also suffered the consequences of being outspoken and independent, both from her family and the art world in general. She was not taken seriously till recently and her work was inaccessible. Women need models of resistance which she provided. There are very few. It makes sense that she would be lauded after age 70 in Mexico, in a way that then had repercussions. I met Carrington mid-1980 and asked her if she felt disappointed to be overlooked historically, and she said the only thing that was important was continuing to do her work.

Kim L. Pace: Currently, there's a re-evaluation of many women artists' contribution to the canon, including Carrington's legacy. Her vision was an expression of interiority that braided ancient thought with immense creativity; her exploration of other realities and alternative worlds is once again timely, as we explore our relations—past and potential—with the earth and nature; particularly through spaces in which the rules of the world no longer apply.

Aleksandra Niemczyk: Her works offer reflections over universal issues, archetypes, and human instincts and conditions, society and its mechanisms, that regardless of the changing world, technology and development of civilisation, stay rooted in what is fundamentally the human mind. I don't think she suddenly feels very relevant now. I think her works were relevant through the years, since creation. But the common knowledge of her existence, her works, were not acknowledged widely by art historians and art critics, museums and such until recent years. Female artists in general, and surrealist female painters as well, were not as widely promoted as their male colleagues. Luckily, slowly we see the rise of critical and artistic works putting a spotlight on and reclaiming the status and importance of artists such as Carrington, allowing many to discover how relevant she was and is.

Elizabeth Cheche: I feel Carrington's legacy is proving so productive because she was such a nonconformist in her life and work, and this appeals to most creatives, we tend to walk a different path than most folks. I also believe that the relevancy of Leonora now, has to do with our much-needed shift in consciousness regarding the importance of women in all endeavours, and of course she was extremely talented, in both her writing and painting.

Anita Elias: It's the goddess quality of women. Divinity and creative forces are always relevant as in the energy of life force. When the spirit speaks through the art of women, we experience the divinity.

4. **Would you describe your practice as feminist in any way? What does this word mean to you?**

Lynn Hershman Leeson: Of course. Feminism to me means EQUALITY. It is a matter of Civil Rights. In fact, I made a film about it called *Women Art Revolution.*

Kim L. Pace: I've always considered myself and my practice as feminist. On my studio wall, I have a Jeanette Winterson quote about writing, which for me is interchangeable with all forms of creative practice and that embodies my thoughts on being a woman artist in 2021: "I was trying to get away from the received idea that women always (write) about 'experience'—the compass of what they know— while men (write) wide and bold; the big canvas, the experiment with form ... In any case, why could there not be experience and experiment?"

Aleksandra Niemczyk: In the sense of subjects and characters, my films are often focusing on the perspective of a female, illustrating the female condition or bringing the subject of an unusual female character or story to the surface. Perhaps that's why many of my films, by their theme, touch feminism. It comes as a natural outcome of my attitude to life, interests, and opinions, not as a calculated mission. I grew up in a family where the female-male dynamics, roles, economy, careers, were very equal, but I see how the world those days—instead of cultivating those values and strengthening balance between the genders even further—is developing tendencies towards a conservative patriarchy and the limitation of women's rights and status. It's worrisome that norms that I grew up with and took for granted are now in jeopardy and regression in many places in the world. At the moment I see, more and more, a need to cultivate, research, and bring to public awareness, strong female role models and to manifest the values of feminism through my choices and my work.

Elizabeth Cheche: I've always embraced the idea and lifestyle of individualism, perhaps thanks to my intellectual parents allowing me to be open-minded; growing up this way never occurred to me to be a feminist trait, but now that's how I see it. I have a really hard time with conventional wisdom or anyone trying to control my path, this to me is true feminism.

Anita Elias: Feminism today, to me, goes back to roots of self within the creation as a creator of life myself. Creating life translates to creating art, creating food, educating, planting, nurturing, all in the path back to source. Goddess is a feminist without the need to proclaim it in a cardboard sign. Hence my work represents femininity as a guiding feminist force. To enlighten, to conceive and grow.

Performance

1. **What is your creative practice, and can you explain how Leonora Carrington has become manifest within it?**

   Lynn Lu: My multidisciplinary practice revolves around participation and collaboration, context and site specificity, and the poetics of absurdity.

   Katharina Ludwig: My practice revolves around (narrative) holes and wounds. It is therefore entangled with the unsayable-ness and unspeakable-ness of trauma and a subsequent but seemingly counter-intuitive eloquence and articulation surrounding it. My current research in the framework of the Art Research programme at Goldsmiths is concerned with narrative holes in women*'s writing and the temporalities of the "wounded text." I try to activate textual holes as a subversive feminist practice of resistance with insurrectional potential that treats the textual wound as a political and writerly strategy in opposition to authoritarian systems. My art practice moved into a mostly text-based direction, which is perforated and truncated by objects (props that act as seemingly ritualistic objects), costumes, performances, and occasional installations.

   Carrington's surrealism, especially her engagement with the unconscious, the unknown, is also relevant for my work/practice, which deals with the unconscious and the Lacanian Real through psychoanalysis. I see the wounds or holes as connecting points between reality and the real, between the conscious and the unconscious. Through these portals I try to channel voices into a collective polyvocality. The character K (as in the phonetic sound of the letter K or C) appears in my written thesis, not as a classic alter-ego, but rather as an amalgamation of voices of different characters, whose names begin respectively with the letter K or C, amongst them Carrington and other radical women* who too often were ignored or occupied only marginalised roles in the (art) historical male canon. Hence Carrington's voice seeps through holes into my text, commenting, conversing, and channelling the unknown/unsayable.

2. **What specifically about Carrington and/or her work interests you? Which of her artworks and/or writings are you particularly drawn to? When did you first become interested in her?**

   Lynn Lu: I love *The Hearing Trumpet*—the marvellous and hilarious old women I aspire to be like, and Carrington's merciless parody of Gurdjieff whom I once greatly admired. I also love her *Portrait of Max Ernst* whose luxuriantly furred fishtailed garb perfectly befits the borderline paedophilic philanderer he was.

   Katharina Ludwig: There were all these men. These men painted women*. Men masters painting mothers, muses, maids. Through their gaze. These women* didn't look or feel like women* (I use this word in the broadest sense possible here), their representation appeared flawed to me. There were books on fairy tales, there were the legends from the area I grew up in, there were my own dreams and things I saw in the darkness. The women* who appeared there didn't match the women* in the paintings of the "masters," didn't match the men's representations of mothers, maids and muses. Yet, next to these men of surrealism there was Meret (Oppenheim)—her fur cup, which I felt drawn to, but how delighted I was when I discovered that there also was Virginia Fur (a character from Carrington's short story 'As They Rode Along The Edge'). In Carrington's stories I found the women* and creatures I was missing. These were the ones that felt strangely familiar in the strange-ness. And so, I entered Carrington's *oeuvre* through her texts, her snarky humour and her un-adapted characters. When I then encountered her paintings, I saw the same characters brought from dreams, nightmares, the unconscious directly onto the canvas. The canvas appeared as a window/opening into a world that usually constitutes the underbelly of reality and hence feels much closer to the Real.

In my own research I continued to work with Carrington's stories and texts. Next to some of her short stories the book *Down Below* provides an excellent example of women*'s writing, trauma literature and hole-y/wounded writing. While we have to be careful not to equate holey writing and the wounded text as symptoms of traumatic experiences and marginalisation, and through this romanticise and idolise serious socio-historical and political impacts and health conditions that negatively affect a person's life, I still believe that texts like *Down Below* also offer a glimpse into not treating the hole as a lack but rather as a portal and hence as a site of political/writerly/personal resistance.

3. **Why is Carrington's legacy proving so productive a site for creative work today? She suddenly feels very relevant again. Why do you think this might be?**

Lynn Lu: The perverse changeling boldly presages the rebellious alchemist.

Katharina Ludwig: I can only speculate on this, but I do believe that during the last couple of years the focus of the art world finally shifted (ever so slightly) to other histories that run beyond the hegemonic canon of white western patriarchy. Consequently, institutional and public interest grew toward the work of women* artists and POC artists. In addition, there seems to be a revived interested in religion(s) and spirituality and a resurrection of the occult (unfortunately not only from the political left …). These are all themes that are quite present in Leonora Carrington's work, that translate well into the present time.

Her work in a male-dominated field (the typical boys' club still present today in the arts), together with the refusal of the role of the muse, her activism with Mexico's Women's Liberation movement show a very distinctive and engaged feminism that probably also resonates with the struggles of many women* (artists) today.

4. **Would you describe your practice as feminist in any way? What does this word mean to you?**

Lynn Lu: Prior to becoming a mother in 2013, I did not actually identify as particularly female (due to Buddhist training) hence did not address gender in particular even though much of my work was autobiographical. Then because my experience of motherhood has been unusually harrowing, I made a series of works that specifically addressed the maternal. And in 2018, I made *Haumapuhia Rising*, which was my first consciously feminist work—made as the mother of a daughter.

To be a feminist in 2020 is to know that we stand on the shoulders of Mary Wollstonecraft, Emmeline Pankhurst, Sojourner Truth, Simone de Beauvoir, Rosa Parks, et al. And while we have come a long way (#MeToo, #TimesUp), equality has yet to be achieved: something abundantly clear in terms of how becoming a parent still generally all but decimates the mother's career while making not so much as a dent on the father's career. And here in Asia, mothers' careers are safeguarded by routinely farming out our children to women who are less privileged—who then are unable to adequately nurture their own children which perpetuates their poverty.

Katharina Ludwig: I couldn't imagine my practice without it being feminist, by which I mean that it is only feminist if it also critically interrogates gender, race, class, and privilege of any sort. If it is not immediately tied into action and practice the word means nothing to me, but if it does it means everything.

Theatre

1. **What is your creative practice, and can you explain how Leonora Carrington has become manifest within it?**

Stacy Klein: I founded Double Edge in 1982 based on the principle of the actor's autonomy in performance creation and a training practice which reflected the growth of the total actor. (Originally sourced in my mentor Rena Mirecka's Teatr Laboratorium plastics/physical, psycho physical, metaphor.) This practice is the basis of long-term ensemble work which now takes place at our farm centre in western Massachusetts and includes performance creation of both indoor performance and outdoor spectacle. The work meets visceral training, source work with image, large objects, vocal and instrumental music, metaphor, and text. In the cycles DE has created, visual artists are used both as source material and inspiration for story and design. This includes Bruno Schulz, in the *Republic of Dreams*, part of the *Garden Cycle*; the *Chagall Cycle*, including *Shahrazad*, *Odyssey*, and the *Grand Parade* (all based on his paintings, with the *Grand Parade* also inspired by his long life throughout the twentieth century), and now the work of Carrington. Finding Leonora has been, for me, a meeting with a visual artist version of my own imagination, a mirror into my art and vision, a reflection, and a guide. Her way of seeing multiple realms and realities together in one world speaks to me in a singular way.

Eldarin Yeong: I am a theatre maker and cross-disciplinary artist. In 2017, I watched a documentary on Carrington. I was shocked to learn that her parents were instrumental in her imprisonment in Spain. It prompted me to research coercive control and honour-based violence, and I later made a performance art responding to it.

Alison Duddle: My work is typically made for performance, so as a director I weave together narratives with puppets, masks, and, more recently, animation. The materials I am repeatedly drawn to are clay, paper, and wood—but the scale and context of the work I am making often determines the materials used.

2. **What specifically about Carrington and/or her work interests you? Which of her artworks and/or writings are you particularly drawn to? When did you first become interested in her?**

Stacy Klein: *The Stone Door* is one of the most meaningful books I have ever read, bringing story into a Kabbalistic vision and undertaking of the spirit. I read three sentences at a time (just like I read the ZOHAR). The words "let me in" still resonate. *Down Below* is profound and honest in a way that I don't normally find, particularly as a woman. The transforming of rape and pain into art, without glamour and without burying is courageous. *The Hearing Trumpet* is wonderful in its characterisation of age, older women. I could go on … And about paintings, there are few that I don't find compelling at the very least. We have a joke that each time we look at Leonora's work (as we did just now in the MARCO Museum) we have new favourites. *Gibbet Birds*, *The House Opposite*, her Kabbalistic work, her sculptures, *Nunscape*, parts of *St Anthony* … Again the way in which animals come alive and dominate (as if we humans aren't always the centre of the universe), her melding of the spiritual with the ordinary, her sense of humour, the water, the fire, the ruins …

Eldarin Yeong: I first came across Carrington's work when I visited the Tate years ago. Her art and stories are very complementary to each other, both fantastical, childlike, and disturbing to the psyche. 'The Oval Lady' is my favourite. For me, her work is uniquely powerful, because not only she depicted extreme human conditions, she lived through them.

Alison Duddle: In addition to being inspired by the painting, I have returned repeatedly to the painting, *The Giantess*, to her sculpture, and to the short stories, which have a wonderful playfulness about them.

3. **Why is Carrington's legacy proving so productive a site for creative work today? She suddenly feels very relevant again. Why do you think this might be?**

Stacy Klein: I think that Leonora had access to many cultures, understood deeply both the pain and the amazement of women, saw war and massacre but at the same time saw the possibilities of the imagination and upheld the environment with the value it should have for all of us. In this she was a prophet (and we still don't listen to our prophets even as we bring to extinction so many species and perhaps the earth itself). She was spiritual and magical and yet she recognised the daily as necessary to the spirit. There is everything in her work. I cannot tell you how many women have said to me, after seeing *La Maga y el Maestro*, that they have never seen a woman mentoring a man on stage, or a woman creating magic, or a woman of her magnitude. Today my doctor's secretary, who saw the show a couple months ago (and who I thought did not like it) went on and on telling me she had gone out afterwards and researched all of Leonora's paintings and she couldn't believe it and that there needs to be more works about women!

Eldarin Yeong: Leonora was born at a time when women were largely expected to follow gender roles. She broke away from traditions, became a feminist and part of the male-dominated surrealist movement. Her achievement was and still is something quite revolutionary.

Alison Duddle: They are mysterious, beautiful, and refuse to explain themselves. Also, her lifetime-long practice throughout all stages of her life is inspirational.

4. **Would you describe your practice as feminist in any way? What does this word mean to you?**

Stacy Klein: YES. Double Edge was founded as a feminist theatre in 1982—a response to the times. I realised in 2016 that little had changed, and I was quite shocked for a while. But now it seems FUNDAMENTAL to everything that women start leading the world, before we don't have one left to lead.

Eldarin Yeong: I don't consider myself a feminist, but I aspire to be an activist. I think being a feminist nowadays is to acknowledge the diversity among women and to understand the complexity of gender equality that can be contributed by race, class, and other factors.

Alison Duddle: My work often explores female narratives or re-imagines the female role in traditional narratives. I would say that my work is informed by my feminist principles, rather than that my practice is feminist.

Animation

1. **What is your creative practice, and can you explain how Leonora Carrington has become manifest within it?**

   Elizabeth Hobbs: I am an animated filmmaker, with a background in printmaking and artist's books. My films tend to be experimental in form and often inspired by real people or events. Previous subjects include the painter Oskar Kokoschka, the Serbian administrator Imperial Provisor Frombald, and the pilot Amy Johnson.

   Eleanor Mulhearn: I work with diverse combinations of materials (particularly clay), to create figurative and animated projected works, often at miniature scale. These pieces draw on animation craft practices, in investigation of animation's pre-filmic making histories and mythological roots. Carrington's work includes examples of beguiling collisions of scale, from the sub-miniature to the gigantic, these worlds sitting together without any need for explanation. Her strange worlds free the viewer from the everyday, metaphorically evoking potential new relationships and new interpretations for coexisting in the world. I am interested in how collaborating with my fellow artists on this project, each of us working at widely differing scales and employing diverse skills, is evolving to produce new imaginary spaces, increasingly through animation, performance, storytelling, and sound.

2. **What specifically about Carrington and/or her work interests you? Which of her artworks and/or writings are you particularly drawn to? When did you first become interested in her?**

   Elizabeth Hobbs: I read Carrington's short story 'The Debutante' in 2015 and approached the literary agent for the Estate for the rights to make an animation based on the story. I was happy to get permission to adapt the story and to be able to begin making the film in 2020 with the support of the BFI's Film Fund. All of her stories are extraordinary, but 'The Debutante' particularly resonates with my own life. Carrington's background isn't so different from my own; she and I both attended St Mary's Convent in Ascot and Chelsea School of Art. I also feel as if I escaped from the life that had been planned for me, so I particularly appreciate the wild, defiant way in which she chose to express her struggle for independence as a young woman.

   Eleanor Mulhearn: I first encountered Leonora through finding her novel, *The Hearing Trumpet*, in a library—which led me to her short stories and diverse artworks. Her painting, *The House Opposite*, which has inspired our project, suggests through its strange architecture, thresholds and movements between our world and others—compelling territory for animators. I am fascinated by Carrington's playful deployment of scale and symbols, both in her artworks and her short stories—which inspire reworkings of mythologies.

3. **Why is Carrington's legacy proving so productive a site for creative work today? She suddenly feels very relevant again. Why do you think this might be?**

Elizabeth Hobbs: Leonora Carrington's voice, her feminism and inclusivity, make her an artist who is very relevant in 2021. In Carrington's world there are no boundaries or hierarchies between humans and animals, and this is also a theme that particularly chimes with us now. I particularly appreciate her practical and unfussy approach to making work in many different mediums over the course of a long and rich life.

Eleanor Mulhearn: Carrington draws on ancient mythologies, also bringing together mythologies of different cultures, which expands the worlds she creates away from the dominant Western influence of her roots, enriching them with magical and potent possibility. I feel this connects with contemporary, multi-disciplinary focus on the search for forms of (re)enchantment.

4. **Would you describe your practice as feminist in any way? What does this word mean to you?**

Elizabeth Hobbs: I wouldn't describe my work as feminist, but as an educator and practitioner I try to be consciously inclusive and I aim to champion other women's work and practices.

Eleanor Mulhearn: My work explores female experience through what is perhaps a contradictory representation somewhere between containment and experimental creative expression. Further embedded within this, my practice often alludes to the responsibility, complexity and joy, both physical and emotional, of bringing up and educating children. I would say that this certainly connects with feminist thought and concerns. I would like to think that the future for children in the world could be taken far more seriously and responsibly than it is at present, with direct reference to climate change.

Textiles

1. **What is your creative practice, and can you explain how Leonora Carrington has become manifest within it?**

Alice Kettle: I work in stitched textiles, making narrative works that form a kind of social commentary. All use stitch as a descriptive medium and material to comment and revision stories and situations. They are located in the real and imaginary world at the same time, where in the work change and even resolution is indicated through the artwork and through the act of making. Carrington with her spaces that are betwixt and between offers a place for change to happen. So, whilst there is no direct reference in my work, she is present in all my work, acknowledging the dissolvable boundary between what is experience and what is experienced through the imaginary.

2. **What specifically about Carrington and/or her work interests you? Which of her artworks and/or writings are you particularly drawn to? When did you first become interested in her?**

   Alice Kettle: The process of making in her work is often ritualistic and draws upon domestic activities. The past, present, and future are interwoven as experiences that are in flux. Nothing is fixed, but objects and people are both archetypal and not human. All of Carrington's work is about self-revelation and self-creation, inner life, hope, desires, and dreams. The stories of ourselves can be reinvented and become real, so that we are reborn. Her work is both non-specific and detailed; it is full of contradictions and moves between the impossible and real. I find this epitomises my thinking. I used her a lot in my PhD, which was called *Creating a Space of Enchantment: Thread as a Narrator of the Feminine*. I referenced *The House Opposite* and it was this painting that I suggested should become the starting point for our work. The house is a stage for a magical world; the home is a site for creation, a liminal space of no time. Carrington uses tiny gestural obsessive marks, much like my stitches.

3. **Why is Carrington's legacy proving so productive a site for creative work today? She suddenly feels very relevant again. Why do you think this might be?**

   Alice Kettle: Because as women we reimagine ourselves as alternative beings, we have a chance to be other, with all the desires and longing to find multiple dimensions we can inhabit. We do not want or need to define ourselves as who we should be. We can become magical beasts. The between-ness is about moving between being everyday and being superhuman, we can be both; we do not need to abandon or explain any part of ourselves.

4. **Would you describe your practice as feminist in any way? What does this word mean to you?**

   Alice Kettle: Yes, I see feminism as being female with all the attributes that we possess. It is about being creatively female and negotiating who we are and want to be, which is not one thing but mutable and changeable. I am not sure I think feminism is even the right word. It is about self-revelation and self-discovery and opportunity to be oneself.

Music

1. **What is your creative practice, and can you explain how Leonora Carrington has become manifest within it?**

    Clara Engel: I sing and write songs, and I also make visual art. I think it's more accurate to call myself a poet and a musician rather than a singer-songwriter. There is a common assumption that a person singing and writing songs is approaching it from a confessional point of view, but that has never been the case with me. Songwriting can be as expansive and otherworldly as painting and film are allowed to be. "Songs For Leonora Carrington" came to be via Wist Rec, a record label that does a whole series in which each participating musician chooses another artist (working in any medium) and writes a series of pieces based on their life and/or work. I chose Carrington because I was intrigued by what I had seen of her work and I wanted to push myself by choosing someone who didn't work in the realm of music.

    Michael Begg: I am a composer, dealing mainly in exploratory/experimental music. In 2016, I was working on a commission with the Scottish National Galleries. Gráinne Rice, their adult education programme co-ordinator, brought Leonora to my attention. Upon following up the lead I learned that she had been briefly in the company of Lee Miller. Lee Miller is a towering figure for me—I have a large, framed image in the hall of Sherman's photograph of her sitting in Hitler's bathtub—and so anyone associated with her immediately arouses further interest from me.

    More recently I was offered a composer residency as part of the UK Mexico Seeing Hearing UK Mexico programme: a three-year collaboration made possible with the support of Anglo Arts, the cultural department of the Anglo Mexican Foundation A.C.; British Council Mexico, CMMAS (Centro Mexicano para la Música y las Artes Sonoras) and Cryptic Glasgow. I jumped at the chance to make Leonora Carrington the subject of the residency, so that is what I proposed as the subject, and the proposal was met positively—and with no small degree of excitement. What I did not expect was the impact she ultimately made on my work more generally. Whilst I came to quickly understand that she was never explicitly a surrealist—and had never read the manifesto, I felt it appropriate to explore surrealist methods in approaching the work.

    As a consequence, recent developments in how I approach not only my work, but my waking day have become somewhat influenced by her. I began to write again, which I hadn't done in many years, and I began to meditate, as a direct consequence of the inward reflective thinking provoked by the other activities; automatic writing, dream recording, and free-association exercises.

2. What specifically about Carrington and/or her work interests you? Which of her artworks and/or writings are you particularly drawn to? When did you first become interested in her?

Clara Engel: I originally found out about her through a friend who is a big Remedios Varo fan. Carrington's sculptures and her novel *The Hearing Trumpet* are what drew me in, and what have stayed with me the most. Her novel in particular was very important for me in creating the song series. I was struck by how she uses humour and surreal imagery to communicate much harder truths, like the way in which patriarchal power structures are destroying the earth. I also love how she creates worlds that are not anthropocentric and that blur the lines between humans and other creatures. She decentres humans and also highlights our absurdity in a way. Her sculpture *The Palmist*—the bird-headed woman with palms outstretched—I found that image extremely powerful and moving. I've only looked at photographs of her art, never seen it in person ... I would really like to see her sculptures in person one day.

Michael Begg: I think I first responded—albeit subconsciously—to the ease with which she throws multiple disparate influences together. She creates coherent worlds from completely unrelated elements and establishes an extraordinary balance in her paintings. By which I mean the horror never becomes horrific; the whimsical never becomes entirely frivolous. There is a great balancing act at play. This echoes my own work as I increasingly turn towards bringing unusual juxtapositions of sound, texture, and source together and work to create some form of unity in the assemblage of sounds. My research process tends to involve reading multiple texts at the one time and allowing them into freeplay in my mind to create resonant—though unfathomable—connections.

It is not surrealism, I don't think. It is—in her case—a coherent figurative art, just not one that can be read prosaically. The works are emotionally coherent in a way that surrealism is not. I believe those who say that she was never really a surrealist but recognised enough commonalities with them, and exploited, to an extent, the tag in order to assist her with gaining her own audience.

I am in the midst—now having recently returned from a two-week residency in Mexico developing soundscapes based on some of her work—of pulling that work together *properly*. It is called *Sonámbulo: un bebedero para pájaros compuesto por dientes para la novia del viento* (Sleepwalker: a birdbath composed of teeth for the bride of the wind). The title was derived as an exercise in surrealism—taking Ernst's nickname for her as a starting point before wandering off on an automatic writing spree. This phrase leapt out from the page. The actual works I sought to represent musically were *Plain Chant, Nine Nine Nine, Ab Eo Quod, Portrait of Max Ernst, Down Below,* and *Garden of Paracelsus.* Why these works? I had photocopied bits of paper with paintings, and work titles which I scattered about the garden. We keep hens, and I noted which names and images were first approached by the birds. I was very happy that *Ab Eo Quod* was selected by the birds, as that is a favourite image. But it is curious to note that a little after the exercise, National Galleries of Scotland announced that it had acquired the *Portrait of Max Ernst*. Surrealism does call into question the nature of coincidence and that would seem to chime here! Again, the Ernst portrait is a favourite—though it took a while for it to become so, and that was down to considering the narrative more deeply rather than the image. For me, it suggests a very honest appraisal of a woman being torn deeply by conflicting emotions. Here, as in many other works, she portrays herself as a horse. My sense is that part of herself is frozen directly on account of her attachment to Ernst. She has put a part of her soul on ice. Yet, there is another part (the lantern) that is (and this is very clever) simultaneously happy to be contained by the relationship, whilst providing a light for him. So very *female* to recognise multiple roles acting in parallel.

This is what I think I am getting at when I imply the unity or coherence achieved by disparate elements. That image is so tender, yet the tenderness is in the way that the different elements rub against each other, rather than a depiction of anything specifically tender. For me, musically, the potential to create resonance from two elements coming together is, I think, entirely the same approach.

3. **Why is Carrington's legacy proving so productive a site for creative work today? She suddenly feels very relevant again. Why do you think this might be?**

Clara Engel: My research was far from exhaustive, and there's a lot about her work and life that I'm not familiar with, but within the scope of what I absorbed, I would say that her work speaks to very timely issues: climate change is threatening life on earth, so many species are disappearing, bees are endangered. There is a pressing need for people to dream on a smaller and less industrial scale and use their intelligence in less greedy and destructive ways. In *The Hearing Trumpet* there is even a call to stop eating animals, which surprised and moved me (as an animal lover and long-time vegetarian) and seemed very ahead of its time.

Michael Begg: To be honest, I haven't personally been aware of other artists making much of her influence. I am certainly aware that she still has a commanding presence in Mexico. All I am really aware of here in the UK is that when she is mentioned it is in relation to her being a singular female—a role model, if you like—rather than an artist. A figure who battled through a male-dominated milieu, endured love, loss, mental breakdown, and a resurgence in exile—as an exotic *Mexican* artist. Curious—that idea of coming into one's own voice far away from one's origin reminds me of Paul Bowles—another significant influence on me. He also, of course, through his association with Gertrude Stein, shared some surrealist sensibilities, along with an appreciation for the importance of magic, allowing the subconscious free creative control of his hand, and a kinship with pagan esoterica over western Judeo-Christian culture. I wonder now what they might have made of each other?

4. **Would you describe your practice as feminist in any way? What does this word mean to you?**

Clara Engel: I can't imagine a world in which feminism is no longer relevant. Sexism and patriarchal value systems still thrive—they are just more insidious a lot of the time. Many female and non-binary artists are written out of art and music or made to be very marginal figures by the people narrating both current events and history. Most art movements and music scenes are boys' clubs. I've noticed that far more people are familiar with Ernst or with Dalí than with Carrington or Varo.

In terms of my own work and what feminism means to me, I feel like the question is so big I could expand it into an exploratory essay (but I won't). Gender is a spectrum, and I've always felt most at home in the grey area, which has often made me feel like a stranger in more black-and-white/this-or-that/man-or-woman worlds. So, from my personal perspective, simply by existing as an androgynous person in the world and putting my work out there in my own voice and on my own terms—there is something challenging about that in and of itself that owes a lot to feminism.

Michael Begg: I am somewhat nervous about even scratching the surface of this. "Should I cut the red wire or the black?" I would not consciously describe my work as feminist. If I am collaborating or taking my place in Clodagh Simonds's Fovea Hex project, the dynamic may change, but in my own work—I work alone and I am not consciously led by matters out of the immediate concerns of the work in hand. I am no longer operating within any kind of academic context and so no longer feel conscious of working within any framework, whether it be feminist, Marxist, or anything else. I am entirely at liberty to follow my own train of thought.

However, the work, whatever I do, arises from a composer who acknowledges and respects the equality of male and female *energy* and the absolute requirement for equality among any coupling or grouping of people. Leonora, I find fascinating in this respect, though I am not entirely sure how much support my own appraisal would gain right now. Yes, she is a hugely important figure in terms of promoting the vital role of the female in society, and it's plain to see—through her struggles to be recognised in and around an artistic movement (surrealism) dominated by males, often with questionable attitudes regarding females—how she fits well into the current climate of challenge, overthrow and revolt. But, intuitively, I simply don't think that she would be in support of the present tone and texture of the activity.

My understanding is that her appreciation for the female role in society began to truly blossom after becoming a mother. There was already the influence of alchemy, and pre-Christian/pagan mythologies with the consequent appreciation for the role of the female in those cultures informing her work, but after motherhood it seems to me, and the sudden urgency of having to personally care and provide meant that these elements began to forge as a coherent vision of how her present linked to the deep, deep past, and how her findings informed her vision more broadly.

Curation

1. **What is your creative practice, and can you explain how Leonora Carrington has become manifest within it?**

Wendi Norris: I am a gallerist. I represent a roster of critically acclaimed modern and contemporary artists for whom my gallery curates and produces exhibitions, publishes books, facilitates museum exhibitions, and cultivates market support. I have worked directly with Carrington and her work since 2002.

Viktor Wynd: My practice is multifaceted. Sometimes I build semi-fictional, semi-autobiographical museums filled with objects of wonder, some collected, some created, bound together by little labels where I tell my stories. I retell old fairy and folk tales, I draw, and I am currently creating a 'Garden of Earthly Delights' out of an enormous array of strange little creatures I am making in bronze and porcelain. I get spurred on and inspired by all sorts of things. Two years ago when I had a vision of my 'Garden of Earthly Delights,' I definitely thought back to the sculpture I saw Carrington working on when I visited her all those years ago, but I also thought of Brueghel and the strange creatures I seemed to see out of the corners of my eyes as I wondered the forest at night.

Cecilia Alemani: I've always been interested in intertwining visual art and literature, and Carrington is a perfect example of an artist who was moving fluidly between the two fields, hybridising both mediums.

Jenna C. Ashton: My work, for the majority, is a form of feminist social practice, focusing on people and social and ecological justice issues. My work combines different methods of research and storytelling, from curation and installation, performance, writing, archiving, and collecting, etc. No project is ever the same. I was invited into the House of Opposites project due to my previous PhD work on childhood and contemporary art (and domestic spaces, and object surrogates), work on Angela Carter, and other projects around women and girlhood.

Carrington's work is rich with the themes and issues I'm concerned about but communicated through surrealist forms. I was interested in how to connect the very real everyday conversations and experiences of domestic space, violence and oppression, and women's relationships, through a form of surrealist feminist storytelling. I want to experiment with that. I've been photographing around the house, thinking about how we occupy and live in/with space: corners, walls, floors, etc. My primary work in the project is writing in response to the visual works being developed by Alice, Alison, and Eleanor; and my writing feeds back into their practice, as do our collective conversations around the installation as a whole.

Helen Nisbet: I'm a curator and have a degree in History of Art; I studied in a time and place when women were scarcely mentioned. When I discovered Carrington I was hooked, but she was so often derided and diminished in order for us to focus on the charismatic and revered men of the movement. The feeling I had then, of frustration and feeling let down – being determined to challenge accepted patriarchal structures stayed with me. I'm in a very different world now, but when I began working as Curatorial Fellow at Cubitt in London in early 2017, I kept coming back to Carrington—to how important she is, that she has still not achieved the status she deserves. She is a part of Art History and yet she is so close to us—her ideas, the people she touched. I was fretting about how my programme might unfold and how to present Carrington in a small contemporary gallery when things fell into place—2017 was the centenary of her birth and I found out that the feminist publishers Silver Press were launching a compilation of her short stories. I worked with the women-led architecture practice vPPR to design a space that held both her drawings and a seated area, bathed in purple light, where audiences could listen to her stories, read by folk including artists, participants in Cubitt's Education programme, and writers.

2. **What specifically about Carrington and/or her work interests you? Which of her artworks and/or writings are you particularly drawn to? When did you first become interested in her?**

Wendi Norris: I read Whitney Chadwick's *Women Artists and the Surrealist Movement* in 2002 and was subsequently introduced to Leonora by Whitney and Susan L. Aberth. I was drawn to Carrington's memoir, *Down Below*, which provided a lens through which I began to appreciate the depth of her work and mastery in its execution. I started collecting Leonora's work soon thereafter and my first acquisitions, *Le Bon Roi Dagobert*, *Bird Bath*, and two small compositionally intriguing gouaches from 1942/43 remain among my favourites today.

Viktor Wynd: In some ways all my creative practice is influenced by her work. It was reading *The Seventh Horse and Other Tales* as a teenager that reopened my eyes to the world of wonder and magic, and I return to them, and *Notes From Down Below*, again and again. I live surrounded by her work, and it is something I go back to again and again. I currently have some drawings on my bedroom wall that she made when she was in the hospital in Santander, one in particular, half horse, half woman, but then I also love the mischievous sense of humour she sometimes has—in my loo hang three works by her depicting badgers conducting séances, somehow the fact that there are not one but three of these makes me laugh and gives me pleasure.

Cecilia Alemani: I love her short stories, and I remember reading 'The Debutante,' and think that she must have had a quite incredible life herself! And while I absolutely love her paintings, I am very drawn by her writings, like *Down Below*, or even *The Milk of Dreams*, which I found so incredibly profound and personal and evocative. And a bit creepy too.

Jenna C. Ashton: Although I knew of Carrington's work prior to our project, I had never fully researched her work. I had never read any of her stories—so that has been exciting to dive into. It has been fascinating to read about her collaborations with Remedios Varo and Kati Horna—so that's a more intangible interest for me: women's creative relationships. I've been thinking a lot about that through this work: how collaborations evolve, the points of exchange with other women artists. Carrington's imagined human-to-animal relationships are fascinating as well—and really wonderful for visualising an eco-feminist discourse (such as Haraway), which decentres the human Anthropocene, towards more entangled relationships between humans and nature.

Helen Nisbet: It's hard to know where to begin. I feel about her like I do about important friendships—excited at the sound of her name. She has a delicacy of touch, a sharp humour that cuts through the pain she suffered in her life, and most importantly, her work—writing and art—is incredible, imaginative, raw, and brave. I love her. She is connected to the surrealist movement but feels like a contemporary artist to me. I love *The Hearing Trumpet*, I had a beautiful first edition of the publication in the show. I'm also partial to 'The Sand Camel,' which was read in my exhibition by my cousin Kristian, recorded by BBC Radio Orkney. I adore her sculpture and painting *How Doth the Little Crocodile*. Female friendship, particularly in old age, is an important feature in her work (and indeed life), so I'm partial to her painting *The Old Maids*.

3. **Why is Carrington's legacy proving so productive a site for creative work today? She suddenly feels very relevant again. Why do you think this might be?**

Wendi Norris: Carrington's work is timeless, weaving in cross-cultural histories, a broad base of religious and occult mythologies and symbols along with a touch of the autobiographical or political. Her work offers an expansive historical and worldview, each of which help us to better comprehend the chaos of today's world.

Viktor Wynd: Her work has been speaking to me, or rather I should say I have been listening to it for almost thirty years. But perhaps it is because she was never a "contemporary" or "fashionable" artist so her work is outside of time and place—which is her greatness. At Dulwich recently in an exhibition on British Surrealism they hung two of her paintings in a room full of old masters, and they sang and held their place; very few other pictures in the show could have done that.

Cecilia Alemani: Part of it is the tendency to "rediscover" forgotten talents like hers. Part of it is that through her life and work she managed to be independent, to shape her own voice, and to not be afraid of portraying a world full of hybridity and transformation, concepts that are extremely timely right now.

Jenna C. Ashton: The themes of women, space, freedoms, oppressions, sexuality, relationships: these ideas are always relevant. Her surrealist forms and mythology are timeless. I think living artists are also kicking back against a certain "contemporary art" aesthetic snobbery that has shown disdain for the sensuous, colourful, intricate and detailed, figurative. I'm keen to connect (reclaim) this type of work for a UK social practice, which sometimes is dominated by an anti-art or anti-beauty discourse—as if socially conscious work can't also be beautiful, pleasurable, playful, evidencing technique, etc.

Helen Nisbet: I think a lot of it is down to the fact that she was never properly appreciated in this country in her lifetime. While artists like Ernst, Dalí, and Breton were ushered into the canon with speed, hyperbole, and reverence, Carrington has not had that honour. Her work and reputation were also damaged by tastemakers of the time, including Peggy Guggenheim, who referred to her mostly via her "madness" and "beauty." As we look to redress and reimagine a male dominated art history, it only makes sense for artists like Carrington to inspire us afresh. And as I said in the previous question, I think of Carrington as a contemporary artist—her concerns, ideas, and multidisciplinary practice. She has so much influence on artists making work today.

4. Would you describe your practice as feminist in any way? What does this word mean to you?

Wendi Norris: If a "feminist practice" is one that advances certain artists and engages with certain thematics based primarily on gender, anatomy, or sexuality—then no. If a "feminist practice" is one that:

a) recognises that women have unique histories, narratives, and visions that arise from their biological and cultural status as women and which have for the most part been excluded from the history of art (to the detriment of both art and women)
b) seeks to reinscribe that history/narrative/vision within contemporary art as a means to broaden the quality, reach, and transformative capacities of art for all human beings, including women but regardless of gender, sex, or anatomy
c) is accompanied by an understanding that
     (c.1) the art comes first and
     (c.2) the status of victimisation and exclusion do not confer excellence or lend value to the creations of the victim or the excluded, simply by virtue of her being victimised or excluded—then yes.

Viktor Wynd: I have always been drawn to the work of the surrealists and dadaists—but many of the most interesting ones did not like being buttonholed as "surrealists," or were not even involved in the movement. Leonora Carrington for example is often described as a surrealist, and her work is as good as surrealism gets, but I think it goes beyond that, besides in a creative career spanning some 70 years her formal involvement with the surrealists was only very marginal for a handful of years and her work hangs just as happily, if not more so, next to the Florentine Masters such as Uccello who were probably just as important an influence on her work as Dalí or André Breton.

Cecilia Alemani: I think the term has become quite loaded and charged these days. I prefer to say that through my curatorial practice I support women artists and writers, and that I try to create a space for helpful conversations about themes of gender and identity.

Jenna C. Ashton: Feminism is a social justice movement that aims to end sexism, sexist exploitation, and oppression—and to change society for the better, for all. For me, that's the real meaning of feminism (not tea-towel quotes of feminism). This is a consistent focus and impetus of my work and working through creative practice to find new models of living and thinking. Climate and land justice, and racial justice, is core to this; so this is increasingly the focus of my work. I find other politically and socially vibrant, and diverse, women artists so wonderful to work with, for inspiration and a richness in conversations. I see my engagement with Carrington's work—and collaborating with Eleanor, Alison, and Alice—as part of that.

Helen Nisbet: My work is absolutely feminist. More importantly, my work is intersectionally feminist—in my research, how I work with others and my personal life solidarity with all oppressed people is paramount.

Notes

1 Clarissa Pinkola Estés, *Women Who Run with the Wolves: Contacting the Power of the Wild Woman* (London: Random House, 1992), 12.
2 Roland Barthes, 'Death of the Author,' *Image, Music, Text*, trans. Stephen Heath (London: Fontana, 1977), 142–148.
3 Lucy Skaer, 'The Transcendence of the Image,' *Tate Etc.* 14 (Autumn 2008): www.tate.org.uk/context-comment/articles/transcendence-image (Accessed 11 March 2020).
4 Katharine Conley, 'Carrington's Kitchen,' *Papers of Surrealism*, 10 (2013): www.research.manchester.ac.uk/portal/files/63517394/surrealism_issue_10.pdf (Accessed 22 May 2020); Jonathan P. Eburne, 'Breton's Wall, Carrington's Kitchen: Surrealism and the Archive,' *Intermediality: History and Theory of the Arts, Literature and Technology*, 18 (Autumn 2011), 17–43: www.erudit.org/en/journals/im/1900-v1-n1-im087/1009072ar.pdf (Accessed 22 May 2020).
5 Jennifer Lee, 'Wonderland Wanderings: Samantha Sweeting,' *Filler* 2:4 (Winter 2011): http://fillermagazine.com/culture/gallery/though-the-looking-glass-samantha-sweeting (Accessed 24 November 2020).
6 China Miéville in conversation with Jordy Rosenberg, *Lannan Podcasts* (18 January 2017): https://podcast.lannan.org/2017/01/22/china-mieville-with-jordy-rosenberg-conversation-18-january-2017-video (Accessed 31 January 2022).
7 Lynn Hershman Leeson donated this Carrington drawing, *Woman on a Bicycle* (n.d.), to the Museum of Modern Art in New York: www.moma.org/collection/works/187412 (Accessed 12 May 2021).

References

Books and articles

Aberth, Susan L. *Leonora Carrington: Surrealism, Alchemy and Art*. Aldershot: Lund Humphries, 2004.

— 'The Alchemical Kitchen: At Home with Leonora Carrington' in *Nierika* volume 1, number 1 (June 2012): 7–15.

— '"An Allergy to Collaboration': The Early Formation of Leonora Carrington's Artistic Vision' in *Leonora Carrington and the International Avant-Garde*. Edited by J. P. Eburne and C. McAra, 20–38. Manchester: Manchester University Press, 2017.

— 'Animal Kingdom' in *Leonora Carrington: Magical Tales*. Edited by Tere Arcq and Stefan van Raay, 243–273. Mexico City: Instituto Nacional de Bellas Artes, 2018.

— 'Programme Notes' in *Leonora: La Maga y el Maestro* (2018): 6.

— *Women and Magic: Hidden Territories of Women's Creative Process* (Ashfield: Double Edge Theatre, 2019): https://vimeo.com/330893013 (Accessed 7 September 2019).

— and Tere Arcq, 'Cauldrons and Curanderas: The Magical Collaborations of Remedios Varo and Leonora Carrington' in *The Story of the Last Egg*. Edited by Wendi Norris, 75–77. New York and San Francisco: Gallery Wendi Norris, 2019.

— and Tere Arcq, 'As in a Mirror with Multiple Facets: Leonora Carrington and the Tarot' in *The Tarot of Leonora Carrington*, 63–111. Somerset: Fulgur Press, 2020.

— and Tere Arcq, 'Magical Reflection: The Creative Collaborations of Leonora Carrington and Remedios Varo' in *The Life and Influence of Leonora Carrington: A Symposium* (New York: Gallery Wendi Norris, 2019): https://vimeo.com/357681039 (Accessed 9 July 2020).

— and Stacy Klein, 'Leonora Carrington and the Theatre: Susan L. Aberth and Stacy Klein in Conversation' (7 March 2021): www.youtube.com/watch?v=gJUTP82shOY (Accessed 28 March 2021).

'About Us' in *i-D Magazine* (2020): https://i-d.vice.com/en_uk/page/i-d-about-us-en-uk (Accessed 4 July 2020).

Adès, Dawn. 'Carrington's Mysteries' in *Leonora Carrington*. 99–122. Dublin: Irish Museum of Modern Art, 2013.

— 'Testimonial' in *Leonora Carrington: Magical Tales*. Edited by Tere Arcq and Stefan van Raay, 443–446. Mexico City: Instituto Nacional de Bellas Artes, 2018.

Allmer, Patricia. 'Feminist Interventions: Revising the Canon' in *A Companion to Dada and Surrealism*. Edited by David Hopkins, 366–381. Chichester: Wiley Blackwell, 2016.

Arcq, Tere. 'In the Land of Convulsive Beauty: Mexico' in *In Wonderland: The Surrealist Adventures of Women Artists in Mexico and the United States*. Edited by Ilene Susan Fort, Tere Arcq and Terri Geis, 64–87. Los Angeles and Mexico City: LACMA and Prestel, 2012.

— 'A World Made of Magic' in *Leonora Carrington*. Translated by Jonathan Brennan, 17–40. Dublin: IMMA, 2013.

— 'Leonora Carrington in Mexico: The Mirror of the Marvelous' in *Annual Stanley and Pearl Goodman Lecture on Latin American Art* (21 November 2019): www.youtube.com/watch?v=eF2PlzMfrVo (Accessed 11 May 2021).

— and S. van Raay, *Leonora Carrington: Magical Tales*. Mexico City: Museo de Arte Moderno, 2018.

—, S. van Raay, and J. Moorhead, *Surreal Friends: Leonora Carrington, Remedios Varo and Kati Horna*. Chichester: Pallant House, 2010.

Aridjis, Chloe. 'An A-Z of Leonora Carrington Memories, Mostly in Quotes, Gathered Over Years of Visits to Her Home' in *Leonora Carrington and the International Avant-Garde*. Edited by Jonathan P. Eburne and Catriona McAra, 17–19. Manchester: Manchester University Press, 2017.

— 'In conversation with Marina Warner' in *London Review of Books* (4 April 2017).

— 'Talking about Leonora Carrington (with Marina Warner and Jennifer Higgie)' in *Houses Are Really Bodies* (London: Cubitt, 2017): www.cubittartists.org.uk/event/houses-are-really-bodies-public-programme (Accessed 17 July 2020).

— 'Reading with…Chloe Aridjis' in *Shelf-Awareness* (22 February 2019): www.shelf-awareness.com/issue.html?issue=3437#m43424 (Accessed 13 May 2021).

— in conversation with Juliet Jacques, *London Review of Books Podcast* (2019): www.lrb.co.uk/podcasts-and-videos/podcasts/at-the-bookshop/chloe-aridjis-and-juliet-jacques-sea-monsters (Accessed 8 May 2020).

— 'Leonora Carrington at Home in the Colonia Roma and the Mexican Underworld' in Centre for Mexican Studies, Kings College London (3 June 2019).

— 'Leonora Carrington and the Secret of the Sacred Feminine' in *Frieze* (18 June 2019): www.frieze.com/article/leonora-carrington-and-secret-sacred-feminine (Accessed 10 July 2021).

Aridjis, Homero. *News of the Earth*. Translated and edited by Betty Ferber. Simsbury, CT: Mandel Vilar Press, 2017.

'The Art Fund helps Hunterian acquire work by Turner Prize-nominated artist Lucy Skaer' in *Art Fund Blog* (24 June 2009): www.artfund.org/blog/2009/06/24/the-art-fund-helps-hunterian-acquire-work-by-turner-prize-nominated-artist-lucy-skaer (Accessed 21 May 2020).

Baddeley, Oriana. 'Frida Redressed' in *Frida Kahlo: Making Herself Up*, 175–186. London: V&A, 2018.

Bal, Mieke. *Quoting Caravaggio: Contemporary Art, Preposterous History*. London and Chicago: University of Chicago Press, 1999.

— 'Dispersing the Image' in *Looking In, The Art of Viewing: Mieke Bal: Essays and Afterword*. Edited by Norman Bryson, 65–91. Amsterdam: G+B Arts International, 2001.

— *Louise Bourgeois' Spider: The Architecture of Art Writing*. Chicago: Chicago University Press, 2001.

— 'Autotopography: Louise Bourgeois as Builder' in *Biography*, volume 25, number 1 (Winter 2002): 180–202.

— *Don Quijote: Sad Countenances*. Växjö: Trolltrumma, 2019.

— and Michelle Williams Gamaker, 'Mrs B: The film analysis of a novel' in *Flaubert [Online], Translations/ Adaptations* (2012): http://flaubert.revues.org/1837 (Accessed 2 November 2019)

Barbier, Laetitia. 'Death and Resurrection as Muse' (6 March 2021).

Barthes, Roland. 'Death of the Author' in *Image, Music, Text*. Translated by Stephen Heath, 142–148. London: Fontana, 1977.

— 'From Work to Text' in *Image, Music, Text*. Translated by Stephen Heath, 155–164. London: Fontana, 1977.

— 'The Metaphor of the Eye' in *Story of the Eye*, 119–127. London: Penguin, 1979.

Bauduin, Tessel M. 'The "Continuing Misfortune" of Automatism in Early Surrealism' in *communication +1*, volume 4, number 10 (September 2015), 2.

—, V. Ferentinou, and D. Zamani (editors), 'Introduction' in *Surrealism, Occultism and Politics: In Search of the Marvellous*, 1–19. New York: Routledge, 2018.

Baum, D. and J. Appignanesi, 'Fluidity, Indeterminacy, Interdependence: A Conversation with Chloe Aridjis' in *Wasafiri*, volume 36, issue 2 (2021): 10.1080/02690055.2021.1879477 (Accessed 23 July 2021).

Baxandall, Michael. *Patterns of Intention: On the Historical Explanation of Pictures*. New Haven, CT: Yale University Press, 1985.

Benjamin, Walter. 'The Work of Art in the Age of Mechanical Reproduction' in *Illuminations*. Edited by Hannah Arendt, translated by Harry Zohn, 219–253. London: Pimlico, 1999.

Benson, Stephen. 'Angela Carter and the Literary Märchen' in *Angela Carter and the Fairy Tale*. Edited by Danielle M. Roemer and Cristina Bacchilega, 30–58. Detroit, MI: Wayne State University Press, 2001.

Bernheimer, Kate. 'Editor's Note' in *Fairy Tale Review: The Green Issue*. Detroit, MI: Wayne State University Press, 2006.

— 'Fairy Tale is Form, Form is Fairy Tale' in *The Writer's Notebook: Craft Essays from Tin House*. Edited by Aimee Bender, Dorothy Allison, and Susan Bell, 61–73. Portland, OR: Tin House Books, 2009.

— 'Power Imagined: Fairy Tales as Survival Strategies' in *Woman Power: The 2020 SBS Downtown Lecture Series* (2 October 2020): www.youtube.com/watch?v=C28-paZlJtA (Accessed 12 May 2021).

Björk, 'Björk Guest-Edit: In Conversation with Maggie Nelson,' *AnOther* (Spring/Summer 2019): www.anothermag.com/design-living/11554/bjork-guest-edit-in-conversation-with-maggie-nelson (Accessed 3 June 2020).

Bloom, Harold. *The Anxiety of Influence*. Oxford: Oxford University Press, 1997.

Boas, Natasha. 'The Leonora Carrington Effect: What We Can Learn From Carrington Today' in *The Life and Influence of Leonora Carrington: A Symposium* (New York: Gallery Wendi Norris, 2019): https://vimeo.com/364355299 (Accessed 9 July 2020).

— 'Projects and Projections: The Leonora Carrington Effect' in *The Story of the Last Egg*. Edited by Wendi Norris, 79–83. New York and San Francisco: Gallery Wendi Norris, 2019.

Boldrick, Stacy. 'Skeletons Within' in *Lucy Skaer*, 56–65. Edinburgh: Fruitmarket Gallery, 2008.

Bonk, Ecke. *The Portable Museum: The Making of the Boîte-en-valise*. London: Thames & Hudson, 1989.

Borrelli-Persson, Laird. 'Bat for Lashes's Natasha Khan is the Vampire Heroine We Need Now' in *Vogue* (2020): www.vogue.com/article/bat-for-lashes-natasha-khan-is-the-ultimate-vampire-heroine (Accessed 14 July 2020).

Bradley, Fiona. 'Introduction' in *Lucy Skaer*, 9–14. Edinburgh: Fruitmarket Gallery, 2008.

Breton, André. 'The Mediums Enter' in *Modernism: An Anthology*. Edited by Lawrence Rainey, translated by Mark Polizzotti, 742–745. London: Blackwell, 2005.

Bryan-Wilson, Julia. 'Letters on Casting' in *Hello Leonora, Soy Anne Walsh*. 77–86. Cambridge, MA: MIT Press, 2019.

Buchloh, Benjamin H. D. 'Beuys: The Twilight of the Idol' in *Neo-Avantgarde and Culture Industry: Essays on European and American Art from 1955 to 1975*, 41–64. Cambridge, MA: MIT Press, 2000.

Carey-Thomas, Lizzie. 'Garlic and Sapphires in the Mud' in *Lucy Skaer*, 28–37. Edinburgh: Fruitmarket Gallery, 2008.

Carrington, Leonora. 'Commentary' in *Leonora Carrington: A Retrospective Exhibition*, 23–24. New York: Center for Inter-American Relations, 1976.

— 'For Alain' in *Alan Glass*, 5. New York: Claude Bernard Gallery, 1991.

— 'What is a Woman' in *Surrealist Women: An International Anthology*. Edited by Penelope Rosemont, 372–375. London: Athlone, 1998.

— 'Female Human Animal' in *Leonora Carrington: What She Might Be*. Edited by Salomon Grimberg, 11–15. Dallas, TX: Dallas Museum of Art, 2008.

Carter, Angela. 'Notes From the Front Line' in *Shaking a Leg: Collected Journalism and Writings*. Edited by Jenny Uglow, 36–43. London: Penguin, 1997.

Cass, Caroline. 'The Mistress of Surrealism' in *Telegraph Magazine* (16 August 1997): 28–34.

Chadwick, Whitney. *Woman Artists and the Surrealist Movement*. London: Thames & Hudson, 1985.

— 'Painting on the Threshold' in *Leonora Carrington: Recent Works*, 2–4. New York: Brewster Gallery, 1988.

— 'El Mundo Mágico: Leonora Carrington's Enchanted Garden' in *Leonora Carrington: The Mexican Years*, 9–31. San Francisco: Mexican Museum, 1991.

— 'Muse Begets Crone: On Leonora Carrington' in *M/E/A/N/I/N/G: An Anthology of Artists' Writings, Theory and Criticism*. Edited by Susan Bee and Mira Schor, 418–422. Durham, NC: Duke University Press, 2000.

Chambers, Selena. 'The Hyena's Escape Plan: Leonora Carrington's Advice on Surviving Brexit' in *The Debutante*, issue 1 (2020): 4.

Cherem, Silvia. 'Eternally Married to the Wind: Interview with Leonora Carrington' in *Leonora Carrington, What She Might Be*. Edited by Salomon Grimberg, 17–43. Dallas, TX: Dallas Museum of Art, 2008.

Cherry, Deborah. 'Troubling Presence: Body, Sound and Space in Installation Art of the Mid-1990s' in *RACAR: Revue D'art Canadienne / Canadian Art Review*, volume 25, issue 1/2 (1998): 12–30. www.jstor.org/stable/42630590. (Accessed 12 May 2020).

Cixous, Hélène. 'The Laugh of the Medusa' in *Signs*, volume 1, number 4 (1976): 875–893.

Colvile, Georgiana M. M. 'Women Artists, Surrealism and Animal Representation' in *Angels of Anarchy: Women Artists and Surrealism*. Edited by Patricia Allmer, 64–73. New York: Prestel, 2009.

Comita, Jenny. 'Tilda Swinton Transforms Again, Into the Legendary Eccentric Edith Sitwell' in *W Magazine* (2018): www.wmagazine.com/story/tilda-swinton-tim-walker-fashion-photos-edith-sitwell (Accessed 14 May 2020).

'Commedia dell'arte' in The Metropolitan Museum of Art (2020): www.metmuseum.org/toah/hd/comm/hd_comm.htm (Accessed 20 May 2020).

Conley, Katharine. 'Carrington's Kitchen' in *Papers of Surrealism*, issue 10 (2013): www.research.manchester.ac.uk/portal/files/63517394/surrealism_issue_10.pdf (Accessed 22 May 2020).

— *Surrealist Ghostliness*. Lincoln and London: University of Nebraska Press, 2013.

Connelly, Frances S. *The Grotesque in Western Art and Culture: The Image at Play*. Cambridge: Cambridge University Press, 2012.

Crenshaw, Kimberlé Williams. 'Demarginalizing the Intersection of Race and Sex: A Black Feminist Critique of Antidiscrimination Doctrine, Feminist Theory and Antiracist Politics' in *University of Chicago Legal Forum*, volume 1989, article 8 (1989): https://chicagounbound.uchicago.edu/uclf/vol1989/iss1/8 (Accessed 23 June 2021).

Crewdson, Gregory. '20 questions with Tilda Swinton and Gregory Crewdson' (14 April 2020): www.youtube.com/watch?v=q0XkPo1P360 (Accessed 10 July 2020).

Das, Jareh. 'Interview with Samantha Sweeting' in *Bomb Magazine* (29 January 2014): https://bombmagazine.org/articles/samantha-sweeting (Accessed 22 April 2021).

'David Cameron visits Mexico,' *The Office of David Cameron* (10 May 2018): www.davidcameronoffice.org/david-cameron-visits-mexico (Accessed 24 June 2021).

de Angelis, Paul. *Leonora Carrington: The Mexican Years*, 33–42. San Francisco: Mexican Museum, 1991.

d'Eaubonne, Françoise. *Le Féminisme ou la Mort*. Paris: Pierre Horay, 1974.

de Beauvoir, Simone. *The Second Sex*. Edited and translated by H. M. Parshley. London: Vintage, 1997.

Demos, T. J. *The Exiles of Marcel Duchamp*. Cambridge, MA: MIT Press, 2007.

de Pressigny, Clementine. 'To Create' in *i-D Magazine* (2017): 188.

Dey, C. and H. Sopinka, *About Horses Atelier* (2020): www.horsesatelier.com/pages/about (Accessed 9 February 2020).

Double Edge Theatre, 'From Allston to Ashfield: Historical Highlights from 1982-Present' in *Medium* (24 April 2019): https://medium.com/@DoubleEdgeTheatre/from-allston-to-ashfield-historical-highlights-from-1982-present-931c35c0714d (Accessed 23 April 2020).

Dunn, Frankie, 'To Create' in *i-D Magazine* (2017): 182–183.

Durón, Maximilíano. 'Paying Tribute to Leonora Carrington, 2022 Venice Biennale Takes the Title "The Milk of Dreams"' in *Art News* (9 June 2021): www.artnews.com/art-news/news/venice-biennale-2022-title-1234595242 (Accessed 29 June 2021).

Dwyer, Kate. 'Why Leonora Carrington's Work Feels So of the Moment' in *W Magazine* (4 February 2022): www.wmagazine.com/culture/leonora-carrington-venice-biennale-books-history (Accessed 14 February 2022).

Eburne, Jonathan P. 'Breton's Wall, Carrington's Kitchen: Surrealism and the Archive' in *Intermediality: History and Theory of the Arts, Literature and Technology*, number 18 (2012): 31; 33. www.erudit.org/en/journals/im/1900-v1-n1-im087/1009072ar.pdf (Accessed 22 May 2020).

— 'The Memory Tower' in *Leonora Carrington Centenary Symposium* (Biblioteca de México, 2017): www.youtube.com/watch?v=K8fTDkN_x8s (Accessed 16 July 2020).

— 'Poetic Wisdom: Leonora Carrington and the Esoteric Avant-Garde' in *Leonora Carrington and the International Avant-Garde*. Edited by J. P. Eburne and C. McAra, 141–162. Manchester: Manchester University Press, 2017.

— *Outsider Theory: Intellectual Histories of Unorthodox Ideas*. London and Minneapolis: University of Minnesota Press, 2018.

— '"All Artwork is a Magical Act,"' *ASAP/J* (10 October 2019): http://asapjournal.com/all-artwork-is-a-magical-act-an-interview-with-susan-aberth-and-stacy-klein-jennifer johnson (Accessed 16 Aprilo 2020).

— 'Preface' in *The Invisible Painting: My Memoir of Leonora Carrington*, vi-xi Manchester: Manchester University Press, 2021.

— and C. McAra, 'Introduction' in *Leonora Carrington and the International Avant-Garde*, Edited by J. P. Eburne and C. McAra, 1–16. Manchester: Manchester University Press, 2017.

— and C. McAra, 'Mujeres conciencia (*Women's Awareness*): Leonora Carrington's Agit-prop,' Manchester University Press Blog (July 2019): https://manchesteruniversitypress.co.uk/articles/mujeres-conciencia-womens-awareness-leonora-carringtons-agit-prop-by-catriona-mcara-and-jonathan-p-eburne (Accessed 23 November 2020).

Elizabeth, S. *The Art of the Occult: A Visual Sourcebook for the Modern Mystic*. London: Frances Lincoln, 2020.

Emre, Merve. 'How Leonora Carrington Feminized Surrealism' in *The New Yorker* (21 December 2020): www.newyorker.com/magazine/2020/12/28/how-leonora-carrington-feminized-surrealism (Accessed 29 December 2020).

— 'NYRB: Leonora Carrington's *The Hearing Trumpet*' (14 January 2021).

Ernst, Max. 'Preface, or Loplop Presents the Bride of the Wind' in *The House of Fear: Notes From Down Below*, 25–26. London: Virago, 1989.

Farago, Jason. 'The Real Story Behind Tilda Swinton's Performance at MoMA' in *The New Republic* (28 March 2013): https://newrepublic.com/article/112782/real-story-behind-tilda-swintons-performance-moma (Accessed 11 July 2020).

Fazio, Vince. *31 Women Artists*. Sedona, AZ: Sedona Arts Center, 2020.

Foster, Hal. *Compulsive Beauty*. Cambridge: MIT Press, 1995.

Foucault, Michel. *The Order of Things: An Archaeology of the Human Sciences*. New York: Routledge, 2002.

Fowkes, Maja. *The Green Bloc: Neo-Avant-Garde Art and Ecology under Socialism*. Budapest: Central European University Press, 2015.

Freud, Sigmund. 'Fetishism' in *Standard Edition of the Complete Psychological Works of Sigmund Freud*. Edited by James Strachey, 152–157. London: Hogarth Press and Institute of Psychoanalysis, 1961.

— *Civilization and Its Discontents*. Translated by David McLintock. London: Penguin, 2002.

Fiduccia, Joanna. 'Fathoming Gestures' in *Lucy Skaer: A Boat Used as a Vessel*, 31–33. Basel: Kunsthalle, 2007.

Gee, Felicity. 'Review: of Gillian Wearing and Claude Cahun: Behind the Mask, Another Mask' in *ASAP/J* (27 April 2017): https://asapjournal.com/a-review-of-gillian-wearing-and-claude-cahun-behind-the-mask-another-mask-felicity-gee (Accessed 12 May 2021).

Giblin, Tessa. *Lucy Skaer: The Green Man* (2018): www.trg.ed.ac.uk/sites/default/files/2020–04/LucySkaerTheGreenMan.pdf (Accessed 16 July 2020).

Grant, C. and K. Random Love, *Fandom as Methodology: A Sourcebook for Artists and Writers*. London: Goldsmiths Press, 2019.

Greenberg, Clement. 'Surrealist Painting,' in *The Collected Essays and Criticism: Perceptions and Judgments, 1939–1944*, volume 1, edited by John O'Brian, 225–231. Chicago: University of Chicago Press, 1986.

Grimberg, Salomon. 'Travelling Toward the Unknown, Leonora Carrington Stopped in New York' in *Leonora Carrington: Magical Tales*. Edited by Tere Arcq and Stefan van Raay, 69–97. Mexico City: Instituto Nacional de Bellas Artes, 2018.

Harad, Alyssa, 'Author Panel on Leonora Carrington's *The Hearing Trumpet*: Alyssa Harad, Porochista Khakpour, Maria Dahvana Headley, Amber Sparks, and Taisia Kitaiskaia' for *Book People Events* (7 April 2021).

Haraway, Donna J. *Simians, Cyborgs, and Women: The Reinvention of Nature*. New York: Routledge, 1991.

— *When Species Meet*. London and Minneapolis: University of Minnesota Press, 2008.

— *A Cyborg Manifesto: Science, Technology and Socialist-Feminism in the Late Twentieth Century*. Minneapolis: University of Minnesota Press, 2016.

Hare, David (editor). 'Concerning the present day relative attractions of various creatures in mythology and legend' in *VVV magazine*, number 1 (1942): 62.

Harris, Caroline I. 'Review: Leonora Carrington and the International Avant-Garde' in *Woman's Art Journal*, Spring/Summer (2019): 56–57.

Harris, Jeremy O. 'Playful, Fantastical, Rare: At Home with Tilda Swinton on Her Highlands Estate' in *Vogue* (14 February 2021): www.vogue.co.uk/arts-and-lifestyle/article/tilda-swinton-interview (Accessed 28 April 2021).

Heathfield, A. and A. Jones, *Perform, Repeat, Record: Live Art in History*. London: Intellect, 2012.

Hentschker, Frank. 'In conversation with Stacy Klein and Stephanie Monseu' in *Segal Talks* (8 May 2020): https://youtu.be/SOzefa8J_Bc (Accessed 12 May 2020).

Hernández Urías, Fernando. '"Without disenchantment there is no change"' in *Chilango* (21 April 2020): www.chilango.com/cultura/chloe-aridjis-monstruos-marinos (Accessed 22 April 2020).

Hewison, James and Michelle Man, 'Imaginarium: Dancing with Carrington' in *Leonora Carrington: Living Legacies*. Edited by A. Cox, J. Hewison, M. Man, and R. Shannon, 61–81. Wilmington, DE: Vernon Press, 2020.

Hicklin, Aaron. 'We'd Sit at Church Looking Down on Children From the Village' in *The Herald Magazine* (2008), 7–9.

'Higgie, Jennifer. How *Female Human Animal* Blends Documentary with Fiction' in *Frieze* (2018): https://frieze.com/article/how-female-human-animal-blends-documentary-fiction (Accessed 8 June 2020).

— 'Alison Goldfrapp on Leonora Carrington' in *Bow Down: Women in Art History* (September 2020) [podcast]

Hogg, Joanna. 'Joanna Hogg, Honor Swinton Byrne and Tilda Swinton on The Souvenir' in *Film at Lincoln Center* (15 May 2019): www.youtube.com/watch?v=xzfBXkmo2Kg (Accessed 18 May 2020).

Holquist, Michael. *Dialogism: Bakhtin and His World*. London and New York: Routledge, 1990.

Hopkins, David. 'The Politics of Equivocation: Sherrie Levine, Duchamp's "Compensation Portrait," and Surrealism in the USA 1942–45' in *Oxford Art Journal*, volume 26, number 1 (2003): 45–68.

— *Dark Toys: Surrealism and the Culture of Childhood*. London and New Haven, CT: Yale University Press, 2021.

Horna, Norah. 'Testimonial' in *Leonora Carrington: Magical Tales*. Edited by Tere Arcq and Stefan van Raay, 406–411. Mexico City: Instituto Nacional de Bellas Artes, 2018.

Horton, Derek. 'Review: Leonora Carrington/Lucy Skaer' in *Corridor 8* (28 July 2016): https://corridor8.co.uk/article/review-leonora-carrington-lucy-skaer-leeds-college-of-art (Accessed 19 June 2020).

Hutcheon, Linda. *A Theory of Adaptation*. New York: Routledge, 2013.

Jodorowsky, Alejandro and Marianne Costa, *The Spiritual Journey of Alejandro Jodorowsky*. Rochester: Park Street Press, 2005.

— *The Way of Tarot: The Spiritual Teacher in the Cards*. Rochester: Destiny Books, 2009.

Jones, Amelia. 'The Return of Feminism(s) and the Visual Arts, 1970–2009' in *Feminisms is Still Our Name: Seven Essays on Historiography and Curatorial Practices*. Edited by Malin Hedlin Hayden and Jessica Sjöholm Skrubbe, 11–56. Newcastle upon Tyne: Cambridge Scholars Publishing, 2010.

— 'Writing as Doing: Performance Arcade…Counternarratives' in *The Live Press: Performance Arcade* (2018): 1–4.

Kérchy, A. and C. McAra, 'Interview with Mieke Bal' in *European Journal of English Studies*, 21, issue 3 (2017): 231–235 10.1080/13825577.2017.1369269 (Accessed 16 July 2020).

Kermode, Mark, 'In Conversation with Tilda Swinton' at British Film Institute (March 2020): www.youtube.com/watch?v=PfaETIdhgcA (Accessed 13 May 2020).

Kettle, Alice. 'House of Opposites' in *Alice Kettle* (13 May 2020): https://alicekettle.co.uk/the-house-of-opposites (Accessed 2 May 2021).

Khakpour, Porochista. 'Surreal Talk: The Otherworldly, Magical Writing of Leonora Carrington' in *Book Forum* (2017): www.bookforum.com/print/2403/the-otherworldly-magical-writing-of-leonora-carrington-18463 (Accessed 23 April 2021).

Kissane, Seán. 'The Celtic Surrealist' in *Leonora Carrington*, 45–70. Dublin: Irish Museum of Modern Art, 2013.

Klein, Stacy. '"All Artwork is a Magical Act"' in *ASAP/J* (10 October 2019): http://asapjournal.com/all-artwork-is-a-magical-act-an-interview-with-susan-aberth-and-stacy-klein-jennifer-johnson (Accessed 16 April 2020).

Kristeva, Julia. *Powers of Horror: An Essay on Abjection*. Translated by Leon S. Roudiez. New York: Columbia University Press, 1982.

— 'Word, Dialogue, Novel' in *Desire in Language: A Semiotic Approach to Literature and Art*. Edited and translated by Leon S. Roudiez, 64–91. New York: Columbia University Press, 1982.

Lawner, Lynne. *Harlequin on the Moon: Commedia dell'Arte and the Visual Arts*. New York: Harry N. Adams, 1998.

Leaver-Yap, Isla. 'Lucy Skaer: Drawing Close' in *Map Magazine*, 10 (June 2007): https://mapmagazine.co.uk/lucy-skaer-drawing-close (Accessed 21 May 2020).

Lee, Jennifer. 'Wonderland Wanderings: Samantha Sweeting' in *Filler*, volume 2, number 4 (Winter 2011): http://fillermagazine.com/culture/gallery/though-the-looking-glass-samantha-sweeting (Accessed 24 November 2020).

Lever, Caroline. 'Tilda Swinton's The Maybe' in *AnOther* (17 April 2013): www.anothermag.com/art-photography/2664/tilda-swintons-the-maybe (Accessed 12 May 2020).

Lindauer, Margaret A. *Devouring Frida: Art History and Popular Celebrity of Frida Kahlo*. Middletown, CT: Wesleyan University Press, 1999.

Lommels, Andreas. *Masks: Their Meaning and Function*. London: Ferndale Editions, 1981.

Lord, Catherine with Michelle Williams Gamaker, 'House of Preposterous Women: Michelle Williams Gamaker re-auditions Kanchi' in *OAR: The Oxford Artistic and Practice Based Research Platform*, issue 3 (2018): www.oarplatform.com/house-of-preposterous-women-michelle-williams-gamaker-re-auditions-kanchi (Accessed 5 June 2020).

Lu, Lynn. 'The Hearing Trumpet' (2011): www.lynnlu.info/projectItem.php?Pid=125&PP=8&NP=10 (Accessed 23 May 2015).

— 'Haumapuhia Rising' in *Lynn Lu* (2018): https://lynnlu.info/haumapuhia-rising (Accessed 24 April 2021).

— 'Creative, Academic, and Personal Responses to Breastfeeding Research' (6 May 2021): www.youtube.com/watch?v=mAIr1nlJXUU (Accessed 15 May 2021).

Lusty, Natalya. *Surrealism, Feminism, Psychoanalysis*. Aldershot: Ashgate, 2007.

Lyon, Janet. 'Carrington's Sensorium' in *Leonora Carrington and the International Avant-Garde*. Edited by C. McAra and J. Eburne, 163–176. Manchester: Manchester University Press, 2017.

Mabey, Robert. 'Introduction' in *The Snow Leopard*, vii–xv. London: Vintage, 2010.

'Magic and Mystery, Fantasy and Fashion: Leonora Carrington in Pop Culture' in *The Art Story Blog* (n.d.): www.theartstory.org/blog/magic-and-mystery-fantasy-and-fashion-leonora-carrington-in-pop-culture (Accessed 3 June 2020).

Maizz Visual (2013; 2018): https://en.maizz.mx/leonoras-dream-gif-collection (Accessed 8 August 2020).

Markova, Lora and Roger Shannon, 'Leonora Carrington on and off Screen: Intertextual and Intermedial Connections between the Artist's Creative Practice and the Medium of Film' in *Arts*, volume 8, number 11 (January 2019): www.mdpi.com/2076–0752/8/1/11 (Accessed 22 February 2020).

Martínez, Elizabeth Coonrod 'Introduction' in *Lilus Kikus and Other Stories by Elena Poniatowska*. Translated by Elizabeth Coonrod Martínez, 1–29. Albuquerque: University of New Mexico Press, 2005.

Marx, Bill. 'Best Stage Productions of 2019' in *The Arts Fuse* (28 December 2019): https://artsfuse.org/192651/theater-feature-best-stage-productions-of-2019 (Accessed 24 April 2020).

Matthiessen, Peter. *The Snow Leopard*. London: Vintage, 2010.

Mavor, Carol. *Aurelia: Art and Literature Through the Mouth of the Fairy Tale*. London: Reaktion Books, 2017.

Miéville, China. In Conversation with Jordy Rosenberg, *Lannan Podcasts* (18 January 2017): https://podcast.lannan.org/2017/01/22/china-mieville-with-jordy-rosenberg-conversation-18-january-2017-video (Accessed 31 January 2022).

Moorhead, Joanna. *The Surreal Life of Leonora Carrington*. London: Virago, 2017.

Morton, Lisa. *Calling the Spirits: A History of Seances*. London: Reaktion Books, 2020.

Mulvey, Laura. 'Pandora's Box: Topographies of Curiosity' in *Fetishism and Curiosity*, 53–64. Bloomington and Indianapolis: Indiana University Press, 1996.

Mulvey-Roberts, Marie and Fiona Robinson, *Strange Worlds: The Vision of Angela Carter*. Bristol: Samson, 2016.

Nicholson, Rebecca. 'Björk: what inspires me' in the *Guardian* (2012): www.theguardian.com/music/2012/may/03/bjork-what-inspires-me (Accessed 18 May 2020).

Nieves, Bianca. '10 Best Books For Teens According To Kendall Jenner' in *Teen Vogue* (17 March 2020): www.teenvogue.com/story/books-for-teens (Accessed 17 April 2021).

Noheden, Kristoffer. 'The Grail and the Bees: Leonora Carrington's Quest for Human-Animal Coexistence' in *Beyond Given Knowledge: Investigation, Quest and Exploration in Modernism and the Avant-Gardes*. Edited by H. Veivo, J. P. Montier, F. Nicol, D. Ayers, B. Hjartarson, and S. Bru, 239–252. Berlin: De Gruyter, 2018.

Norris, Wendi. 'An Endlessly Unfolding Gift' in *The Story of the Last Egg*. 7–9. New York and San Francisco: Gallery Wendi Norris, 2019.

— 'Michaela Carter in conversation with art expert Wendi Norris' (6 April 2021): www.youtube.com/watch?v=obywWxBprkY (Accessed 13 April 2022).

Opie, Iona and Peter Opie. *The Oxford Dictionary of Nursery Rhymes.* Oxford: Oxford University Press, 1997.

Orenstein, Gloria. 'Art History and the Case for the Women of Surrealism' in *Journal of General Education*, volume 27, number 1 (Spring 1975): 31–54.

Patrizio, Andrew. *The Ecological Eye: Assembling an Ecocritical Art History.* Manchester: Manchester University Press, 2019.

Penrose, Antony. 'Testimonial' in *Leonora Carrington: Magical Tales.* Edited by Tere Arcq and Stefan van Raay, 403–405. Mexico City: Instituto Nacional de Bellas Artes, 2018.

Penrose, Roland. 'Letter to Leonora Carrington' (4 March 1960). Collection of the Scottish National Gallery of Modern Art, Edinburgh.

Peterson, Ryan. 'Young Londoners, Straight Up' in *i-D Magazine* (2016): https://i-d.vice.com/en_uk/article/j583qp/young-londoners-straight-up (Accessed 2 July 2020).

Pinkola Estés, Clarissa. *Women Who Run with the Wolves: Contacting the Power of the Wild Woman.* London: Random House, 1992.

Plunkett, Tara. 'Dissecting *The Holy Oily Body*: Remedios Varo, Leonora Carrington and *El Santo Cuerpo Grasoso*' in *Leonora Carrington and the International Avant-Garde.* Edited by J. P. Eburne and C. McAra, 72–89. Manchester: Manchester University Press, 2017.

Pollock, Griselda. *Vision and Difference: Feminism, Femininity and the Histories of Art.* London and New York: Routledge, [1988] 2003.

— 'Professor Griselda Pollock: Graduation Speech' (London: Courtauld Institute of Art, 2019): https://courtauld.ac.uk/professor-griselda-pollock-graduation-speech-2019 (Accessed 25 October 2019).

Prim: A Nursery Story [Unpublished family catalogue].

Rawsthorn, Alice. 'Stranger Than Paradise' in *W Magazine* (May 2013): 135–140.

Rich, B. Ruby. 'The Time Travellers' in *Aperture*, issue 235 (Summer 2019), 41–45.

Rohmann, Chris. 'Love Letter to a Nightmare' in *Valley Advocate* (4 February 2020): https://valleyadvocate.com/2020/02/04/love-letter-to-a-nightmare (Accessed 14 April 2020).

Rosemont, Penelope. *Surrealism: Inside the Magnetic Fields.* San Francisco: City Lights, 2019.

Russo, Mary. *The Female Grotesque: Risk, Excess and Modernity.* New York: Routledge, 1994.

Scanlan, J. and T. Swinton. 'The Maybe: Modes of Performance and the "Live"' in *Perform, Repeat, Record: Live Art in History.* Edited by A. Heathfield and A. Jones, 469–481. London: Intellect, 2012.

Schechner, Richard. 'Double Edge Theatre in Its Ashfield Community: An Interview with Stacy Klein' in *TDR/The Drama Review*, volume 64, issue 4 (December 2020): 44–71.

Scott Fox, Lorna. 'Swimming Under Cemeteries' in *Times Literary Supplement* (May 2017): www.the-tls.co.uk/articles/public/leonora-carrington (Accessed 6 April 2021).

Shackleton, Holly. 'Editorial: The Creativity Issue' in *i-D Magazine* (Summer 2017): 34.

Shandler Levitt, Annette. 'The Bestial Fictions of Leonora Carrington' in *Journal of Modern Literature*, volume 20, number 1 (Summer 1996): 65–74.

Sills, Leslie. 'Leonora Carrington' in *Visions: Stories About Women Artists*, 20–31. Morton Grove, IL: Albert Whitman, 1993.

Skaer, Lucy. 'The Transcendence of the Image' in *Tate Etc.* (September 2008): www.tate.org.uk/context-comment/articles/transcendence-image (Accessed 11 March 2020).

Smith, Ali. 'Introduction' in *The Hearing Trumpet*. v–xv. London: Penguin, 2005.

Solway, Diane. 'Stranger Than Paradise' in *W Magazine* (May 2013): 129.

Sopinka, Heidi. 'Interview with Leonora Carrington' in *The Believer*, issue 94 (November/December 2012): 80–86.

— 'Hey Necromancer!' in *Paris Review* (18 September 2018): https://theparisreview.org/blog/2018/09/18/hey-necromancer (Accessed 11 February 2020).

— 'Master Pieces' in *Brick*, issue 102 (January 2019): https://brickmag.com/master-pieces (Accessed 29 April 2020).

—, N. Matutschovsky and A. Piercy, 'Resurrecting Leonora Carrington's World' in *Lenny Letter* (18 September 2018): www.lennyletter.com/story/resurrecting-leonora-carringtons-world (Accessed 25 October 2019).

Stallard, Natasha. 'In Conversation with Chloe Aridjis' in *Tank Magazine*, issue 77 (2018).

Stansfield, Ted. 'Teen artist removes his nipples and sells them as art' in *Dazed* (2016): www.dazeddigital.com/artsandculture/article/31032/1/teen-artist-removes-his-nipples-and-sells-them-as-art (Accessed 2 July 2020).

Stevens, Isabel. 'Smoke and Mirrors and Make-Believe' in *Sight and Sound Magazine* (April 2020): 24–33.

Stewart, Susan. *Nonsense: Aspects of Intertextuality in Folklore and Literature*. Baltimore, MD and London: Johns Hopkins University Press, 1979.

— *On Longing: Narratives of the Miniature, the Gigantic, the Souvenir, the Collection*. Durham, NC and London: Duke University Press, 1993.

Stoddart, Helen. *Rings of Desire: Circus History and Representation*. Manchester: Manchester University Press, 2000.

Suleiman, Susan Rubin. *Subversive Intent: Gender, Politics, and the Avant-Garde*. Cambridge, MA and London: Harvard University Press, 1990.

Sullivan, Rosemary. 'On Leonora Carrington and P. K. Page' in *A Manner of Being: Writers on Their Mentors*. Edited by A. Liontas and J. Parker, 132–138. Amherst: University of Massachusetts Press, 2015.

Sweeting, Samantha. [Anon.] 'Samantha Sweeting,' *Rebel Magazine* (2010): http://therebelmagazine.blogspot.com/2010/10/interview-with-samantha-sweeting.html?m=1 (Accessed 19 June 2020).

—'Still waiting for you to come back to me' (2010): www.samanthasweeting.com/performanceinstallation/stillwaitingforyou.html (Accessed 19 June 2020).

— 'The Hearing Trumpet' (2011): www.samanthasweeting.com/performanceinstallation/hearingtrumpet.html (Accessed 23 May 2015).

— *Encounters with Animals* (29 April 2013): https://encounterswithanimals.wordpress.com/page/3 (Accessed 15 April 2021).

— 'Artist's Statement' (2014): www.samanthasweeting.com (Accessed 19 June 2020).

— 'Familiars and Shape Shifters: On Fur and Foxes' (2020). Unpublished.

Swinton, Tilda. *Creative Camera* (August–September 1995): 50.

— 'Another Email from Tilda Swinton to Amelia Jones, 29 April 2008' in *Perform, Repeat, Record: Live Art in History*. Edited by A. Heathfield and A. Jones, 473–478. London: Intellect, 2012.

— 'Introduction' in *Orlando*. ix–xvi. Edinburgh: The Canons, 2012.

— *Aperture*, 235 (Summer 2019).

Tanning, Dorothea. *Between Lives: An Artist and Her World*. London and New York: W. W. Norton, 2001.

Thackara, Tess. 'Carolee Schneemann's Lifelong Love Affair with Her Cats' in *Artsy* (14 February 2018): www.artsy.net/article/artsy-editorial-carolee-schneemanns-lifelong-love-affair-cats (Accessed 15 April 2021).

Tickner, Lisa. 'A Strange Alchemy: Cornelia Parker' in *Difference and Excess in Contemporary Art: The Visibility of Women's Practice*. Edited by Gill Perry, 46–73. London: Blackwell, 2004.

Toderash, Courtney. 'An Intimate Discussion with Claudia Dey and Heidi Sopinka: Designer-Novelists, and the Duo Behind Horses Atelier,' *Kobo* (18 December 2018): www.kobo.com/blog/claudia-dey-and-heidi-sopinka-horses-atelier (Accessed 9 February 2020).

Turner, Lynn. 'When Species Kiss: Some Recent Correspondence Among Animots' in *Humanimalia: A Journal of Human/Animal Interface Studies*, volume 2, number 1 (Fall 2010): 60–86.

Walker, Tim. *Tim Walker: Wonderful Things*. London: V&A, 2019.

Walsh, Anne. *Hello Leonora, Soy Anne Walsh*. Cambridge, MA: MIT Press, 2019.

Warner, Marina. 'Back from Below' in *The Independent* (22 July 1989): 42–45.

— 'Introduction' in *The House of Fear: Notes From Down Below*, 1–21. London: Virago, 1989.

— 'Introduction' in *The Seventh Horse and Other Tales*. London: Virago, 1989.

— 'Leonora Carrington's Spirit Bestiary; or the Art of Playing Make-Belief' in *Leonora Carrington: Paintings, Drawings and Sculptures 1940–1990*. Edited by Andrea Schlieker, 10–23. London: Serpentine Gallery, 1991.

— *From the Beast to the Blonde: On Fairy Tales and Their Tellers*. London: Chatto & Windus, 1994.

— 'Leonora Carrington: Badger' in *Leonora Carrington in the Viktor Wynd Collection*. Edited by Catriona McAra, 23–26. Leeds: Leeds Arts University, 2016.

— 'From high society to surrealism: in praise of Leonora Carrington—100 years on' in the *Guardian* (6 April 2017): www.theguardian.com/books/2017/apr/06/leonora-carrington-from-high-society-to-surrealism-in-praise-of-100-years-on (Accessed 15 April 2020).

— 'Leonora's Storytelling Imagination' in *Leonora Carrington: Magical Tales*. Edited by Tere Arcq and Stefan van Raay, 291–315. Mexico City: Instituto Nacional de Bellas Artes, 2018.

Watz, Anna. *Angela Carter and Surrealism: 'A Feminist Libertarian Aesthetic.'* New York: Routledge, 2017.

— '"A Language Buried at the Back of Time": *The Stone Door* and Poststructuralist Feminism' in *Leonora Carrington and the International Avant-Garde*. Edited by J. P. Eburne and C. McAra, 90–104. Manchester: Manchester University Press, 2017.

Weisz Carrington, Gabriel. 'A Celtic Window' in *Leonora Carrington*. Edited by Seán Kissane, 12–13. Dublin: Irish Museum of Modern Art, 2013.

— 'Shadow Children: Leonora as Storyteller' in *Leonora Carrington and the International Avant-Garde*. Edited by. J. P. Eburne and C. McAra, 126–140. Manchester: Manchester University Press, 2017.

— 'In Conversation with Gabriel Weisz Carrington' in *Leonora Carrington: Living Legacies*, Edited by A. Cox, J. Hewison, M. Man, and R. Shannon, 209–217. Wilmington, DE: Vernon Press, 2020.

— 'Leonora's Inner Compass' in *The Tarot of Leonora Carrington*, 8–15. Lopen, Somerset: Fulgur Press, 2020.

—. *The Invisible Painting: My Memoir of Leonora Carrington*. Manchester: Manchester University Press, 2021.

Young, Serenity. *Women Who Fly: Goddesses, Witches, Mystics and Other Airborne Females*. Oxford: Oxford University Press, 2018.

Fiction

Aridjis, Chloe. *Book of Clouds*. London: Vintage, [2009] 2010.

— *Asunder*. London: Chatto & Windus, 2013.

— *Sea Monsters*. London: Chatto & Windus, 2019.

Aridjis, Homero. *The Child Poet*. Translated by Chloe Aridjis. London: Archipelago Books, 2016.

Carrington, Leonora. 'As They Rode Along the Edge' in *The Debutante and Other Stories*, 26–37. London: Silver Press, [1941] 2017.

— 'The Seventh Horse' in *The Debutante and Other Stories*, 82–87. London: Silver Press, [1941] 2017.

— *The Hearing Trumpet*. London: Penguin, [1974] 2005.

— *The Stone Door*. New York: St Martin's Press, [1976] 1977.

— *The Milk of Dreams*. New York: New York Review of Books, 2013.

— *Down Below*. New York: New York Review of Books, 2017.

Carter, Michaela. *Leonora in the Morning Light*. New York: Avid Reader Press, 2021.

Christensen, Susanne. *Leonora's Journey*. Translated by Matt Bagguley (2019). Unpublished manuscript.

Conrad, Joseph. *Heart of Darkness*. London: Penguin, [1899] 1994.

Flores, Fernando A. 'The Performances of Liliana Krauze' in *Death to the Bullshit Artists of South Texas*, 67–96. Austin, TX: Host, 2018.

Miéville, China. *Last Days of New Paris*. London: Picador, 2016.

Poniatowska, Elena. *Leonora: A Novel*. Translated by Amanda Hopkinson. London: Serpent's Tail, [2011] 2015.

Sopinka, Heidi. *The Dictionary of Animal Languages*. London: Scribe, 2018.

Smith, Ali. *Artful*. London: Penguin, 2012.

Waugh, Evelyn. *Vile Bodies*. London: Penguin, [1930] 2012.

Films, documentaries and music

Appignanesi, Josh. *Female Human Animal* (2018).

Bowie, David. 'The Stars (Are Out Tonight)' in *The Next Day* (2013).

Evans, Kim. *Leonora Carrington and the House of Fear* (BBC Omnibus, 1992).

Garrone, Matteo and Maria Grazia Chiuri, *Le Mythe Dior* (2020): www.youtube.com/watch?v=yxBFwqRbI8c (Accessed 9 July 2020).

Moorhead, Joanna. *Leonora Carrington—Britain's Lost Surrealist TateShots* (2015): www.youtube.com/watch?v=lqXePrSE1R0 (Accessed 1 April 2020).

Skaer, Lucy. *Lucy Skaer*, DVD (Edinburgh: Fruitmarket Gallery, 2008).

Social media

Dean, Claire. @claireddean (20 September 2018). [Twitter]

Elkin, Lauren. @lauren_elkin_ (9 June 2021). [Instagram]

Gee, Felicity. @fiandshoegaze (14 March 2018). [Twitter]

Goodyear, Rachel. @rachel_goodyear (7 June 2021). [Instagram]

Hobbs, Mary Anne. @maryannehobbs (4 November 2020). [Twitter]

Hodson, Chelsea. @chelseahodson (7 November 2019). [Twitter]

Horses Atelier. @horsesatelier (28 June 2020). [Instagram]

Ndzube, Simphiwe. @simphiwe_ndzube (18 November 2020). [Instagram]

Thomas, Leah. @greengirlleah (28 May 2020). [Instagram]

Weisz, Daniel. @leonoracarringtonestate (28 June 2020). [Instagram]

Index

EU authorised representative for GPSR:
Easy Access System Europe, Mustamäe tee 50,
10621 Tallinn, Estonia
gpsr.requests@easproject.com